Lake Dwellings
after Robert Munro

Sidestone Press

Lake Dwellings after Robert Munro

Proceedings from the Munro International Seminar:
The Lake Dwellings of Europe 22nd and 23rd October 2010,
University of Edinburgh

Edited by
Magdalena S. Midgley & Jeff Sanders

© 2012 Individual Authors

Published by Sidestone Press, Leiden
   www.sidestone.com

ISBN 978-90-8890-092-1

Illustration cover: "Lake Village with Blue Mountain" by Ernest Griset (1844-1907);
   Lubbock family archives (reproduced with permission of the Lubbock family.
Cover design: K. Wentink, Sidestone Press
Lay-out: F. Stevens & P.C. van Woerdekom, Sidestone Press

Contents

Acknowledgments	7
List of contributors	9
List of figures	11
Preface	15
1 Munro and the emergence of archaeology *Magdalena S. Midgley and Jeff Sanders*	17
2 A man changed by Darwin *David Clarke*	37
3 Research on Neolithic and Early Bronze Age wetland sites on the north European plain *Johannes Müller*	55
4 All in good tradition? some thoughts on cultural markers in a late Neolithic lakeside dwelling from Switzerland *Thomas Doppler, Sandra Pichler, Brigitte Röder, Jörg Schibler*	93
5 Copper artefacts of the Mondsee group and their possible sources *Carolin Frank and Ernst Pernicka*	113
6 Forging a chronological framework for Scottish crannogs: the radiocarbon and dendrochronological evidence *Anne Crone*	139
7 Crannogs as buildings: the evolution of interpretation 1882 - 2011 *Graeme Cavers*	169

Acknowledgments

The organisers of the Munro International Seminar would like to thank the Munro Trust, University of Edinburgh; the College of Humanities and Social Sciences, University of Edinburgh; and the Society of Antiquaries of Scotland, for providing financial support.

Warms thanks are due to the speakers who contributed so much to making the Symposium a success. Thanks for helping to run the event smoothly are due to a number of student volunteers from Archaeology, School of History, Classics and Archaeology, University of Edinburgh; and also to Vasilki Koutrafouri, Erin Osborne-Martin and Simon Gilmour from the Society of Antiquaries of Scotland.

Particular thanks are due to the Lubbock family for permission to use in our publicity, and subsequently as the cover for this volume, the image "Lake Village with Blue Mountain" (Lubbock family archive) and to Marie-Louise Kerr, Curator, Bromley Museum Service, for permission to use the image "Lake Village" (Bromley Museum Service). Both images are from the collection of paintings illustrating scenes of life from prehistory, commissioned from Ernest Griset (1844-1907) by the pre-eminent prehistorian Sir John Lubbock (1834-1913).

List of contributors

Graeme Cavers
AOC Archaeology Group
Edgefield Industrial Estate
Loanhead
Midlothian EH20 9SY
Scotland

David Clarke
David Clarke
Former Keeper of Antiquities
National Museums of Scotland
Edinburgh
Scotland

Anne Crone
AOC Archaeology Group
Edgefield Industrial Estate
Loanhead
Midlothian EH20 9SY
Scotland

Thomas Doppler
Institute for Prehistory and
Archaeological Science
Basel University
Spalenring 145
4055 Basel
Switzerland

Carolin Frank
Institut für Ur- und Frühgeschichte
und Archäologie des Mittelalters,
Universität Tübingen
Germany

Magdalena S. Midgley
Archaeology
School of History, Classics and
Archaeology
The University of Edinburgh
William Robertson Wing
Teviot Place
Edinburgh EH8 9AG
Scotland

Johannes Müller
Institut für Ur- und Frühgeschichte
Christian-Albrechts-Universität
D-24118 Kiel
Germany

Ernst Pernicka
Institut für Ur- und Frühgeschichte
und Archäologie des Mittelalters,
Universität Tübingen
Germany

Sandra Pichler
Institute for Prehistory and
Archaeological Science
Basel University
Spalenring 145
4055 Basel
Switzerland

Brigitte Röder
Institute for Prehistory and
Archaeological Science
Basel University
Spalenring 145
4055 Basel
Switzerland

Jeff Sanders
The Society of Antiquaries of
Scotland
National Museums Scotland
Chambers Street
Edinburgh EH1 1JF
Scotland

Jörg Schibler
Institute for Prehistory and
Archaeological Science
Basel University
Spalenring 145
4055 Basel
Switzerland

List of figures

Figure 1.1	Lake Village.	27
Figure 2.1	Robert Munro.	38
Figure 2.2	Munro at Hyndford Crannog.	50
Figure 2.3	Excavations at Ardoch.	51
Figure 3.1	Neolithic and Early Bronze Age wetland settlements in Central Europe.	56
Figure 3.2	Circum-Alpine pile dwellings and wetland sites.	58
Figure 3.3	"House 1" Hunte 1 at the Dümmer.	60
Figure 3.4	Neolithic sites in the Oldenburger Graben, East Holstein.	62
Figure 3.5	The settlement at Oldenburg-Dannau.	63
Figure 3.6	Burial from the settlement at Oldenburg-Dannau.	65
Figure 3.7	Posts in the wet area of Oldenburg-Dannau.	65
Figure 3.8	Human skull from the wet area in Oldenburg-Dannau.	66
Figure 3.9	Middle Neolithic mace head with a decorated wooden shaft from Oldenburg-Dannau.	66
Figure 3.10	The well from the settlement of Oldenburg-Dannau.	67
Figure 3.11	Belau. The opening up of landscape reflected in the record of Lake Belau.	68
Figure 3.12	Sum calibration curves from six regions in the Netherlands to Central Southern Sweden.	69
Figure 3.13	Bad Oldesloe-Wolkenwehe: reconstruction of houses.	70
Figure 3.14	Posts from the old excavation in 1950-52 by Schwabedissen.	71
Figure 3.15	Settlements, single finds, votive deposits and burial places in the Mittlere Travetal.	72
Figure 3.16	The excavation of the Early Bronze Age site Bruszczewo 5.	74
Figure 3.17	Aerial photograph of the excavation.	75
Figure 3.18	Houses in the eastern wet area.	78
Figure 3.19	Details of wooden constructions in the eastern part of Bruszczewo 5.	79

Figure 3.20	Early Bronze Age wooden artefacts from Bruszczewo.	80
Figure 3.21	The eastern woodworking area.	81
Figure 3.22	The local oak-dendro-curves and single oak-curves from Bruszczewo 5.	81
Figure 3.23	The settlement burial of a young, hardworking man.	82
Figure 3.24	Eastern shore fortification.	83
Figure 3.25	Reconstruction of socio-economic activities and political institutions.	85
Figure 3.26	Diagram of the overall development in Bruszczewo 5.	86
Figure 4.1	Location of the Neolithic lakeside settlement Arbon Bleiche 3.	95
Figure 4.2	Dendrochronologically dated house plans.	96
Figure 4.3	The ceramics found in Arbon Bleiche 3.	97
Figure 4.4	Internal division of Arbon Bleiche 3 according to archaeozoological data.	99
Figure 4.5	Distribution of animal bones.	100
Figure 4.6	Horizontal distribution of foreign ceramics.	102
Figure 4.7	Example of a canonical correspondence analysis.	104
Figure 5.1	Sites of the Mondsee group around the lakes of Mondsee and Attersee.	114
Figure 5.2	C-14 dates for the sites of the Mondsee group.	115
Figure 5.3	Chemical characteristics of the copper used in Mondsee artefacts.	121
Figure 5.4	Chemical characteristics of the copper used in Mondsee artefacts.	123
Figure 5.5	Chemical "fingerprint" of the copper used in Mondsee artefacts.	123
Figure 5.6	Lead isotope ratios of artefacts of the Mondsee group.	125
Figure 5.7	Ore districts in the east Alpine area.	125
Figure 5.8	Lead isotope ratios of eastern Alpine copper ore.	126
Figure 5.9	Lead isotope ratios of artefacts of the Mondsee group.	129

Figure 5.10	Comparison of the chemical characteristics of the copper used in Mondsee artefacts.	129
Figure 5.11	Serbian artefacts.	130
Figure 5.12	Daggers of Cucuteni type and hooked spirals of Hlinsko type.	131
Figure 6.1	Distribution of all known crannogs in Scotland.	148
Figure 6.2	The chronological distribution of the radiocarbon dataset.	149
Figure 6.3	Crannogs with both later prehistoric and Early Historic radiocarbon dates.	151
Figure 6.4	The two crannogs in Dall Bay, Loch Tay.	152
Figure 6.5	Summary plans showing dendro-dated phases on Buiston.	156
Figure 6.6	Chronological relationships from the major contexts at Buiston.	157
Figure 6.7a	Dorman's Island.	158
Figure 6.7b	Dendrochronological results from Dorman's Island.	159
Figure 6.8a	Cults Loch promontory crannog.	160
Figure 6.8b	Dendrochronological results from Cults Loch.	161
Figure 7.1	Plans of Buiston and Lochlee.	172
Figure 7.2	Plan of Milton Loch.	174
Figure 7.3	Armit, Piggott and Feachem reconstructions.	175
Figure 7.4	Dumbuck crannog, depicted by Donnelly.	177
Figure 7.5	Lochan Dughaill.	179
Figure 7.6	One of the structures at Cults Loch crannog.	180
Figure 7.7	Ballycagen, Isle of Man.	181

Preface

Dr Robert Munro (1835-1920) was a distinguished medical practitioner and, from the 1870s onwards, also a keen archaeologist with a particular interest in the lacustrian settlements in Scotland and on the Continent. Upon his retirement from medical practice in 1885, Robert Munro undertook a review of all lacustrian research in Europe, travelling widely across the Continent studying collections and visiting most of the then known lake-dwelling localities. The results of this work formed the Society of Antiquaries of Scotland Rhind Lectures, delivered in Edinburgh in 1888 and published two years later as *The Lake-Dwellings of Europe*.

In 1910 Robert Munro offered the University Court of the University of Edinburgh a financial gift with which to fund lectures – the Munro Lectures on Anthropology and Prehistoric Archaeology – with the specific aim to "deal systematically with the general field of Anthropology, especially with the antiquity of man and his physical and mental evolution as evidenced by his fossil remains and handicraft works" (Munro 1921, 74; the Munro Bequest, University of Edinburgh). Robert Munro, at the request of the University Court, delivered the first series of these on the subjects of "Palaeolithic Man in Europe" and the "Terremare"; they were a great success and attracted large audiences.

Over the past century the Munro Trust has been supporting an annual series of lectures in Anthropology and Archaeology which, in their breadth and depth, reflect Munro's original wish. In 2010, the year of the centenary of the Munro Trust, the University of Edinburgh and the Society of Antiquaries of Scotland jointly celebrated the occasion with a small gathering of continental and British scholars at the Munro International Seminar on The Lake Dwellings of Europe, which took place on 22nd and 23rd October.

The seminar provided an opportunity to reflect on the life work of Robert Munro, covering the lake-dwellings as well as his other interests in the fields of Anthropology and Archaeology. In offering this small volume, we hope that the selection of papers presented at the Seminar will form a fitting tribute to Robert Munro's scholarly achievements in his quest of "making some investigations into the mysteries of life and human civilisation" (Munro 1921, 38).

Magdalena S. Midgley and Jeff Sanders

References

Munro, R. 1890, *The Lake-Dwellings of Europe: being the Rhind Lectures in Archaeology for 1888*. London: Cassell & Company, Limited.

Munro, R. 1910, *The Munro Bequest*. Edinburgh: University of Edinburgh.

Munro, R. 1921, *Autobiographic Sketch of Robert Munro M.A., M.D., LL.D, 21st July, 1835 - 18th July, 1920*. Glasgow: MacLehose, Jackson and Co.

Chapter 1

MUNRO AND THE EMERGENCE OF ARCHAEOLOGY

Magdalena S. Midgley and Jeff Sanders[1]

Abstract

Robert Munro's contribution to the study of lake-dwellings, as well as other fields of archaeology, followed the time of dramatic changes in a host of disciplines which were developing from the mid-nineteenth century onwards. Public and scholarly imagination was fired by fascinating archaeological discoveries, new methodological approaches to excavation, interpretation of finds and a close relationship between archaeology and other fields of enquiry such as geology, biology and anthropology.

These developments, together with contributions from key archaeological and other scientific figures of the period, provide the intellectual framework for the appreciation of Robert Munro's contribution to archaeology, within Scotland as well as the wider European context.

Key words: Antiquity of man, Three Age System, evolution, lake-dwellings, shell middens, Munro, Lubbock, Wilson

Introduction

Dr Robert Munro's (1835-1920) Rhind lectures in 1888, and the subsequent publication of these in 1890 as *The Lake-Dwellings of Europe*, marked a seminal moment not just in lake settlement studies, but also in prehistoric archaeology in general. Munro had previously

---

1 Magdalena S. Midgley, School of History, Classics and Archaeology, University of Edinburgh, Magda.Midgley@ed.ac.uk; Jeff Sanders, Society of Antiquaries of Scotland, scarf@socantscot.org

synthesised knowledge on lake settlements in Scotland with his *Ancient Scottish Lake Dwellings* (1882). Prior to Robert Munro, crannog studies in Scotland, and lake dwellings work in Europe, could be characterised as enthusiastic, albeit unsystematic and of variable quality. The publication of Munro's Rhind lectures meant that a framework was now in place for future research on both a Scottish and a European scale. The importance of Munro's syntheses in allowing new research to be systematised had implications far beyond Scotland. In doing so he helped lake dwellings join the pantheon of established archaeological topics of investigation, alongside other phenomena including shell middens and megaliths.

Munro became an active archaeologist in the 1870s, following a couple of decades during which archaeology had changed significantly, in parallel with other scientific fields of enquiry. A number of key archaeologists, sites, and important publications had been emerging from many different strands of archaeology as well as other disciplines. Munro was not operating within a vacuum, even as he helped open up and systematise one particular field of enquiry. Most of the mid-nineteenth century controversies had by then been solved, and the then new concepts and ideas now form the backbone of archaeology as a modern discipline. However, what preceded his involvement had a profound impact on the development of archaeology. It was a period of fascinating discoveries, of new ideas, new approaches and unprecedented, indeed, ground-breaking *rapprochement* between different fields of science, creating a new intellectual climate which drew together an astonishing array of passionate individuals, with drive and with the conviction that they were creating a whole new world of knowledge.

This introduction therefore offers a brief analysis of those turbulent but exciting years around the middle of the century, when (r)evolution turned antiquarianism into the modern discipline of archaeology. The broader context from which Munro's work developed, at a time when archaeology itself was emerging, is a story of individuals and events as well as broader processes. These unfolded over Europe, within Britain and locally in Scotland.

The emergence of archaeology

Robert Munro, by then into his forties, came to archaeology in the 1870s, and during his lifetime its emergence as a modern discipline can be traced. His work contributed in part to this transition from an 'essentially dilettantist avocation' to 'an organised discipline' (Chapman, 1989, 34), ultimately providing an early exemplar work of synthesis and thus a framework for the incorporation of future knowledge.

The work of earlier and contemporary archaeologists paved the way for Munro's own work. Alongside the archaeological innovation certain antiquarian themes continued, and the social, economic and cultural milieu played a central role. Broader themes and influences, which form the wider context in which Munro develops as an archaeologist, are therefore also important to understanding the development of his thought as well as his archaeological contribution.

The emergence of archaeology in the middle of the nineteenth century owes much to developments in sister disciplines, especially geology and biology. The publication of Charles Lyell's (1797-1875) *Principles of Geology* over 1830-33 and Charles Darwin's (1809-1882) *On the origin of species* in 1859, represent the most important influences. Wresting archaeology free from history was an unintended consequence of the recognition of the deep time of prehistory, and the development of methodological tools to sort the remains from this time. The concepts of evolution itself already pervaded some of the earlier science writing, with evolutionary theories of the earth, plants and animals being put forward from the eighteenth century onwards, for example by James Hutton (1726-1797), Erasmus Darwin (1731-1802) and Lamarck (1744-1829) (Hobsbawm 1962). But it was really only when Sir Charles Lyell published his *Principles of Geology* (1830-1833) that the climate was created for the concept of evolution to enter intellectual debate in a wider sense. Geology demonstrated the very great length of time over which the processes of erosion and accumulation shaped the earth and - vitally from the point of view of archaeology - geological strata showed an evolution of plants and animals preserved as fossils in different layers. Archaeological evidence was interpreted in light of evolutionary theory and came to fuel its development as new discoveries were made.

For the acceptance of the antiquity of man, the year 1859 is rightly considered an important point of convergence, when several events came together, but earlier discoveries were already preparing the way. The most famous is the 1856 recovery of human remains in a cave in the Neander valley in Germany, although finds of artefacts and fossil bones were made even earlier by Jouannet in France and Schmerling in Belgium (Coye 1997); other finds of ancient tools and human fossils followed in the later part of the nineteenth century. Both Darwin and Lyell were very much part of a network that included early archaeologists, Sir John Lubbock (1834-1913) being a pivotal figure.

In 1859, the claims of an eccentric and persevering Romantic French antiquary Boucher de Perthes that his *antédiluviens* deposits, containing flint implements and bones of extinct animals, were a proof for the existence of a fossil man, were finally confirmed in the field, during a visit by two British scientists, the geologist Joseph Prestwich and an archaeologist John Evans, and subsequently presented at various London learned societies. William Pengely's excavations at Brixham near Torquay and the verification of earlier finds, made by Frere at Hoxne in 1797, provided further confirmation. Like other archaeological controversies of the period this one was solved by a coming together of several developing disciplines – geology, archaeology, palaeontology, and even infant photography, with the famous photograph showing the *in situ* find of an axe in the gravel pit at St Acheul (Daniel 1981; Cohen and Hublin 1989; Trigger 2006; Gamble and Kruszynski 2009, Fig. 2). Lyell also considered the evidence from the Swiss lake dwellings in support of the antiquity of humankind (1863, 39-40). Through his correspondence with Charles Adolphe von Morlot (1820-1867), a Swiss antiquarian and geologist who also corresponded with Darwin, Lyell received botanical samples from the sites at Robenhausen and Moosseedorf (Leckie 2010).

These types of stunning archaeological discoveries were providing a vehicle for the ideas of people such as Darwin and Lyell to communicate beyond the scientific and antiquarian communities. In effect they became a 'battle-ground of evolutionary theory' (Sherratt 2004, 268). These debates were also played out within antiquarian circles in Europe, for example at the 1877 Congress of the *German Anthropological Society* in Munich (Sklenář 1983, 119). Munro himself was convinced by Darwin's ideas to the extent that he chose to become a doctor rather than a minister (Munro 1921, 7-10; Clarke, this volume). It is interesting to note that Munro, working within an evolutionary paradigm, is active at a time where in archaeology this begins to give way to culture-history – the facts arranged 'not in time but in space' (Sklenář 1983, 129; Trigger 2006, chapter 6).

Archaeology's emergence can also be traced through the intellectual and supportive networks in which archaeologists moved. This operated at a number of levels, from personal connections (see below), via learned, social or didactic societies, to full blown institutions. There was also a tradition of medical and clerical professionals with archaeological interests (Levine 1986, 10). This tended to promote what today would be called a 'multi-disciplinary' approach. The heady mix of scientific and religious outlooks held by individuals, however, could easily be masked, or reconciled, within a slice of society with similar social standing, education background and outlook. Liberal-minded antiquarians could easily mix with those of a more conservative outlook within an encompassing social milieu.

Romanticism also continued to exert an influence over the new science of archaeology. The universalising elements of Enlightenment and evolutionary thought, and the specific richness or 'spirit' of a particular area as characterised in Romantic thought, produced a tension, but one that could be productive, especially in the case of lake dwellings (Sherratt 2004; Kaeser 2004). Lake dwellings effectively became a 'cultural phenomenon' (Sherratt 2004, 272) that could be explored as part of a canon, marrying specific data with broader analogy and high theories from different periods or locations.

Romanticism is also associated with nationalism, complicated by both regional and Imperial identities. For those antiquarians from, or working within, countries such as Switzerland, Scotland or Denmark, this national context would have been pervasive, and an influence on the writing of the past (Zimmer 2003; Rowley-Conwy 2007, chapter 5). This would also affect subsequent developments and the popularity of culture-history (Trigger 2006, chapter 6). Romanticism is also an important thread in the portrayal of the prehistoric past: from Caspar David Friedrich's depictions of the megaliths around the turn of the nineteenth century (Vaughan 1994) to the peaceful idylls represented by such paintings as Albert Anker's "*Die Pfahlbauerin*" painted in 1873 or Carl von Häberlin's "*Pfahlbauromantik*" painted as late as 1904 (Weber 2010, Figures on pages 288 and 289). Romanticised images such as these helped fuel the fashion for lake dwellings across Europe (Sklenář 1983, 74).

The early archaeologists were also caught up in this mix of Enlightenment principles and Romanticism, albeit to varying degrees. For example, Bruce Trigger contrasts the depictions of aboriginal people by Daniel Wilson (1816-1892, see below) to those in the publications of John Lubbock (Trigger 2002, 55). By Munro's time, archaeology was not used as much to 'prove' the Whiggish conception of history by illustrating various natural phases of human society in sequence (Rowley-Conwy, 2007, 139). Rather, it was used more on its own terms, reconstructing past societies fleshed out with emerging ethnography as well as classical analogy. However, nineteenth-century ethnography had an underlying racism, and looking to the past from the perspective of tracing the origin of the present was still prevalent.

Archaeology as a discipline was also producing its first 'textbooks', including the translation of Christian Thomsen's *Guide to Northern Antiquities* (first published in 1836, translated into English in 1843), J. J. A. Worsaae's *Primeval Antiquities of Denmark* (first published in 1843, translated into English in 1849), Daniel Wilson's *The Archaeology and Prehistoric Annals of Scotland* in 1851, James Fergusson's *Rude Stone Monuments in all Countries* in 1872, and William Greenwell's *British Barrows* published in 1877. The Three Age System provided the methodological tool to apply fundamental evolutionary principles to what was becoming the science of archaeology. The fact the Robert Munro was from and worked in Scotland was of importance in this, in that Scotland embraced this approach more readily than many other countries (Rowley-Conwy 2007, chapter 5).

Fieldwork was making an impact, moving from the retrieval of artefacts in order to add to collections - sometimes to highlight evolutionary principles, often for more aesthetic tastes - to structured retrieval of information on the past. Work had been undertaken on Swiss lake dwellings (Keller 1866) and the preservation conditions had allowed considerable reconstruction of past life. Work in Switzerland had inspired a generation of antiquarians, of which Munro came to be one of the most prominent. The work of early archaeologists such as William Greenwell (1820-1918) and General Augustus Lane-Fox Pitt-Rivers (1827-1900) was also providing a series of exemplars of field recording.

Fieldwork on other types of monument, notably megaliths (within their world context as well as Europe), was also providing a range of examples of how archaeology could be undertaken. Munro himself professed these to have had "a peculiar fascination for my mind; so much so that the itinerary of many a country ramble had to be arranged so as to include any of these striking landmarks which happened to be in the vicinity" (Munro 1921, 52). At that time the approach to the megaliths was on a global scale. The Dutchman Nicolaus Westendorp's (1773-1836) inspection of the Dutch and some German megaliths resulted in a sort of "mental map" based on description of their locations throughout Europe and he dated them firmly to the Stone Age (Bakker 2010, 110). Similar maps were later compiled by a French scholar Alexandre Bertrand and the Swiss aristocrat Baron de Bonstetten in his famous 1865 *Essai sur les dolmens* (interestingly published the same year as Lubbock's *Prehistoric* Times; Bertrand 1863, Bonstetten 1865).

This global approach, unsurprisingly, created its own problems of universality and origins, of the routes of spread (both Bertrand and Bonstetten believed that "megalithic people" and the tradition of tomb building spread from north to south). It posited questions on chronology, although the only serious dissenter, after 1865, from the view that they belonged to the Stone Age was the architect James Fergusson, who had a poor understanding of the concept of the Three Age System and assigned megalithic tombs to the much more recent Christian era (Fergusson 1872); other questions were those of function – were all megaliths tombs or were some temples? – and of details of construction, especially the presence or absence of covering mounds. It was characteristic of Munro to determine to settle some of these questions by personal inspections in the field – an approach as clear from his short but very well-informed paper "*Megalithic monuments of Holland, and their relation with analogous remains in Northern Europe*" published in the Proceedings of the Society of Antiquaries of Scotland in 1884, as from other works such as *Prehistoric Scotland and its Place in European Civilization* (1899, 326).

The popular appreciation of archaeology was also changing, driven and in part reflected by accounts such as Austin Layard's *Nineveh and its Remains* in 1848-9 or the first edition (of seven) of John Lubbock's *Prehistoric Times* in 1865. Stunning archaeological finds such as those by Schliemann in Troy and Mycenae in the 1870s and 1880s, and of the Swiss lake dwellings by Keller and Aeppli in the 1850s were also catching the public's attention. Work on infrastructure projects, notably the railways in Britain and elsewhere in Europe, was also unearthing considerable amounts of archaeological material. At the same time, technologies for recording and reproducing images of this material was also improving, and becoming cheaper.

The discovery and subsequent popularisation of the Swiss lake dwellings had a considerable effect on the public in Switzerland and abroad. The translations of Ferdinand Keller's work in 1866 unleashed an interest in crannogs that had been growing since the 1850s and inspired many investigations (Coles, 2004, 101). That the crannog at Lochlee attracted the attention of the Archaeological Association for Ayrshire and Wigtonshire, and the subsequent involvement of Munro, should not be surprising (Clarke, this volume).

Danish shell middens and Swiss lake villages

Kristiansen (2002, 11) drew attention to the fact that, while most of the mid-nineteenth-century archaeological writings have a distinctly "antiquarian" character, there are others which even today appear "modern"; he linked this to the emergence of new methodologies and new ways of thinking, within the developing disciplines of the period, which are a part of the scientific tradition we recognise as our own. These disciplines, as already noted, involved geology, biology, zoology; and the influence they had within an archaeological context was particularly dramatically demonstrated at the excavations of the shell-middens in Denmark, and of the lake dwellings in Switzerland. Both were of intense interest to the international scientific community of the time and made an important contribution to the development of archaeological methodology and practice.

They are further significant in the context of the present discussion because the lake dwellings, in their broadest sense, were the subject of the Rhind lectures delivered by Robert Munro in 1888 and published two years later. Munro did not study the shell middens in any great detail, but they nevertheless attracted his attention sufficiently to encourage him, after travels in Scandinavia, to write a short paper on the subject, published in the Society's Proceedings in 1884. The importance of the mid-nineteenth-century research on the Danish shell-middens (known in Danish as *køkkenmødding*, or in its older English spelling of *Kjökkenmödding(s)* used by both Lubbock and Munro) to the development of archaeology has been well discussed in literature on the history of the discipline (Klindt-Jensen 1975, Gräslund 1987, Bahn 1996, Fischer and Kristiansen 2002) but it is still worthwhile to be reminded of some of the significant aspects of this work. The establishment, in 1848, of an interdisciplinary archaeological project to investigate, with the help of geology and zoology, the mounds of shells found in Jutland and on Zealand was an important landmark in the progress of archaeology. Again, the multi-disciplinary nature of the approaches is apparent.

Irrespective of the subsequent debates on the interpretation of these sites from an economic and functional, or technological and comparative, point of view (problems which have not yet altogether left modern debating agendas), it put in motion a series of new approaches; investigation in the field; documentation based on observations of stratigraphy, context and typological development; and, very importantly, full-scale contributions from the natural sciences. This was a wholly new way of tackling archaeological problems and, having established beyond doubt the existence of the period known as Stone Age, was of enormous interest to scholars in other parts of Europe. The results were swiftly disseminated among the scientific community, with the reports being widely available, and J.J.A. Worsaae himself travelled to France to meet such scholars as Lartet, Boucher de Perthes and Prosper Mereimeé (the latter by then a well-travelled Inspector of Ancient Monuments; Kristiansen 2002, 13).

Within the British scholarly establishment the Danish middens certainly fired John Lubbock's imagination and he visited southern Scandinavia on two occasions in order to see the excavations for himself: in 1861 he went to Denmark and, in 1863, he travelled in Denmark, Sweden and Norway (Patton 2007, 54, 62). His 1861 visit when, in the company of the distinguished Danish zoologist Japetus Steenstrup, he had a chance to inspect the shell middens around the Isefjord, in North Zealand, quickly led to a paper published in the first issue of the *Natural History Review*. That journal had just been acquired, under the powerful drive of Thomas Huxley, by a group of leading British scientists, to provide a forum for scientific discussion and dissemination of original research (Desmond 1998, 284). It was thus an ideal venue to report on the results of that trip and, in one short article, Lubbock was able to draw attention to the importance of Danish inter-disciplinary researches and put them on an equal footing with similar practices, already familiar from the more publicised work on the Swiss lake-dwellings; he further emphasised the significance of the Three Age System in providing a structuring framework for the prehistoric chronology (Lubbock 1861). The following year (1862) Lubbock published another paper for the *Natural History Review*, this time devoted to the scientific investigations of the Swiss lake dwellings which he had also been investigating.

In parallel with the investigation at the Danish shell middens, Swiss research was based on a series of inter-connected methods: a stratigraphic approach was used to prove the integrity of archaeological layers; the chronology of individual sites, based on typology of finds, could thus be established and this methodology fully supported the Three Age System model that the Swiss investigators adopted from Scandinavia (Coye 1997, 193-208). Palaeontological research, apart from identifying ancient types of plants and animals, was an important criterion in the wider chronological scheme, placing the Stone Age lake dwellings relatively recently within the Stone Age - which Lubbock was also hinting at in 1862, and what he was to call in 1865 the 'Neolithic'.

Archaeology and Anthropology

Anthropology, together with its sub-fields ethnology and ethnography, was a close sister discipline emerging at a similar time, with Edward Tylor's (1832-1917) *Anthropology* first published in 1881. With the growing separation of prehistoric archaeology from history, ethnography (also known as comparative method) was being used as a source to increase knowledge of prehistoric times. The use of ethnographic comparisons formed an important aspect of the lake dwelling research; Keller's ethnographic sources included, among others, those of Captain Cook and Dumont d'Urville, and they provided models for the interpretation of ways of life at lake villages. Reconstruction of the village at Obermeilen followed d'Urville's descriptions and sketches of lake villages in New Guinea, and it is interesting to note that this image served as frontispiece in Lyell's book *The Antiquity of Man* (1863).

The link between European prehistoric communities and contemporary "savages" known from ethnographic accounts, first mooted in Daniel Wilson's *Prehistoric Annales of Scotland*, was another strong stimulus for establishing links, as indeed was the confirmation of the antiquity of man. Within the next decade the two disciplines were influencing one another in many fields, for example through the work of medical practitioners Joseph Davis and John Thurnam on craniology leading to *Crania Britannica* (1865), although anthropology was also identifying its own direction to study the "whole nature of man" (Stocking 1971). Wilson was also a champion of craniological approaches, which Munro himself highlights (Simpson 1963, 6), and which had become accepted practice by the 1850s and 1860s (Morse 1999). Effectively this formed another dating tool complementing the Three Age System, and built on work including *Crania Britannica*, Richard Knox's *Races of Man*, and taken on by the work of Thurnam (1849), George Rolleston, and others (Rowley-Conwy 2007, 164-5).

The greatest populariser of the ethnographic approach in Britain at that time was John Lubbock, with *Prehistoric Times* (1865) and *The Origin of Civilisation* (1870) offering a model of social and cultural evolution. Lubbock was fully committed to an evolutionary explanation of human origins, and believed that technological progress seen in the archaeological record was accompanied by cultural progress and that comparisons with modern primitive peoples could shed light on the lifestyles of prehistory. However, in contrast to Daniel Wilson, who upon his emigration to Canada in 1854 did study at first hand Canadian native communities and used this insight in his work, Lubbock had no direct knowledge of the peoples he was writing about. Like many other Victorian scholars he relied upon accounts of travellers, explorers and others to expound his ideas. Such images of "savages" were thus inevitably out of their historical and cultural context and, seen against the social, political and intellectual frameworks of the time, they carried a political message entirely in keeping with the values of the mid-nineteenth-century Victorian middle classes.

Figure 1.1 "Lake Village". One of two images of a lake village commissioned by John Lubbock from the Victorian illustrator Ernest Griset (courtesy Bromley Museum Service).

The commitment to different disciplines is, however, also apparent in a collection of images "on the life of savages" which Lubbock commissioned for private purposes from a talented French naturalist painter Ernest Griset. As Murray recently observed (2009, 491) the majority were of ethnographic inspiration and this most undoubtedly includes the two images of lake villages (cover image and Figure 1.1) but, equally, they also represent archaeological prehistoric sites that Lubbock visited in the course of his travels in Switzerland.

Key figures

Key figures influential to Munro's work came from both home and abroad. The contemporary intellectual and social milieu within which he moved involved networks of knowledge operating over a number of scales, and with various societies and acquaintances offering opportunities for Munro to become engaged with archaeology. This would not only create openings, but also define the intellectual framework he was working within (and would later contribute to further develop). A key characteristic of this network of archaeologists is the social element or sense of community amongst a generally professional (although not yet in its archaeological sense) group with both regional and national interests. The national is often highlighted, although regional interests were often a stronger pull. Another key element is the cross-over between disciplinary interests, with an often diverse set of interests being combined.

Societies and institutions were pivotal in the development of archaeology, as well as the cultivation of Munro's own interests in the past (Piggott 1976, Levine 1986). Local connections were particularly important with a range of antiquarian and natural science societies, with local interests, present across Scotland. The *Archaeological Association for Ayrshire and Wigtownshire*, for example, which Munro joined at its inception in 1877, provided him with access to other like-minded individuals and introduced him to the local archaeology, including crannogs. Munro had previously served as President of the *Philosophical Institution* and had strong natural sciences interests, which was not unusual for nineteenth-century professionals. National societies were also important, providing a stage for the dissemination of knowledge as well as a network of contacts (and the opportunity to cultivate these socially and through correspondence).

The *Society of Antiquaries of Scotland* was important in a Scottish context, not least through the series of Rhind lectures and the society journal: *Proceedings of the Society of Antiquaries of Scotland*. Munro contributed to both, and was an office bearer in the Society over a number of years. Scottish connections were facilitated through the *Society*, of which Daniel Wilson and his successor at the National Museum of Scotland, Joseph Anderson, were particularly influential. Wilson's mix of Enlightenment principles and Romanticism has seen him considered as belonging to the same 'intellectual movement' of antiquarians such as Thomsen (Trigger 1992, 60), who was another with a variety of interests, including geology. Wilson's *The Archaeology and Prehistoric Annals of Scotland* (1851) pushed back the antiquity of man to prehistory (a term forever associated with him), providing the conceptual space for successive archaeologists. Wilson was also the prime mover for the adoption of a Three Age System in Scotland (Rowley-Conwy, 2007, chapter 5), reorganising the Society's collections according to this scheme in 1848. Wilson therefore provided the structure for approaching prehistory as well as creating the conceptual space to accommodate the idea of the antiquity of man. By 1853, when Wilson had moved to Canada, he had been instrumental in setting up the *Proceedings* and retained an interest in Scottish prehistory. In 1862 Wilson published *Prehistoric Man: Researches into the Origin of Civilisation in the Old and New*

Worlds, including a detailed application of New World ethnography to prehistory (Simpson, 1963, 4).

Beyond Scotland, the *Society of Antiquaries of London* was one of several national institutions that exerted considerable influence over the development of archaeology at the time. Antiquarians such as Wilson, Greenwell and Rhind were active over both sides of the border (Simpson 1963). Continental connections are also apparent; for example, when the *Society of Antiquaries of Zurich* alerted the *Society of Antiquaries of London* to the need for help with the lake dwellings (Wylie 1860), it was in the knowledge that enthusiastic scholars with independent means might help, either collectively, or individually. A predecessor to Munro in the field of lake dwellings, William Wylie wrote *On Lake-Dwellings of the Early Periods* in 1860. Wylie used classical analogy and framed discussion in terms of Classical texts, particularly Herodotus, and used these as a source of ethnographic parallel for comparison (1860, 177). It is clear from his writing that Wylie viewed lake dwellings as primarily defensive (ibid. 187), though also domestic in character and a normal part of the wider settlement system. He also compared the crannogs of Ireland and the Swiss lake dwellings and regarded them as one phenomenon (spread over considerable periods of time). There is an unmistakeable culture-historical theme running through his work, with the Swiss dwellings razed by successive invaders possessing superior military technology (ibid. 182) as part of a historic narrative. In his article, the lake dwellings were dated by artefacts using the Three Age System, though also reinforced by the geological age estimates of the silting of lakes. The Swiss antiquarian community was obviously important in the particular field of lake dwelling studies, with notable early archaeologists including Ferdinand Keller (1800-1881) and Frédéric Troyon (1815-1866); the latter provided estimates of population size and building techniques, and dated sites by the silting of the lake. Morlot was another influential figure in Swiss archaeology who corresponded with Darwin among many others, but was also heavily involved in archaeology outside Switzerland; for example, he provided translations of the results of the Danish kitchen middens.

Ferdinand Keller was one of the main popularisers of the Swiss lake dwellings after highlighting discoveries in 1854. When the first translations of his work into English came out it had a similar effect as *Prehistoric Times*. However, Keller sounds a note of caution regarding the application of the Three-Age scheme, recognising it as a heuristic device, rather than necessarily as a reflection of past life (1866, 12-13). In the translated version of Keller's work on the Swiss lake dwellings, there is also a short section by John Stuart of the *Society of Antiquaries of Scotland* titled 'Notice of the Scotch crannogs' (1866, 389-392). In this, the *Society's* role as a forum for early crannog research is apparent (Stuart's role as Secretary to the Society is highlighted under the paper title). Stuart notes the inspiration drawn from the presentation of papers at Society meetings from early workers including Joseph Robertson, and a presentation to the *British Association* on the finds resulting from the drainage of Loch Dowalton, Wigtonshire by Lord Lovaine (Stuart 1866, 389-90). This inspired Stuart to put together a paper attempting a synthesis of recent finds in order to afford comparison, and in Keller's book he provides a brief overview of crannog classifications and types of finds (ibid. 390). According to Stuart, at this time there were 35 crannogs known in Scotland, and in a footnote he draws upon classical accounts for potential evidence of crannog use (ibid. 392). Putting the Scottish crannogs on a footing to allow comparisons with the Continent is clearly an important consideration, and there is also a section on Irish crannogs (Keller 1866, 380-388), largely abridged from the work of Wilde. The need to synthesise Scottish and Irish examples in order to compare with continental examples was clearly felt, emphasised by the additions to the translation of Keller's work.

This network of early archaeologists both had regional foci and operated on a Europe-wide level, and the number of mutual influences that would have impacted upon the thinking of any antiquarian at the time of Munro is challenging to unpick. John Evans (1823-1908) and Augustus Franks (1826-1897) were also contemporaries, and both provided Munro with letters of introduction where needed for his travels. What was certain is that, by the time Munro began his archaeological work, a network of early archaeologists was firmly established across Europe, shuttling information back and forth and enthusing the public at large with an appreciation of prehistory.

Conclusion

Through establishing the broader background to the development of archaeology in the middle of the nineteenth century, it is easier to understand and evaluate Munro's work. Munro's systematic approach, travel, publication and influences from a range of different countries should be emphasised, though more for their extent rather than for their uniqueness. And while Munro made a number of contributions to the study of the past, he was building on foundations already established in archaeology, and these continuities can be traced throughout his work.

Munro's work represents the apogee for earlier and contemporary work on crannogs and lake settlement - for the extent of coverage, the systematic presentation of findings, and the systematic comparison with lake dwelling sites on the Continent, drawing lake-dwelling studies in individual countries into a Europe-wide context. Building on earlier traditions of fieldwork and establishing comparanda, Munro provided a textbook example (both metaphorically and literally) of good archaeology, and publicised his findings and ideas, of which the Rhind lectures represented a particularly high point. Munro's status built not only on his synthesis publication and presentation feats, but also on his field experience. As well as visiting a large number of sites, Munro worked on several crannog sites. Amongst peers, Munro came to be seen as a father figure and an arbiter of disputes. The controversy surrounding the findings from Dumbuck crannog is an example of this role within contemporary archaeology (Hale & Sands 2005). Munro's subsequent publication of *Archaeology and False Antiquities* (1905) set out his (correct) belief that a number of artefacts had been 'seeded' onto the site.

In the development of archaeology a number of key concepts, important figures and publications provided the broader framework within which Munro's work developed. The intellectual climate was matched by the social milieu, allowing ideas and information to flow between like-minded people in a number of different countries. It is within this context that the real importance of Munro's work is best understood.

References

Bahn, P. (ed.) 1996, *The Cambridge Illustrated History of Archaeology*. Cambridge: Cambridge University Press.

Bakker, J. A. 2010, *Megalithic Research in the Netherlands, 1547-1911. From 'Giant's Beds' and 'Pillars of Hercules' to accurate investigations*. Leiden: Sidestone Press.

Bertrand, A. 1863, Les monuments primitifs de la Gaule, monuments dits celtiques, dolmens et tumulus. *Revue Archéologique* 7: 217-237.

Bonstetten, B. A. de 1865, *Essai sur les Dolmens*. Geneva: Jules-Guillaume Fick.

Chapman, W. 1989, The Organisational Context in the History of Archaeology: Pitt-Rivers and Other British Archaeologists in the 1860s. *The Antiquaries Journal* LXIX: 23-42.

Cohen, C. and Hublin, J.-J. 1989, *Boucher de Perthes, les origines romantiques de la Préhistoire, (Un savant, une époque)*. Paris: Belin.

Coles, B. 2004, The development of wetland archaeology in Britain. In: F. Menotti (ed.) *Living on the Lake in Prehistoric Europe: 150 years of Lake Dwelling Research*. London: Routledge, 98-114.

Coye, N. 1997, *La Préhistoire en Parole et en Acte. Méthodes et enjeux de la pratique archéologique 1830 - 1950.* Paris: L'Harmattan.

Daniel, G. 1981, *Towards a History of Archaeology.* London: Thames & Hudson.

Darwin, C. 1859, *On the Origin of Species by Means of Natural Selection.* London: John Murray.

Davis, J. B. and Thurnam, J. 1865, *Crania Britannica. Delineations and Descriptions of the Skulls of the Aboriginal and Early Inhabitants of the British Islands: With Notices of their Other Remains*, 2 vols. London: Printed for the Subscribers.

Desmond, A. 1998, *Huxley: From Devil's Disciple to Evolution's High Priest.* London: Penguin Books.

Fergusson, J. 1872, *Rude Stone Monuments of All Countries; Their Age and Uses.* London: John Murray.

Fischer, A and Kristiansen, K (eds). 2002, *The Neolithisation of Denmark: 150 Years of Debate.* Sheffield: J. R. Collis Publications.

Gamble, C. and Kruszynski, R. 2009, John Evans, Joseph Prestwich and the stone that shattered the time barrier. *Antiquity* 83: 461-475.

Gräslund, B. 1987, *The Birth of Prehistoric Chronology. Dating methods and dating systems in nineteenth-century Scandinavian archaeology.* Cambridge: Cambridge University Press.

Greenwell, W. G. 1877, *British Barrows.* Oxford: Clarendon Press.

Hale, A and Sands, R. 2005, *Controversy on the Clyde, Archaeologists, Fakes and Forgers: The Excavation of the Dumbuck Crannog.* Edinburgh: RCAHMS.

Hobsbawm, E. 1962, *The Age of Revolution. Europe 1789-1848.* London: Abacus imprint of 2008 (Little, Brown Book Group).

Kaeser, M-A. 2004, Archaeology and the Identity Discourse: Universalism versus Nationalism: Lake-Dwelling Studies in 19th Century Switzerland. In: A. Gramsch and U. Sommer (eds.) *A History of Central European Archaeology. Theory, Methods and Politics.* Bonn: Habelt, 143-160.

Kehoe, A. B. 1991, The Invention of Prehistory. *Current Anthropology* 32: 467-476.

Keller, F. 1866. *The lake dwellings of Switzerland and other parts of Europe.* Translated into English by J.E. Lee. London: Longmans.

Klindt-Jensen, O.K. 1975, *A History of Scandinavian Archaeology.* London: Thames and Hudson.

Kristiansen, K. 2002, The Birth of Ecological Archaeology in Denmark: history and research environments 1850-2000. In: A. Fischer and K. Kristiansen (eds.) *The Neolithisation of Denmark: 150 years of debate*. Sheffield: J.R. Collis Publications, 11-31.

Leckie, K. 2010, Specimens as gifts: Charles Lyell, Adolf von Morlot and a Swiss lake dwelling collection. *Antiquity* 84 Project Gallery: http://www.antiquity.ac.uk/projgall/leckie324/ <accessed on 10 March 2012>

Levine, P. 1986, *The Amateur and the Professional*. Cambridge: Cambridge University Press.

Lubbock, J. 1861, The Kjökkenmöddings: Recent Geologico-Archaeological Researches in Denmark. *Natural History Review* 1: 489-504.

Lubbock, J. 1862, On the Ancient Lake Habitations of Switzerland. *Natural History Review* 2: 26-52.

Lubbock, J. 1865, *Prehistoric Times, as illustrated by Ancient Remains, and the Manners and Customs of Modern Savages*. London: Williams and Norgate.

Lubbock, J. 1868, On the Origin of Civilisation and the Primitive Condition of Man. *Transactions of the Ethnological Society of London* 6: 328-341.

Lubbock, J. 1870, *The Origin of Civilisation and the Primitive Condition of Man: Mental and Social Conditions of Savages*. London: Longmans, Green & Co.

Lyell, C. 1830-1833, *Principles of Geology, Being and Attempt to Explain the Former Changes of the Earth's Surface by Reference to Causes Now in Operation*. vols. 1-3, London: John Murray.

Lyell, C. 1863, *The Geological Evidences for the Antiquity of Man* London: John Murray.

Menotti, F (ed.) 2004, *Living on the Lake in Prehistoric Europe: 150 years of Lake Dwelling Research*. Routledge: London.

Morse, M. 1999, Craniology and the Adoption of the Three-Age System in Britain. *Proceedings of the Prehistoric Society* 65: 1-16.

Munro, R. 1882, *Ancient Scottish Lake Dwellings, or Crannogs*. Edinburgh: David Douglas.

Munro, R. 1884a, Megalithic monuments of Holland, and their relation with analogous remains in Northern Europe. *Proceedings of the Society of Antiquaries of Scotland* 18: 19-35.

Munro, R. 1884b, Danish Kjökkenmöddings, their facts and inferences. *Proceedings of the Society of Antiquaries of Scotland* 18: 216-225.

Munro, R. 1890, *The Lake-Dwellings of Europe*. London: Cassell & Company, Limited.

Munro, R. 1899, *Prehistoric Scotland and its Place in European Civilization*. Edinburgh: Blackwood and Sons.

Munro, R. 1905, *Archaeology and False Antiquities*. London: Methuen.

Munro, R. 1921, *Autobiographic Sketch 21st July, 1835 - 18th July, 1920*. Glasgow: Maclehose, Jackson & Co.

Murray, T. 2009, Illustrating 'savagery': Sir John Lubbock and Ernest Griset. *Antiquity* 83: 488-499.

Patton, M. 2007, *Science, Politics and Business in the Work of Sir John Lubbock*. Aldershot: Ashgate.

Piggott, S. 1976, *Ruins in a Landscape: Essays in Antiquarianism*. Edinburgh: Edinburgh University Press.

Rowley-Conwy, P. 2007, *From Genesis to Prehistory: The Archaeological Three Age System and its Contested Reception in Denmark, Britain and Ireland*. Oxford: Oxford University Press.

Ruoff, U. 2004, Lake-dwelling studies in Switzerland since 'Meilen 1854. In: F. Menotti (ed.) *Living on the Lake in Prehistoric Europe: 150 years of Lake Dwelling Research*. London: Routledge, 9-21.

Sherratt, A. 2004, The importance of lake-dwellings in European history. In: F. Menotti (ed.) *Living on the Lake in Prehistoric Europe: 150 years of Lake Dwelling Research*. London: Routledge, 267-275.

Simpson, D. 1964, Sir Daniel Wilson and the *Prehistoric Annals of Scotland*: A Centenary Study. *Proceedings of the Society of Antiquaries of Scotland* 96, 1-8.

Sklenář, K. 1983, *Archaeology in Central Europe: the First 500 Years*. New York: Leicester University Press.

Stocking, G. W. Jr 1971, What's in a Name? The Origins of the Royal Anthropological Institute (1837-71). *Man* 6: 369-390.

Stuart, J. 1866, Notice of the Scotch Crannogs. In: F. Keller *The lake dwellings of Switzerland and other parts of Europe*. Translated into English by J.E. Lee. London: Longmans, 389-392.

Trigger, B. 1992, Daniel Wilson and the Scottish Enlightenment. *Proceedings of the Society of Antiquaries of Scotland* 122: 55-75.

Trigger, B. 2006, *A History of Archaeological Thought* (Second Edition), Cambridge: Cambridge University Press.

Tylor, E. B. 1881, *Anthropology*. London: MacMillan and Co.

Vaughan, W. 1994, *German Romantic Painting*. New Haven and London: Yale University Press.

Weber, K. 2010, Pfahlbauromantik. Urgeschichte in der Malerei des.19. Jahrhundert. In: Badischen Landesmuseum Karlsruhe (eds.) *Jungsteinzeit im Umbruch. Die "Michelsberger Kultur" und Mitteleuropa vor 6000 Jahren.* Darmstadt: Badischen Landesmuseum Karlsruhe, 285-291.

Wilson, D. 1851, *The Archaeology and Prehistoric Annals of Scotland.* Edinburgh: Sutherland and Knox.

Worsaae, J. J. A. 1849, *The Primeval Antiquities of Denmark.* Translated by W.J. Thoms. London: Parker.

Wylie, W. 1860, On Lake-Dwellings of the Early Periods. *Archaeologia* 38: 177-187.

Zimmer, O. 2003, *A Contested Nation: History, Memory and Nationalism in Switzerland 1761-1891.* Cambridge: Cambridge University Press.

Chapter 2

A MAN CHANGED BY DARWIN

David Clarke

Abstract

In a short autobiographical sketch, Robert Munro divided his life into three phases: in his youth there was a struggle for education, his prime was devoted to public duty as a medical practitioner in the west of Scotland and, finally, early retirement led to an extraordinary new career spurred on by a passion for archaeology. While still practising medicine in the west of Scotland, Munro's involvement in the activities of the Ayr and Wigtown Archaeological Association paved the way to excavations of local crannog sites. His scholarly reputation was established in 1882 through the publication of *Ancient Scottish Lake Dwellings*. It was this reputation, as well as recently inherited family wealth, that encouraged him to retire early from the medical practice and devote the rest of his life to the pursuit of archaeology. While his Scottish archaeological interests never waned and he was closely associated with and active in the Society of Antiquaries of Scotland, he spent much time travelling in Europe gathering materials on the then buoyant researches into lacustrine settlements. *The Lake-Dwellings of Europe*, initially delivered as Rhind Lectures in 1888 and published two years later, sealed his reputation as a serious scholar. Subsequently Munro played an important role in British archaeology, either through his involvement with national organisations, for example the British Association for the Advancement of Science, or association with important archaeological projects, such as excavations at Glastonbury. In 1910 Robert Munro endowed a series of lectures at the University of Edinburgh, a tradition which continues to this day.

Key words: Munro, crannogs, lake dwellings

Introduction

Much of this volume is about lake dwellings, an area of study with which Robert Munro's name remains synonymous nearly a century after his death. What I have chosen to do here is to look briefly at the circumstances that brought about this link. Concentrating on this aspect inevitably involves having to ignore other areas that interested Munro. But I do so because I feel that had Munro not established himself as an expert on lake dwellings and had he not become recognised as such across Europe, the opportunities to investigate other areas might well not have been open to him. And equally important, it is not at all clear that without this recognition Munro (Figure 2.1) would have chosen to offer the University the endowment whose centenary we celebrated in the conference that led to this volume.

Figure 2.1 Robert Munro (Munro 1921, frontispiece).

To understand how Munro became *the* expert on lake dwellings, we need to look at his whole life. In doing so, we will see that Munro achieved this position through a series of opportunities that were seized, but not initiated, by him. His was very much a life in three parts. Indeed, as he began the final period of his life, he characterised it in just such a way:

> *I divide my life into three periods, during the first I struggled hard for my education, during the second I served the public to the best of my ability, and for the rest of my life I mean to please myself. (Munro 1921, 33).*

His early life and the accompanying struggle for education was a particularly formative time for Munro. He was born in Assynt on 21 July 1835, the only son of Donald and Catherine Munro. He was the second child in a family of four children. His was a farming family based in the neighbouring parishes of Alness and Kiltearn on the Cromarty Firth. His father, Donald Munro, is first described as a farm servant but subsequently as a farm grieve or manager. He died at Alness in 1907. His mother, Catherine Munro, appears to have died after the 1851 Census but before the introduction of the statutory registration of deaths in 1855.

Curiously, Munro's own *Autobiographic Sketch* provides no useful information about his parents. All we learn is:

> *My mother was descendant of a branch of the Munros of Foulis ... Her people, so far as I knew them, were a tall blond race, with a florid complexion, light eyes, fair hair and aquiline noses. On the other hand, the physical characters of my father's folk were moderate stature, dark hair and eyes, flat noses, long bodies, short limbs and a swarthy complexion.*

And we only learn this because it provides a preface to;

> *Hence I have always regarded myself from the standpoint of ethnology as a pure mongrel, more especially as I retain in my own person some of the physical characteristics of both these types of humanity. Those on the male side, which probably were derived from the Iberian pre-Celtic races, have, however, a decided predominance in my constitution. (Munro 1921, 5-6).*

Even for the early decades of the twentieth century this seems a very detached presentation of his parents. Indeed, of his sisters he tells us nothing at all. Perhaps though, this is just a consequence of the circumstances surrounding the creation of the *Autobiographic Sketch*. John Horne, in a preface to the volume, tells us that it "was written the year before he passed away while suffering from indifferent health" (Munro 1921, vi). It was, says George Macdonald, "the last piece of work to which he set his hand" – "a short sketch of his own life, which was composed for the information of his closest friends, and which has since been printed for private circulation" (1921, 163). These comments suggest that Munro probably focussed on matters he believed to be of most interest to his select group of readers and that he may not have written in the expectation of publication. Whatever the motivation or constraints affecting its production and notwithstanding that it is the work of an old and ill man, it does provide many important insights into his attitudes and interests.

The struggle for education

Munro received his early education at the Free Church school in the parish of Kiltearn. From there he went on to spend two years at the Royal Academy at Tain, "one of the leading educational institutions in the North of Scotland". He was so successful there, winning many prizes that "my parents actually began to entertain the idea of my going to college – of course as a preliminary step to the ministry" (Munro 1921, 6). The principal barrier to achieving this ambition was a lack of money. Munro overcame this difficulty by turning to teaching. Accepting an initial invitation from a country schoolmaster to act as his replacement while he attended college, Munro quickly realised that teaching offered a source of "finance and congenial occupation". The Disruption of the Church of Scotland in 1843 had led to the establishment of two schools in each parish instead of the previous one. Teachers were in short supply and unqualified individuals, like Munro, found employment easy to obtain. "Accordingly, the next dozen years of my life were devoted to public and private teaching, during which I found time to attend the arts classes in the University of Edinburgh, where I graduated as MA in 1860" (Munro 1921, 7).

The crucial event of this period was the appearance in 1859, before Munro's graduation, of Charles Darwin's *The Origin of Species* with its suggestion that the natural processes affecting plants and animals also applied to humans. From boyhood, Munro had been interested in science, particularly geology. He read Darwin's book and was totally convinced by its arguments. This was a fundamental challenge to all of his plans. For it was "to change the whole tenor and prospects of my future life" by ending the idea of ministry in the Free Church:

> *I considered it dishonest to become a member of a profession in which I could not publicly hold and teach the Darwinian doctrines without making myself liable to be tried by the Church Courts*

> *for heterodoxy. ... As I could not summon sufficient hypocrisy to cross this Rubicon by adopting the Church side of the problem, the practical question I had to face was whether I should continue on the somewhat uncertain fringe of education and literature, or join the medical profession.* (Munro 1921, 7-10).

He did not rush to make a decision. Instead he took a post as a tutor "to a young gentleman of great ability who, owing to a delicate constitution, was unable to attend a University to complete his education". This second involvement in teaching convinced him that medicine would be "more congenial to my quasi-scientific tastes". So, in 1862 he enrolled again at Edinburgh University, this time to study medicine (Munro 1921, 10). His study though did not follow the usual course. After two years, he took time out to accompany an ill friend and fellow student spending a winter on the Riviera. There, on walks with his friend, he found the geology particularly interesting. This seems to have been the first experience that Munro had of travelling abroad, something that became such a feature of the final phase of his life. He resumed his studies in 1865 and "completed them by taking the degrees of C.M. and M.B. in 1867, and M.D. a few years later" (Munro 1921, 12).

A life of public service

Following graduation his first appointment was as assistant to Dr Lawrence who had a large practice among the mining communities of Cumnock. The change from university life was considerable:

> *The sudden transition from a scholastic atmosphere and the teaching of medical science in lecture rooms and well-equipped hospitals to the practice of the healing art among a mining population was to me like coming into a new world. Therapeutic theories and book-learning had to be tested by action there and then. Sometimes the setting of a broken bone had to be done under the most primitive circumstances, bandages, splints, and dressing being improvised from such materials as could be procured in a humble cottage.* (Munro 1921, 15-16).

Early in his time in Ayrshire he made the acquaintance of Dr James Aitken who had a well-established practice in Kilmarnock. Dr Aitken's age and health had encouraged him to consider easing himself into retirement with Munro taking over. But before they could come to an agreement Munro was asked to accompany the son of Archibald Finnie on the Victorian equivalent of the Grand Tour. With his appetite for travel whetted by his previous visit to the Riviera, it was an offer Munro could not decline:

> *I accepted the offer, on condition that our travels were to be of an informatory and semi-scientific character, comprising, besides the usual natural scenery, visits to famous monuments of antiquity, museums, art galleries, etc. (Munro 1921, 18).*

Starting in November 1868, the pair visited Paris, Bordeaux, Marseilles, Genoa, Milan, Florence, Rome, Naples, Messina, Syracuse, Malta, Egypt and the Nile up to the first cataract, Jaffa, Jerusalem, Hebron, the Dead Sea, Jericho, Damascus, Baalbeck, Athens, Constantinople, Varna, Rustchuk (the modern Ruse), Budapest, Vienna and home via Munich and the Rhine. The trip resulted in Munro's first book, *Notes on a Tour in the East* (1875) based on lectures he had given in Kilmarnock.

Back in Ayrshire, he immediately struck an agreement with Dr Aitken. He moved in to Dr Aitken's town house and "soon became possessed of a large and lucrative practice". Munro rapidly became a key member of Ayrshire, and particularly Kilmarnock, society. In part this was aided by his involvement with the Philosophical Institution. He lectured regularly on a wide range of subjects. These were mainly on science but also included a course of lectures on his travels. He served several terms as President. Interestingly, none of his lectures at this time seem to have been concerned with archaeology.

On 6 Sept 1875, by now a successful Kilmarnock doctor, he married Anna Taylor, "an event of great and lasting importance to my domestic comfort and future well-being". The marriage lasted thirty-two years until Anna's death in 1907 and "the acme of domestic happiness was realized to its full extent". Her contribution was significant: "she took part in all my archaeological studies and wanderings, and did most of the drawings illustrating my book on *The Lake-Dwellings of Europe*" (Munro 1921, 37). Equally important though, it was through Anna that Munro gained access to the wealth that enabled him to give up medicine.

The crucial event that ensured Munro's interest in archaeology took place on 19 October 1877. A meeting, chaired by the Earl of Stair, Lord Lieutenant of the county, was held at Ayr with the intention 'to form an Archaeological Association for Ayrshire and Wigtonshire' (Cochran-Patrick 1878, xvii-xviii). Munro was among the 300 members who signed up to join the Association that had wide-ranging interests with a strong historical and records component. The Archaeological section wanted to be active and to engage in fieldwork. Attention turned to the crannog at Lochlee.

Earlier drainage of the site had revealed timbers and two canoes. The drainers involved in the work frequented the shop of James Brown, a provision merchant at Tarbolton. Brown mentioned the discoveries to several local gentlemen who he thought would be interested but they did nothing. In 1878 renewed drainage works revived Brown's interest. He wrote to a gentleman at Ayr but again failed to elicit any response. In the apparent absence of local interest, he wrote to Joseph Anderson at the National Museum. Anderson was certainly interested and wrote to Cochran-Patrick, the Secretary of the newly formed Ayr and Wigtown Archaeological Association. Cochran-Patrick visited the site and, recognising its importance, wrote to J H Turner, the Duke of Portland's factor, advocating the value of an excavation. Meanwhile, Turner has told Munro about the discoveries (Munro 1882b, 68-71). Munro's interest in lake dwelling material had already been aroused by "a holiday visit to some of the Continental museums containing lacustrine relics, especially that at Zurich" which had taken place just before the rediscovery of the crannog at Lochlee (Munro 1921, 27-28). With the support of Cochran-Patrick and the Ayr and Wigtown Archaeological Association excavations started in October 1878 and concluded in 1879. Part way through they lost

> ... the active services of Mr Cochran-Patrick, who hitherto took notes and sketches of each day's proceedings. In consequence of his absence, owing to a protracted illness, and the inability of the other gentlemen to attend, this duty now fell on my inexperienced shoulders; and in giving this short account of the work, I have only to say that, however imperfectly done, I have endeavoured during very inclement weather, to procure as correct and faithful a record of the explorations as possible. (Munro 1882b, 76-77).

It is not clear whether Cochran-Patrick had always envisaged Munro taking over the work of writing up the excavations or whether this came about only because of his illness. Munro noted that "being resident in Kilmarnock, the duty of taking charge of the relics which turned up from day to day at Lochlee, while the excavations were in progress, was entrusted to me" (1921, 28).

What does seem clear is that Munro, by now well established in his medical practice at Kilmarnock, was looking for an area of study in which he might hope to make a mark. By this period, it was unlikely that a country doctor would do so in laboratory-based science or in medicine. Munro's account of his boyhood is largely described in terms of outdoor activities and their appeal seems to have stayed with him throughout his life. Archaeology appears to have caught Munro's interest as much through circumstance as the result of any conscious deliberation. He could just as easily have chosen geology or natural history with a different turn of events. Munro was opportunistic enough to latch on to whatever the area provided. Having decided on archaeology the key archaeological sites in Ayrshire were crannogs.

The involvement of Joseph Anderson, however indirect, was clearly important in encouraging Munro's interest in archaeology. His influence, having been alerted to the crannog at Lochlee, was undoubtedly sufficient to bring in Cochran-Patrick and the Ayr and Wigtown Archaeological Association. That initiative was key in bringing Cochran-Patrick and Munro together. But Anderson played a further role:

> *The task of describing so many novel relics of bygone days made me a frequent visitor to the Museum of National Antiquities in Edinburgh, for the purpose of comparing the newly discovered objects with analogous relics in that museum. Thus I made the acquaintance of the late Dr Joseph Anderson, Curator of that museum, whose unrivalled knowledge of Scottish Archaeology was of great assistance to me in classifying the Lochlee relics. (Munro 1921, 28).*

These trips and the consequent meetings with Anderson were probably crucial in ensuring Munro's election as a Fellow of the Society of Antiquaries of Scotland in 1879.

In many ways Cochran-Patrick and Munro needed each other. Cochran-Patrick was anxious to encourage archaeological activity in south-west Scotland, particularly with the framework of the newly created Association. Munro had the energy and commitment to be a key figure in such developments. The work at Lochlee was the start of an important relationship and Cochran-Patrick was a strong influence on Munro in the early years of his burgeoning interest in archaeology. Cochran-Patrick was a firm believer in induction; in the first volume of the *Archaeological and Historical Collections relating to the counties of Ayr and Wigton*, he wrote,

> *The authors of the various papers in the present volume have confined themselves to giving accurate descriptions and carefully ascertained facts, believing that at the present time archaeological science will be best served by local societies permanently recording, in an authentic and reliable shape, the various objects of antiquity belonging to their district. (Cochran-Patrick 1878, xix).*

Munro seems to have kept Cochran-Patrick's belief in the importance of 'giving accurate descriptions and carefully ascertained facts' as his guiding principle.

As he prepared the work at Lochlee for publication Munro realised that lake dwellings in Britain were a subject ripe for investigation. "The favourable reception given to [the report on the excavations at Lochlee] was", he felt, "partly the means of bringing to light a number of other crannogs in the South-West of Scotland, some of which were excavated under the guidance of the same [Ayr and Wigtown Archaeological] Association" (Munro 1921, 29). Among these were the important sites at Buiston and Lochspouts. Although Munro noted that "the reports on the excavations of both these crannogs also fell to my pen" (1921, 29), it is unclear what his role was in the work. At Buiston, the parish schoolmaster, Duncan McNaught, had discovered the site and he was subsequently to claim that he excavated it together with Cochran-Patrick without making any mention of Munro (Crone 2000, 11-12). Munro's own account is interesting in that he does not claim to have been present when the excavations began, saying only,

> *By general consent, at least nem. con., I was appointed custodier of the relics; and now, acting on the old saying that possession is nine points of the law, I have assumed the role of historian. (Munro 1882b, 193).*

Nevertheless, it seems likely that Munro was a regular visitor to the site but it would be wrong to characterise him as the Director; by all accounts Cochran-Patrick was still an important figure. Certainly, recording techniques had improved since Lochlee. The Buiston report is illustrated with figures drawn from photographs by a Mr Lawrie. And the recent excavator of Buiston notes that "the records and plan Munro published are ... sufficiently accurate and detailed to enable comparisons with results of the recent excavations" (Crone 2000, 12).

At the same time as he was preparing these excavation reports for publication, he began a survey of earlier discoveries. He published initially in articles in the *Archaeological and Historical Collections relating to the counties of Ayr and Wigton* (Munro 1880; 1882a). But this, of course, was just a local journal with a distribution limited to not much more than the 300 members of the Association. Even the reading of the Lochlee report at a meeting of the Society of Antiquaries of Scotland in March 1879 would not have done much more than mark Munro out as a country doctor with serious antiquarian interests. What really transformed his reputation was the publication of *Ancient Scottish Lake Dwellings* in 1882. In his preface, Munro explained how it had come about:

> *In publishing this work few prefatory remarks are required, beyond an explanation of the circumstances which led to its assuming the present form. The primary object contemplated was to place before general readers a record of some remarkable discoveries made in the south-west of Scotland, in a department of Archaeology hitherto*

little known, and of which carefully prepared reports have already appeared in the second and third volumes of the Collections of the Ayrshire and Wigtownshire Archaeological Association.

As it was at the instigation of R W Cochran-Patrick, Esq, MP, that the explorations which led to these discoveries were originally undertaken, so it was also with him that the proposal to issue these reports in a handy volume originated. It occurred, however, to me, that, considering how little had been known of Scottish Lake-dwellings in general, and even this little was only accessible to the members of a few learned Societies, it would be a more satisfactory undertaking to incorporate with the original reports, a résumé of the observations made by previous writers and explorers, so as to present to the public a complete compendium, as it were, of the whole subject. (Munro 1882b, v-vi).

Later in the preface, Munro makes clear that Cochran-Patrick had done much more than just suggest the volume:

To R W Cochran-Patrick, Esq., LL.D., F.S.A., M.P., I am under the deepest obligations for valuable advice and assistance received in all stages of the researches – explorations, engravings, reports, etc., - all being subject to his critical supervision. For the knowledge which he thus so freely and unselfishly placed at my disposal, as well as for much encouragement kindly given during the progress of the entire work, I now beg to express my warmest thanks. (Munro 1882b, vii).

David Douglas, the Edinburgh publisher, who also produced the *Archaeological and Historical Collections relating to the counties of Ayr and Wigton*, published it. And notwithstanding his plea for indulgence over shortcomings because "it is the result of the occupation of such scraps of time as could be spared during the last two or three years from the active duties of a busy professional life", the book established an immediate reputation for him, something that would have taken much longer to garner through publication in the journals of learned societies. The book was, he noted, "received with much commendation by the antiquarian press, as well as by private critics" (Munro 1921, 30).

Pleasing himself

It was, I believe, the growing reputation occasioned by the publication of *Ancient Scottish Lake Dwellings* that helped Munro to make the decisions that led to the third period of his life, a time, as he put it, "to please myself". Of course, a growing reputation as a Scottish archaeologist would not in itself have provided adequate grounds for a decision to give up his medical practice soon after his fiftieth birthday in 1885. What it did do, though, was to show him that he could make an important contribution in an area unrelated to medicine. He was clearly finding the practice of medicine an increasingly routine affair and suffering from what we would now probably describe as a stress-related illness. Yet it had been sufficiently rewarding financially for him to have sizeable savings. But the key factor in enabling Munro's retirement had been death of his father-in-law, William Taylor, in 1879. Munro "became a shareholder in two small local engineering companies of which he [Mr Taylor] was one of the financial promoters". They expanded rapidly and frequently required additional capital. Munro "took up [his] *pro rata* shares in every increase of fresh capital, and so became ultimately one of the largest shareholders". The companies were merged in 1899. From an initial combined value of £30,000, they had grown to be worth £425,000 when Munro resigned as a Director in 1917. It was the wealth provided by the success of this company that underpinned his decision to please himself (Munro 1921, 78-80).

Having taken this decision in the full expectation of travelling, Munro needed to consider what else he might do:

> *In looking around as to what branch of science I could best cultivate as a hobby, during our contemplated peripatetic wanderings, there could be no doubt that anthropology was the most suitable to my quasi-scientific attainments. Also that the branch of this science, which demanded some immediate elucidation, was an epitomised survey of lake-dwelling researches in Europe. the antiquities brought to light by the explorations of the Swiss Lake-Dwellings, then indiscriminately stored in the museums of Western Europe, had yet to be correlated with the industrial objects of present-day civilization. Keller's book on the subject [1866; 1878] consisted of disconnected monographs on different stations, without giving any idea of the chronological and relative value of the remains illustrated. Hence the idea occurred to me that a brief review of lacustrine research was a desirable object, and a subject which I might undertake with some prospect of success. (Munro 1921. 33-34).*

The remarks here about linking past and modern objects are, of course, reflecting the ideas of Pitt-Rivers and others. It is unclear, but likely, that Munro had already met Pitt-Rivers by this time.

Munro went first to Rome in January 1886 on account of his health. There he recuperated rapidly from his illness and consequently had sufficient time and inclination to study lake dwelling material from the Po Valley. A key part of this study was provided by his wife's sketches..

On his return to Scotland in 1886 he found awaiting him an invitation from the Society of Antiquaries of Scotland to give the Rhind Lectures for 1888 on the Lake Dwellings of Europe. This invitation he "accepted with less hesitation, seeing that by this time [he] had gained some practical assurance of being able to bring the widely scattered materials of lacustrine research into something like systematic order" (Munro 1921, 38).

In preparation he armed himself with letters of introduction from the President and Councillors of both the Society of Antiquaries of Scotland and the Royal Anthropological Institute as well as notable individuals including John Evans and A W Franks. These letters informed their recipients that Munro "was especially interested in Lake-dwelling Research, being already the author of a standard work on that subject" (Munro 1921, 34). He and his wife made repeated visits to museums and private collections at home and abroad – 51 museums in 9 countries; 18 private collections in 7 countries (Munro 1890, x-xi).

> *Our visits to the Continent, which seldom exceeded two or three months at a time, were intercalated with similar periods of quiet residence somewhere in Britain, often in the vicinity of the British Museum, so as to have the benefit of its library in arranging our notes. (Munro 1921, 40).*

The lectures were duly delivered in 1888 and the resulting volume, *The Lake-dwellings of Europe*, was published in 1890 by Cassell & Co, a publisher with offices in London, Paris and Melbourne. The delay between lectures and book was in part occasioned by the production of the illustrations.

> *Our pencil drawings had to be redrawn in sepia, often on a different scale, and grouped on sheets according to the provenance of the relics – all of which was done by my wife. These sheets were then sent to Vienna, where blocks were made from them of the proper size for printing in the text. (Munro 1921, 44-45).*

Munro was now established as the senior figure. The book, translated by Paul Rodet, was published in a French edition in 1908 (Munro 1890; 1908).

As a result Munro was now able to use his reputation to good effect. In 1892 he visited the newly discovered site at Glastonbury.

> *Just as I was leaving Glastonbury, Mr Bulleid incidentally mentioned that he had sent a short account of the discovery of the lake-village to a London weekly journal, which occasionally lends*

its columns to archaeological subjects, but that it was declined. [Was this perhaps the Illustrated London News?]. As an appeal to the public was, at the time, the only feasible means of procuring funds for continuing the excavations, publicity of the exceptionally interesting character of this trouvaille, became an urgent necessity. So, on my return to Edinburgh, I sent a note to the editor of The Times, briefly mentioning what I had seen at Glastonbury, and offering to contribute a descriptive notice of the discovery to his paper. The offer was accepted, and the communication, which appeared in The Times of Oct 24, 1892, at once disseminated precise information as to the nature and exceptional importance of the Glastonbury Lake-village throughout the civilised world. (Munro 1911, 7).

Subsequently, Munro played a key role in securing funding for the work from the British Association for the Advancement of Science.

Being President-elect of the Anthropological section of the British Association for 1893, I had no difficulty in persuading the local committee at Glastonbury to send a selected assortment of the village relics for exhibition at the Association meeting to be held at Nottingham. The recommendation was carried out in grand style, the selection of relics being large and varied, and well displayed in appropriate cases. The gratifying result was that a grant of £40 was made by the excavation fund, under the charge of the following committee: Dr. R. Munro (Chairman), Mr. A. Bulleid (Secretary), Professor Boyd Dawkins, General Pitt-Rivers and Sir John Evans, with power to add to their number. (Munro 1921, 54-55).

Later still, after the work at Glastonbury had been suspended but not completed, Munro intervened again. The excavations became

the subject of a post-prandial conversation between Mr W Howard Bell, FSA, and myself [at the Worcester Congress of the Archaeological Institute in July 1906]. On learning how matters stood, Mr Bell generously offered to pay all the additional expenses requisite to complete the excavations. (Munro 1911, 9).

As a result of all this effort, Munro was invited to contribute an introductory chapter to the final report (Munro 1911).

Throughout the first half of his retirement Munro and his wife were inveterate travellers. Their journeys included a round-the-world trip that took in en route the British Association meeting at Toronto in 1897. Gradually though, "the charm of travelling in search of interesting monuments, whether ancient or modern, began to wane" (Munro 1921, 71). They had seen most of the monuments of Western Europe and perhaps more important they were feeling the effects of age. Munro had moved to Manor Place in Edinburgh in 1890 and it remained his main home until 1903 when he started to live more and more at Largs enabling him and his wife "to participate in the more sedentary amenities of a country life" (Munro 1921, 71). This country life replaced the travels of earlier years.

But for his travelling and the expansion of interests that accompanied it, Munro's commitment remained always centred on Scotland. He became very active in the Society of Antiquaries of Scotland. The same year as he delivered the Rhind Lectures, 1888, he became one of the Secretaries of the Society, a post he retained until 1899. It is in this role that he figures in the stained glass window in the present Scottish National Portrait building that illustrates the Council and Officers of the Society at the time of the opening of the Museum half of the building (Clarke 1990). He was a member of Council in 189-1902 and Vice President from 1902 to 1905.

As such he became a member of the Committee that oversaw fieldwork, particularly the extensive series of Roman excavations that the Society was undertaking at this time (Figure 2.3). He also took a keen interest in other excavations more obviously linked to

Figure 2.2 Munro and others visiting the excavations at Hyndford Crannog, 15 November 1898 (author's private archive).

Figure 2.3 Excavations at Ardoch: "Returning to Plate I, to get some idea of the north-east angle, we see Mr Ely with his 10-foot rod standing behind the outer ridge of the trenches, with the beginning of the additional ridge of the north face on his left, Behind him Mr Cunningham stands on the platform ..., from which rises the flanking rampart of the outer ravelin, on which sits Dr Munro" (Christison et al. 1898, 417).

his own interests, for example the investigation of the crannog at Hyndford, Lanarkshire, undertaken by Andrew Smith (Figure 2.2). Munro published this work (1899). Not surprisingly, an interest in crannogs remained with Munro throughout his life. "The last of the practical researches in Scottish archaeology," he wrote, "in which I took a part was a visit of inspection to the crannog in the Loch of Kinellan in Ross-shire, which was then being investigated under a small grant from the Carnegie Research Fund made to myself" (Munro 1921, 75).

This close involvement with a wide range of Scottish fieldwork was particularly important. Munro was a Vice President of the Society of Antiquaries of Scotland when John Abercromby resigned as a Secretary to the Society and withdrew from providing financial support for the Society's excavations. It was this quarrel that ultimately prompted Abercromby to endow the Abercromby Chair of Archaeology in the University of Edinburgh (Piggott & Robertson 1977, item 90). Munro would certainly have been privy to all the details of this dispute and he may well have known of Abercromby's intentions long before they became reality. It may be that his bequest to the University is in part to be read as endorsing Abercromby's position.

It is interesting that as first interpreted the Munro Lectureship involved 10 lectures by a single individual. It is reasonable to see this endowment as Munro's last archaeological act of any significance. The death of his wife in 1907 had been a severe blow leaving him "lonely and helpless at the entrance to the valley of the shadow of death" (Munro 1921, 72). Macdonald in his obituary makes an interesting remark:

> *During the next year or two [after the establishment of the lectureship] he watched with all a parent's solicitude the development of the experiment he had initiated. (Macdonald 1921, 163).*

It gives, I think, an intimation of what the Lectures meant to Munro. He was childless and certainly smart enough to know that his academic work could not stand unchallenged in the future. The endowment is him looking to his future in the scholarly world he so much enjoyed and with it the maintenance of name that we normally associate with children.

References

Christison, D. et al. 1898, Account of the excavation of the Roman station at Ardoch, Perthshire undertaken by the Society of Antiquaries of Scotland in 1896-97. *Proceedings of the Society of Antiquaries of Scotland* 32: 399-476.

Clarke, D. V. 1990, The National Museums' stained-glass window. *Proceedings of the Society of Antiquaries of Scotland* 120: 201-24.

Cochran-Patrick, R. W. 1878, Preface. *Archaeological and Historical Collections relating to the counties of Ayr and Wigton* 1: xvi-xxii.

Crone, A. 2000, *The History of a Scottish Lowland Crannog: Excavations at Buiston, Ayrshire 1989-90*. Edinburgh: Scottish Trust for Archaeological Research.

Keller, F. 1866, *The Lake-Dwellings of Switzerland and other parts of Europe*. London: Longmans, Green & Co.

Keller, F. 1878, *The Lake-Dwellings of Switzerland and other parts of Europe*. 2nd edition. 2 volumes. London: Longmans, Green & Co.

Macdonald, G. 1921, Obituary notice: Robert Munro, MA, MD, LLD. *Proceedings of the Royal Society of Edinburgh* 41(2): 158-69.

Munro, R. 1875, *Notes on a Tour in the East*. Kilmarnock: T Stevenson.

Munro, R. 1880, Ayrshire crannogs. *Archaeological and Historical Collections relating to the counties of Ayr and Wigton* 2: 17-88.

Munro, R. 1882a, Ayrshire crannogs (second notice). *Archaeological and Historical Collections relating to the counties of Ayr and Wigton* 3: 1-51.

Munro, R. 1882b, *Ancient Scottish Lake-Dwellings or crannogs, with a supplementary chapter on Remains of Lake-Dwellings in England*. Edinburgh: David Douglas.

Munro, R. 1890, *The Lake-Dwellings of Europe*. London: Cassell & Co.

Munro, R. 1899, Notes on a crannog at Hyndland, near Lanark, recently excavated by Andrew Smith. *Proceedings of the Society of Antiquaries of Scotland* 33: 373-87.

Munro, R. 1908, *Les stations lacustres d'Europe aux âges dela pierre et du bronze*. Paris: Librairie C Reinwald.

Munro, R. 1911, Introductory chapter. In: A. Bulleid and H. St. George Gray, *The Glastonbury Lake Village: a full Description of the Excavations and the Relics discovered, 1892-1907.* vol 1 Glastonbury Antiquarian Society, 1-35.

Munro, R. 1921, *Robert Munro, M.A., M.D., LLD: Autobiographic Sketch*. Glasgow: MacLehose, Jackson & Co.

Piggott, S. and Robertson, M. 1977, *Three Centuries of Scottish Archaeology*. Edinburgh: Edinburgh University Press.

Chapter 3

RESEARCH ON NEOLITHIC AND EARLY BRONZE AGE WETLAND SITES ON THE NORTH EUROPEAN PLAIN

Johannes Müller[1]

Abstract

Despite intensive research for nearly one hundred years in wetland areas of the north European plain, Neolithic and Early Bronze Age domestic sites are infrequent. This is due to the ecological setting of lakes and shores in north-central Europe which is quite different from that of the circum-Alpine area. Nevertheless, in the case of sites with settlement features in water-logged conditions, the recovered data is of high quality, adding in many aspects to the evidence from dry soil areas. Recently investigated sites from Holstein, Germany, and from Greater Poland provide examples discussed in this paper.

Key words: wetland settlements, wetland environments, fortifications, Neolithic, Bronze Age, Bad Oldesloe-Wolkenwehe, Bruszczewo, Oldenburg Dannau, Oldenburger Graben.

Research history and the wetland archives

Since the nineteenth century research of water-logged sites or *Pfahlbauten* in Central Europe is mainly linked to the *Pfahlbauforschung* in the circum-Alpine region. After the dramatic discoveries of Ferdinand Keller in 1854 it soon became clear that

---

[1] Institut für Ur- und Frühgeschichte, Christian-Albrechts-Universität, D-24118 Kiel, Germany

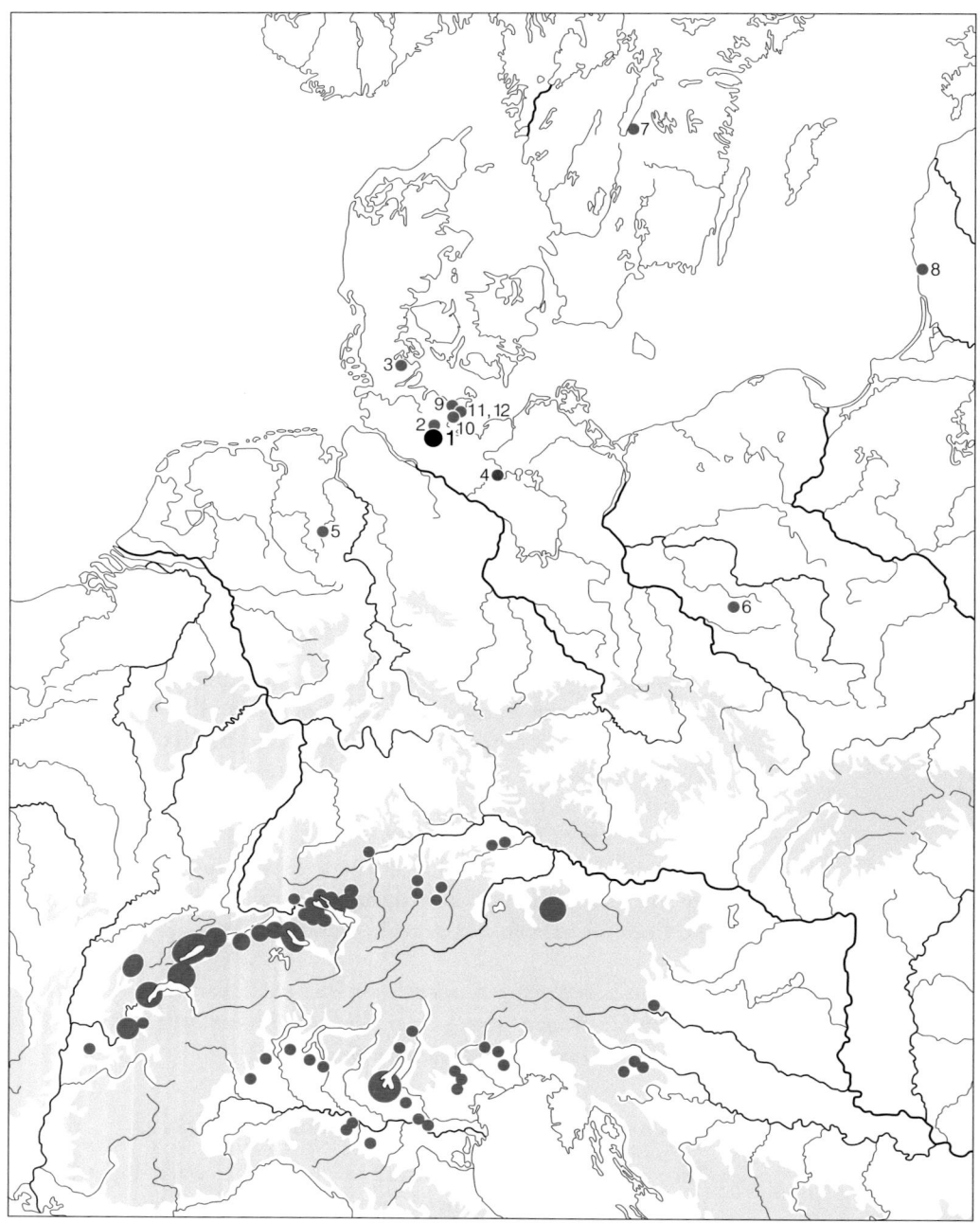

Figure 3.1 Neolithic and Early Bronze Age wetland settlements in Central Europe. 1 Bad Oldesloe-Wolkenwehe, 2 Seedorf-Heidmoor, 3 Satrup peat bog sites, 4 Parchim-Löddigsee, 5 Dümmer, 6 Bruszczewo, 7 Alvastra, 8 Svontoji, 9 Wangels, 10 Neustadt, 11 Grube-Rosenhof, 12 Grube-Rosenfelde, 13 Wangels LA 77. Main sites discussed in the text are in italics (source: Hartz et al. 2004/2005 (2007), 8, Fig. 1); the many sites of the circum-Alpine region are mapped after Schlichtherle 1997.

on the shores of the Alpine and pre-Alpine lakes, wooden posts and cultural layers of many Neolithic and Bronze Age sites were preserved (Schlichtherle, 1997; Figure 3.1).

The Alpine Lakes are bound to the water regime of the glaciers and thus linked to different cyclical climatic effects. The annual cycle leads to severe fluctuations in water level, in some cases by several metres. Furthermore, cosmic solar activities with their own middle and long-term cycles seem to have an influence on the main trends of glacier melting and thus on water levels in the lakes (Magny et al. 2005). Thus during the annual cycle the lake shores could be under water in the summer, and above in the winter. Furthermore the mid- and long-term cycles, resulting in higher and lower lake-water levels, influence the accessibility of the shores with different effects over the centuries. In general high lake-levels are typical of Mesolithic times while in the middle Neolithic, and for many centuries afterwards, the lake shores are accessible for domestic activities.

With the exception of severe breaks (e.g. during the Beaker times), pile dwellings are chronologically concentrated between 4300-1600 cal BC and again between 1100-800 cal BC (e.g. Billamboz 2005). The extraordinary wetland archives for these time periods, were uncovered during the last 150 years of circum-Alpine archaeological research. In consequence chronologies are available which, in many projects, are on a yearly and sometimes even seasonal scale. The quality of information about economy, architecture and disposal behaviour - to mention only some aspects - is excellent. Nevertheless, real settlement processes are still difficult to disentangle: while research has concentrated on these fascinating archives at recent or prehistoric lake shores, that of the hinterland was neglected (Ebersbach 2003). In consequence, it is still unclear whether or not whole villages, small groups or individuals were moving from the shore to the hinterland settlements, whether during the times of the rising lake levels whole settlements were dismantled and relocated to higher altitudes, or whether lake sites were linked to hinterland sites at all. But beside these research tasks, which could also be solved by concentrating on surveys of dry soils and excavations of domestic sites in poor dry soils in the circum-Alpine region, the pile-dwelling archaeology is one of the most successful stories of archaeology worldwide.

In contrast to environmental conditions of the circum-Alpine region, lake (and sea) history in the north European plain is quite different. Despite huge peaty areas and despite the great length of lake (and sea) shorelines, the kind of water-level changes which affect the Alpine lake shores are not found in North-Central Europe (Dörfler and Müller 2008). In general the north European peat bogs started their growth much later than during the Neolithic or Early Bronze Age (Behre 2004, Behre and Kucan 1994). Lake water level changes were never bound to anything like the Alpine glaciers. Clear patterns of flooding or not flooding the lake shores, and therefore of their usefulness for domestic activities, did not exist. In consequence, possible advantages for prehistoric settlers on the lake shores, for example tree- and shrub-free areas which have been reconstructed for the circum-Alpine lakes, did not exist in such a manner in North Germany.

Nevertheless, and probably due to advantageous water supplies or communication routes, prehistoric settlements were also placed on North-Central European islands, peninsulas of lakes close to the sea shores. If research was carried out on such, mostly elevated, topographical places then domestic structures were discovered at nearly every lake on the north European plain. Nevertheless, the topographical situation is quite different to southern Central

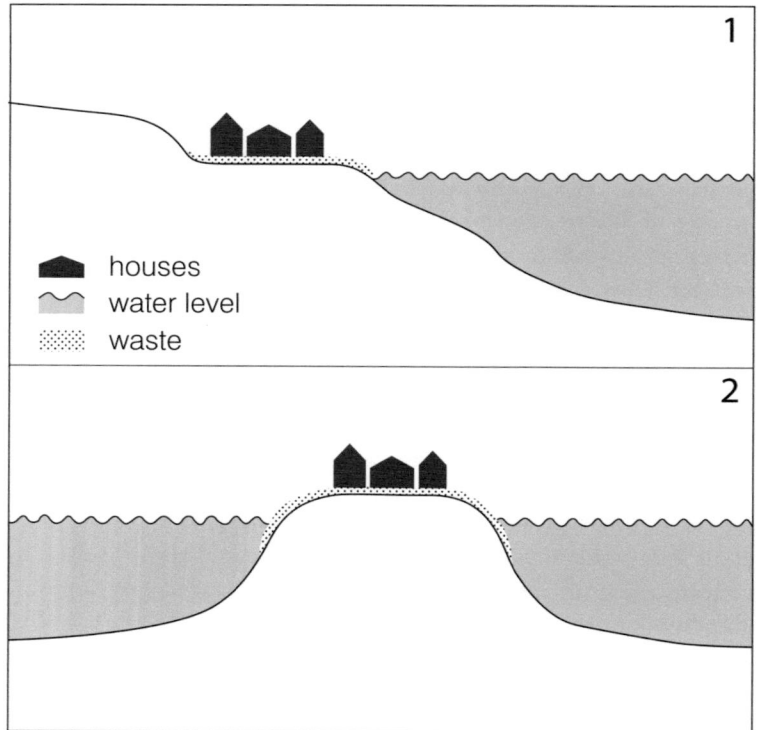

Figure 3.2 Different topographical settings of circum-Alpine pile dwellings (1) and wetland sites of the North European plain (2). The shores of the circum-Alpine lakes are often flooded and preserve domestic structures under wet conditions. The elevated position of the North European sites on islands results in wet preservation only at the edge of the settlements and the waste areas close to the shore (graphics: Ines Rees, Kiel).

Europe: a large lake shore which was subject to annual high waters, in general does not exist (Figure 3.2). We are dealing with *Holme*, sandy islands or peninsulas, formed mainly under peri-glacial conditions after the last glaciation. They are characterised by slopes around the core elevation, created by aquatic or wind erosion, for example in glacial river systems. While there is a good chance of finding prehistoric domestic remains on the elevated area of these islands and peninsulas under dry conditions, the probability of water-logged domestic structures is rather small.

After first discoveries of pit dwellings in the Alpine regions, different research approaches were applied in North-Central European countries to recover similar features. It was the German archaeologist Hans Reinerth (incidentally, deeply involved in fascist rule and promoting fascist ideology in German archaeology before and during the Third Reich) who used his research infrastructure for huge projects in water-logged areas (Reinerth, 1939, Kossian, 2007). Beside his important discoveries in and near the South German Lake Federsee, he was able to locate the then only known area on the north European plain, where waterlogged houses and sites were discovered (Figure 3.1). In the peaty surroundings of Lake Dümmer, near Hannover, the especially flat location at the confluence of the Hunte is an exception to many northern lake environments. On the river fringes, a couple of domestic sites were found under water-logged conditions. Within these conditions Reinerth excavated the Neolithic site of *Hunte Dorf* 1, with Funnel Beaker culture and Single Grave culture remains. He applied, for the first time, a wide range of scientific methods and was able to acquire a lot of information about human-environment relations. The excavated sites were in a good state of preservation but, after the Second World War - mainly because of Reinerth's involvement in Nazi archaeology - research never really started again in this area. It is to the credit of Kossian that he re-examined the old documentation and disentangled the settlement structure of the site after re-evaluation (Kossian, 2007). Until now, no other Neolithic domestic site of such quality has been discovered (Figure 3.3). Since then, only smaller test excavations took place in this area. No real domestic structures, similar to those that Reinerth excavated beside Hunte 1, have been discovered. In contrast, the results of drainage were visible in the deterioration of the condition of the remains. In future, it is necessary to commence a new research project to check, and perhaps recover, an archive which seems to be partly comparable to the one in the Alpine area. During the last decades, beside the question of domestic sites, a lot of Neolithic and Bronze Age trackways were discovered and

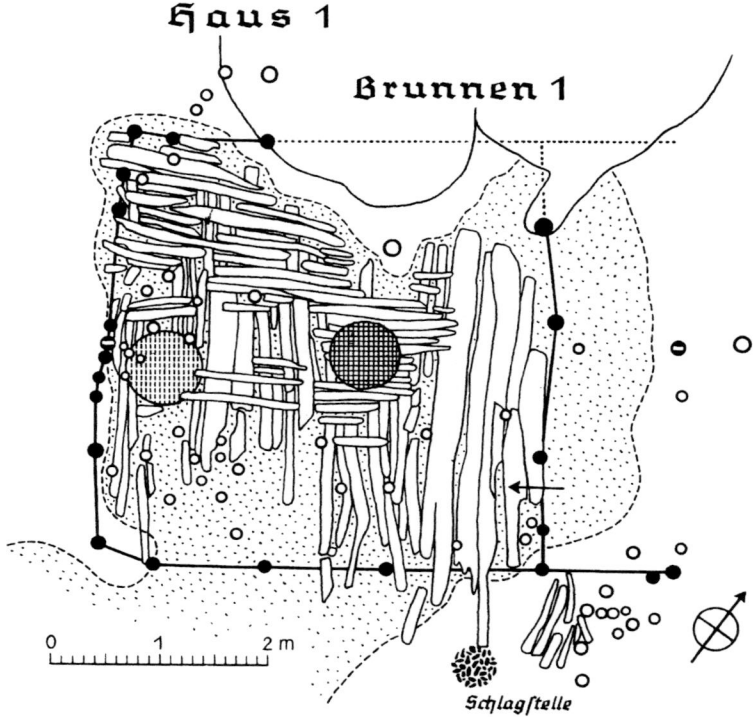

Figure 3.3 "House 1" of the Late Funnel Beaker/Early Single Grave culture site Hunte 1 on the Dümmer (Kossian 2007, 77, Fig. 38). Despite problematic interpretations of other features on the site by Reinerth, for the time being this is the best-preserved house structure of the Neolithic on the north European plain.

recorded in a huge rescue research effort by the Landesdenkmalamt Niedersachsen (Burmeister 2004).

One decade after Reinerth's investigations at the Dümmer, Schwabedissen started his research programme in the wet areas in North Germany. He was able to identify, mainly in Schleswig and Holstein, many sites in peaty areas, some of which he excavated on a large scale (Schwabedissen 1940, 1951, 1953). Beside the Mesolithic sites, and earliest Neolithic layers on the Mesolithic sites, he was able to identify Neolithic domestic remains of the Funnel Beaker and Single Grave cultures at four sites in Schleswig-Holstein. Recently, different research projects within the Priority Program "Early Monumentality and Social Differentiation" began with re-excavations of such places, which were not documented properly by Schwabedissen (Müller 2011). Further research was carried out by Sönke Hartz at the mainly Mesolithic underwater sea site of Neustadt, near the Baltic shore (Hartz et al. 2000) (Figure 3.1). The latest phase on this site is earliest Neolithic but, again, the excavation identified a waste disposal area and not the real domestic structures. The same is true for the Mecklenburg site of Parchim-Löddigsee where, on the shoreline of a former peninsula, different wooden posts and waste layers were preserved under waterlogged conditions (Becker and Benecke 2002).

In general, most features of the North-Central European Neolithic wetland sites were influenced by the alternating wet and dry conditions of the area under investigation (Figure 3.2). As a result no "cultural layers" with organic preservation, such as are known from the circum-Alpine lake sites, were discovered. Figure 3.1 displays the present day situation. Only a few domestic Neolithic sites could be labelled as wetland sites, with a concentration on the western Baltic. On the map the Swedish site of Alvastra and the Latvian site of Švontiji mark the possibility of water-preserved domestic remains in other areas of the Baltic or Southern Scandinavia. Nevertheless, real domestic structures with houses were not discovered; in Alvastra we are dealing with wooden platforms whose purpose is not really known (Hulthen 1998).

Concerning the Early Bronze Age, the situation on the north European plain is not much different. Until now the site of Bruszczewo, 60km south of Poznań, investigated by both a Polish and a German team, represents the only site with structures from both wet and dry conditions (Czebreszuk and Müller 2004a, Müller et al. 2010, Kneisel et al. 2008). Placed on a promontory, which originally was a peninsula in a former lake, not only structures of fortification, but also domestic structures, were preserved in waterlogged conditions. The site demonstrates the potential which still exists on the north European plain but, as yet, no other Early Bronze Age waterlogged sites have been discovered. In consequence I would like to use two typical wetland sites of Holstein and the Bronze Age site of Bruszczewo, to illustrate the research situation on waterlogged sites in the area under discussion.

Neolithic domestic sites: East Holstein

One of the most prominent Neolithic find regions in North Germany and Southern Scandinavia is the Oldenburger Graben, on the way from Hamburg to Fehmarn (Figure 3.4). The area is marked by an east-west oriented depression, the drained *Graben*, which formerly linked two bays of the Baltic Sea and whose geological history could be identified by geological and geomorphological surveys (Hartz et al. 2004). During Mesolithic times it was, in fact, a fjord separating the Northern Wagrien as an island from the mainland. The eustatic rise of the land and the bay situation changed the fjord at the beginning of the Neolithic into a lagoon with brackish water, giving

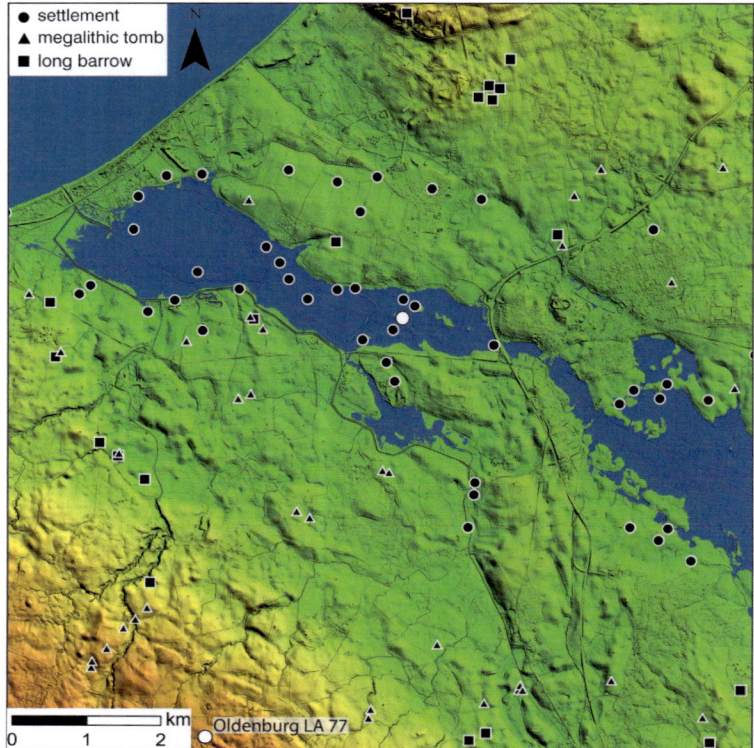

Figure 3.4 Neolithic sites in the Oldenburger Graben, East Holstein (after Brozio 2011, Müller 2011, 57 Fig. 30). The spatial division between domestic sites on lower ground and on islands, and megaliths in the hinterland can be observed. The original watershed is reconstructed from the available palaeo-ecological data.

rise to many peninsulas and islands. Most of these locations were used for settlements during the early and middle Neolithic (Brozio 2010, Müller 2011). One of the projects of the Priority program, about the megaliths and Funnel Beaker culture, is focussing on these sites as well as a comparable inland situation 80km to the south.

During the Neolithic the spatial distribution of sites shows a clear pattern. While megalithic burials are placed preferably in the "hinterland" of the Oldenburger Graben, domestic sites cluster on the aforementioned peninsulas and islands. The large increase in the number of domestic sites in the western Oldenburger Graben (as compared with the Mesolithic) indicates a population rise during the early and, especially, during the middle Neolithic.

Oldenburg-Dannau LA77 was chosen for further excavations (Figures 3.4 and 3.5). Here the archaeological remains are associated with the eastern part of a small former peninsula, today a minor

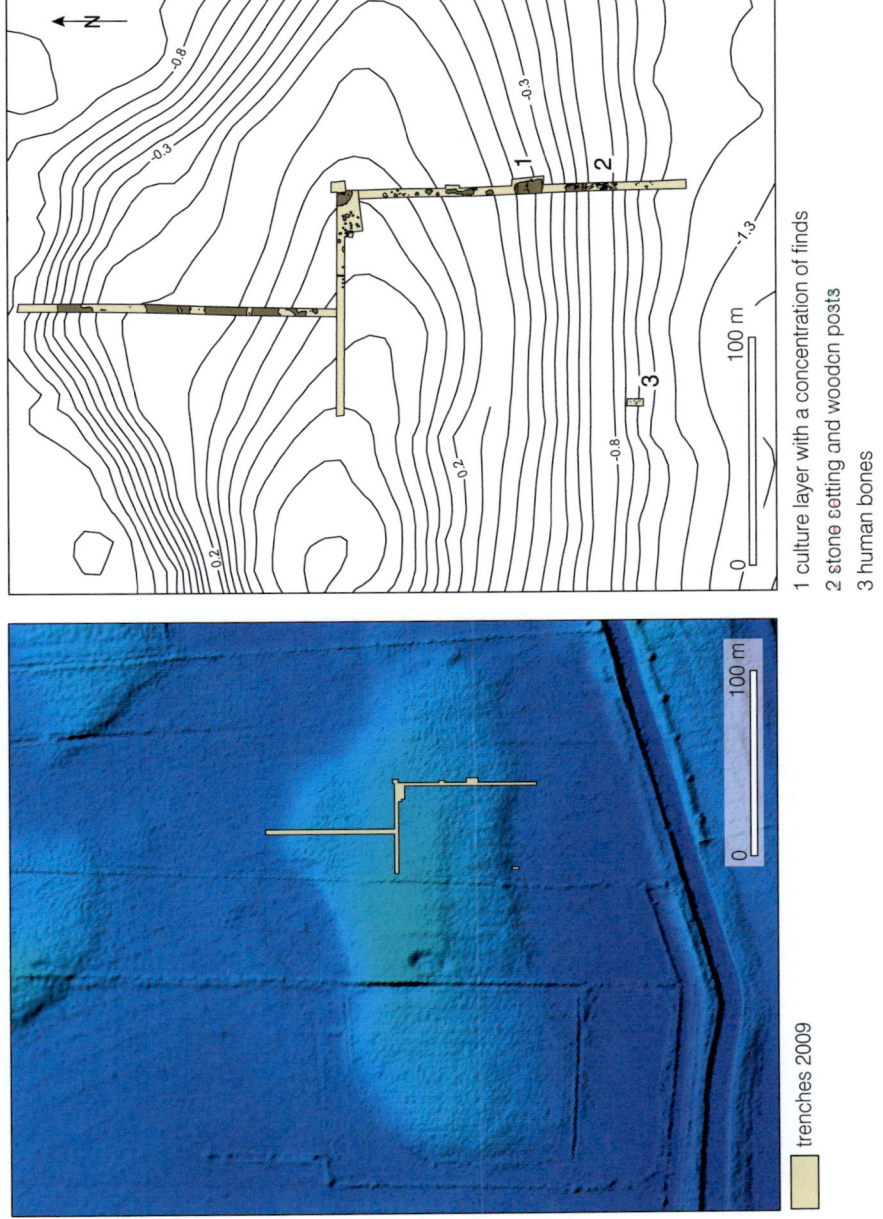

Figure 3.5 The settlement at Oldenburg-Dannau LA77, on the former island (lida-plus scan; after Brozio 2010).

elevation in the peaty area (Brozio 2011, 2010; Müller 2011). The excavations so far have indicated that the dry conditions (on the more elevated parts of the islands) are relatively new. Just eighty years ago, the drainage destroyed the wet conditions on the whole site; still, the bone preservation in the dry areas is quite good, in contrast to other organic material. Despite this, today we have to label the main area of this site as "dry and not wet condition". The actual preservation changes as soon as we come nearer to the old shore line of the island. In deeper-lying parts of the settlement, wooden posts and other wooden material are still preserved; this is even better at the low water area where mainly domestic waste, including animal and human bones, is preserved in waterlogged conditions.

To tell the story of the site under the present conditions is quite challenging; a combined interpretation of both dry land and wetland features is necessary. The hitherto oldest feature is the burial of a mature woman placed in a more or less stretched position and without any clear burial offerings, in a pit in the centre of the site (FN II, 3500-3300 cal BC) (Figure 3.6). The domestic area yielded so far three SW-NE oriented double-aisled Funnel-Beaker culture houses, partly with sunken floors, dating mainly to the MN (3300-3100 BC).

The houses of Oldenburg-Dannau are mainly preserved in the dry soil area of the site, on the higher elevated ground of the former peninsula. Beside the two-aisled constructions, pits and further postholes and stone-packings indicate other activities at the site during the middle Neolithic. At the border with the wet area and the Neolithic shore, different wooden posts are preserved which indicate some form of shore fortification during middle and late Neolithic times (Figure 3.7). In the low water area itself, the deposition of both domestic rubbish and probably some ritual activities took place. Remains of two individuals were found in the wet areas, dating around 2800 cal BC (Figure 3.8). The disarticulations of the human bones are comparable with the disarticulated distribution of animal bones beside other, organic and non-organic leftovers from daily life. The wet layers are also an important archive of ecological information, which is currently under analysis. Beside mainly broken tools, waste from production processes was found, including from the working of wood. Examples are hoes and a decorated shaft of a middle Neolithic mace head (Figure 3.9); the latter was found near a fishing weir.

While domestic activities at the site took place mainly during the middle Neolithic, a second phase of activities has to be associated with the latest middle Neolithic/earliest younger Neolithic transition period. The aforementioned fortification at the shoreline, as well as the ritual depositions of human bones and skulls in the nearby brackish water, are radiocarbon dated to this period. The activities probably took place when the main phase of domestic site was already over. Two wells, in the centre of the settlement, were filled around 3100 cal BC with domestic waste and a lot of deliberately broken querns. One of the wells, up to 2.3m deep, was dug only

Figure 3.6 Burial from the settlement at Oldenburg-Dannau (source: Brozio 2011; Müller 2011 55, Fig. 28). The 40-year-old woman was placed in a pit and later, as a result of secondary manipulation, the femur was taken away.

Figure 3.7 Posts in the wet area of Oldenburg-Dannau - middle Neolithic.

Figure 3.8 Human skull from the wet area in Oldenburg-Dannau (Brozio 2011).

Figure 3.9 Middle Neolithic mace head with a decorated wooden shaft from Oldenburg-Dannau.

Figure 3.10 The well from the settlement of Oldenburg-Dannau (after Brozio 2011). Beside many archaeological artefacts the femur of the nearby burial was also found (Müller 2011, 56, Fig. 29).

2m distant from the above-mentioned late Early Neolithic burial (Figure 3.10). Within the infill, the femur from the single burial, dug out deliberately, was deposited within a secondary small pit. Obviously, consciously and not accidentally, the destruction of the wells, and probably of the middle Neolithic settlement, included a symbolic takeover of the bone of the "female grand ancestor" of the village.

Both the filling of the well and the archaeobotanical and palynological remains from the wet area, allow a reconstruction of the environmental conditions and land use around 3100 cal BC (Kirleis et al. 2011b). Beside small patches of agricultural areas with emmer, einkorn and barley, beside gardens with fennel and leguminous plants, the large amounts of fruits, especially apples, indicate a process of care and domestication of apple trees. Recovered animal bones identify the life cycles of mainly cattle, but also pig and sheep/goat as the principal domestic animals. The conditions of single human bones indicate a conscious use of such bones in the settlement; they had to have been kept in the domestic area in such a way as not to be destroyed, for example by dogs.

Oldenburg-Dannau LA77 is one of the typical North German sites with wetland preservation. While most domestic structures are preserved under dry conditions on higher elevations, only parts of the domestic activities left traces in the waterlogged, deeper areas or low water parts of the site. The site itself was affected by the rising water level of the Oldenburger Graben. While on the one hand the aquatic resources were more and more accessible, on the other hand the pollen record displays a change in the economic base.

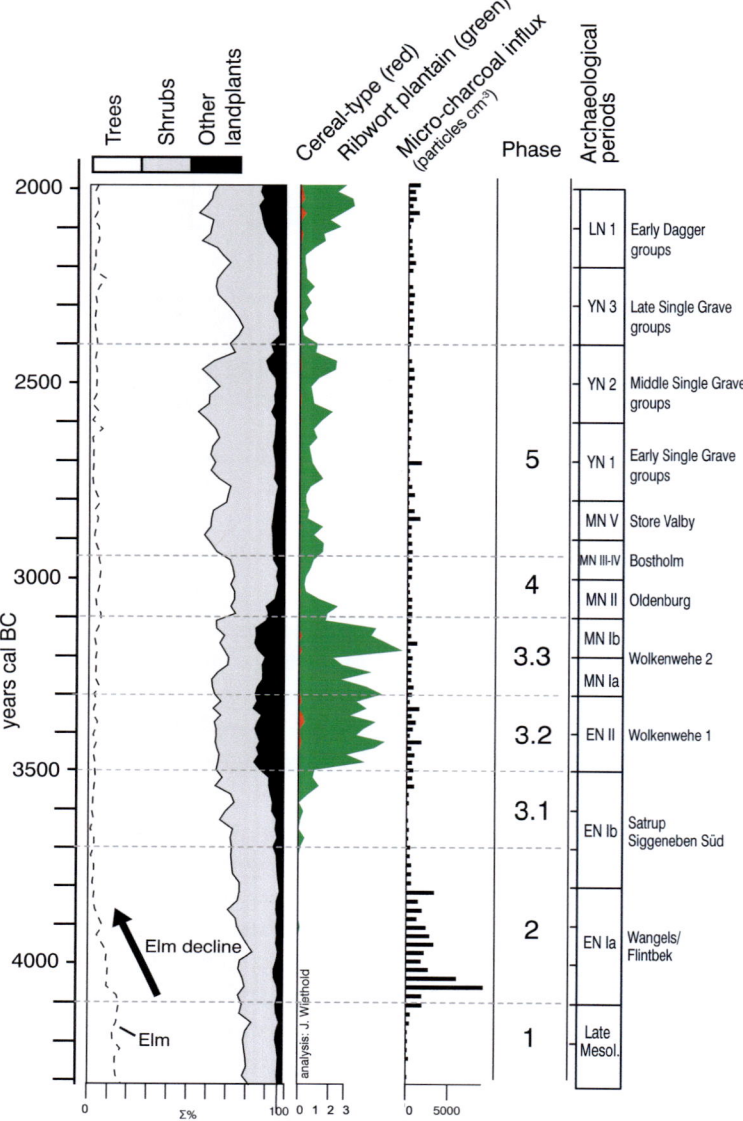

Figure 3.11 Belau. The opening up of landscape reflected in the record of the Lake Belau (Kirleis, Feeser, Kooß 2011). After a period in which charcoal played an important role, around 3500 BC, the imprints of a new agricultural system on the vegetation are visible (Müller 2011, 63 Fig. 31).

The introduction of the plough, linked to the opening up of the landscape, is associated with the peak of the settlement activities, while the observed decrease in human activities all over the southern area of the Northern TRB group is reflected in the destruction at the site (Figures 3.11 and 3.12).

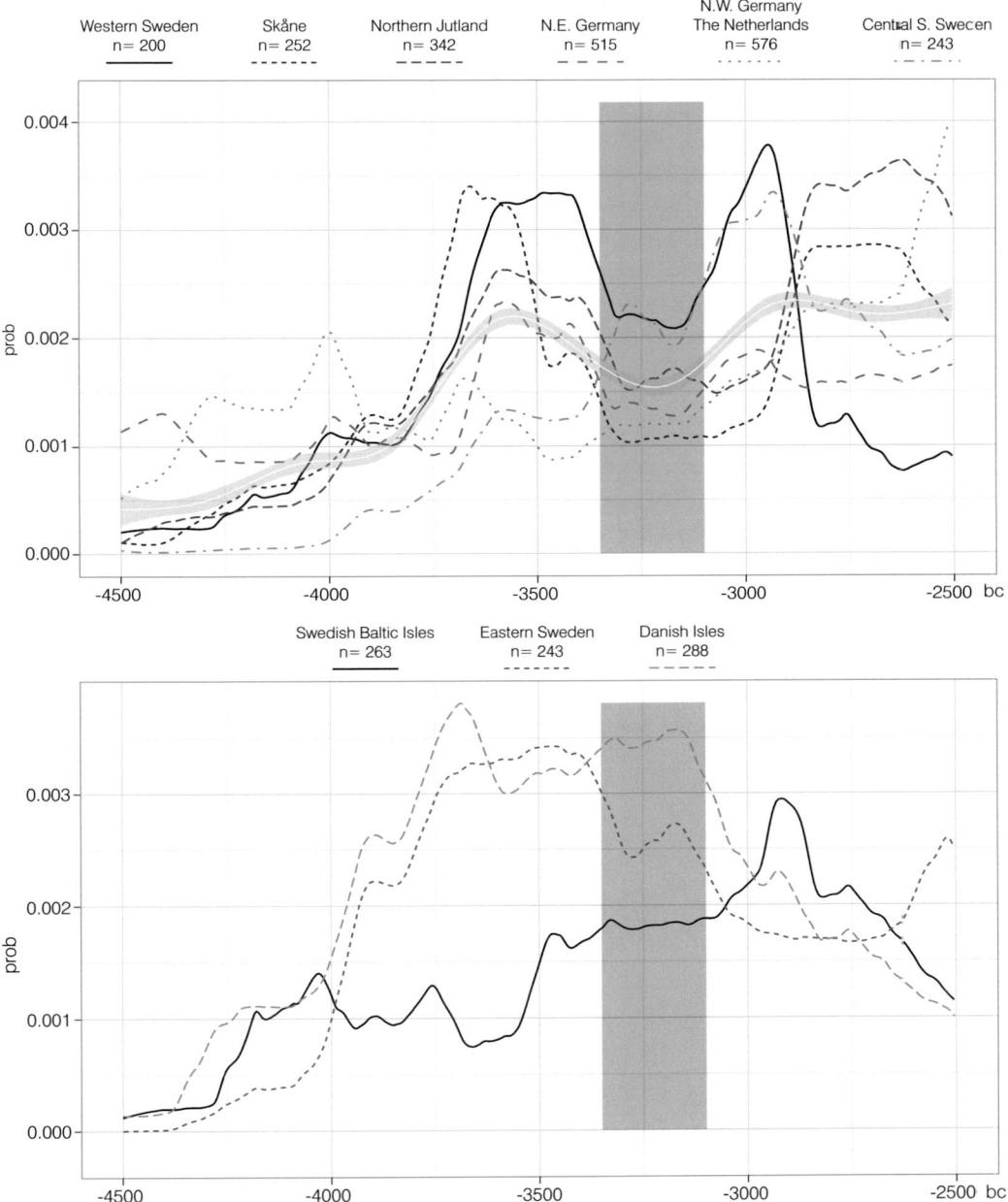

Figure 3.12 Sum calibration curves (from six regions in the Netherlands to central southern Sweden) display similar tendencies. Beside an increase around 3800/3700 cal BC, a decrease around 3400/3350 cal BC and a second increase around and after 3000 cal BC are visible. Despite these patterns a lack of data after 2700 cal BC and before 4200 cal BC should also be taken into consideration (Hinz et al. 2012).

In contrast to the more or less typical site of Oldenburg-Dannau LA 77 (e.g. also Dannau, Neustadt, Parchim-Löddigsee), Bad Oldesloe-Wolkenwehe LA 154 (Figure 3.1) is quite different. In this case the centre of the site is also preserved in at least partly wet conditions (Hartz et al., 2004/2005 (2007), Mischka et al. 2003/2004 (2007), Schwabedissen 1959, Brozio 2010).

Wolkenwehe is one of the sites already excavated by Schwabedissen in the 1950s. Situated in the Mittlere Travetal basin, this site, like many other domestic sites in the area, lies near the river Trave. Again, the distribution pattern indicates domestic activities associated with the depression, and ritual activities, including the construction of megaliths and the deposition of adzes, with terraces and higher areas of the landscape (Figure 3.15).

Wolkenwehe was re-excavated in 2007-2010 to verify the few results which could be reconstructed from the documentation left by Schwabedissen. Actually it became clear that the setting of about 550 posts and the clusters of boulders belonged to a middle Neolithic activity area, which was "settled" only during summer times; pollen and sedimentological analyses proved that high winter waters were regularly flooding the small island of Wolkenwehe during the time between 3300 and 2800 cal BC. Nevertheless, the spatial distribution of wooden posts probably indicates the remains of several two-aisled houses, which are linked to the remains of fireplaces, indicated by

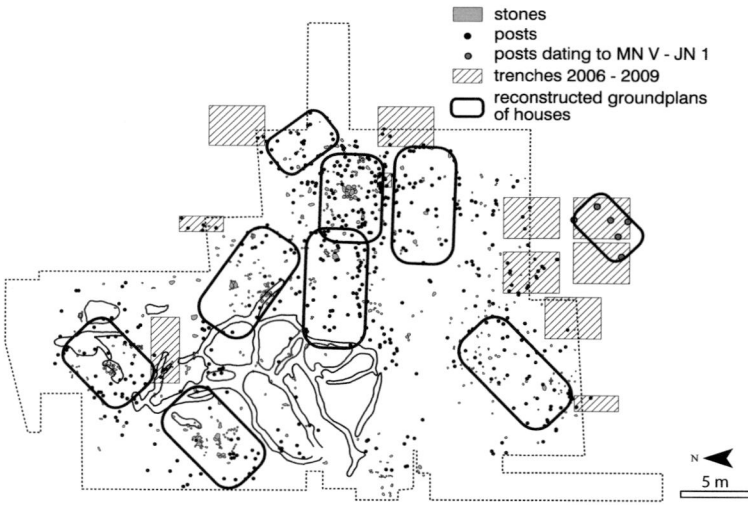

Figure 3.13 Bad Oldesloe-Wolkenwehe: reconstruction of houses represented by wooden posts and stone concentrations and the ditch system of the middle Neolithic site; between 2 and 3 houses existed contemporaneously (Brozio 2011; Müller 2011, 53, Fig. 27).

Figure 3.14 Posts from the old excavation in 1950-52 by Schwabedissen (Hartz et al. 2004/2005 (2007),14, Fig. 8), ditch system (right) and posts (left).

the boulders. A closer dating was not possible, as the posts were too small for dendro-dating (Figure 3.13).

Nevertheless, the purpose and function of the site is not entirely clear. There are no remains of cereal processing and, in the local pollen record, there are no signs of an opening of the landscape for horticultural or agricultural purposes. The location itself, in a peripheral area of the landscape, the depth of the lowland by the river Trave flooded in Neolithic times, indicate that the main purpose of the site could not have been for subsistence. The animal bones indicate consumption of meat but no other special activities.

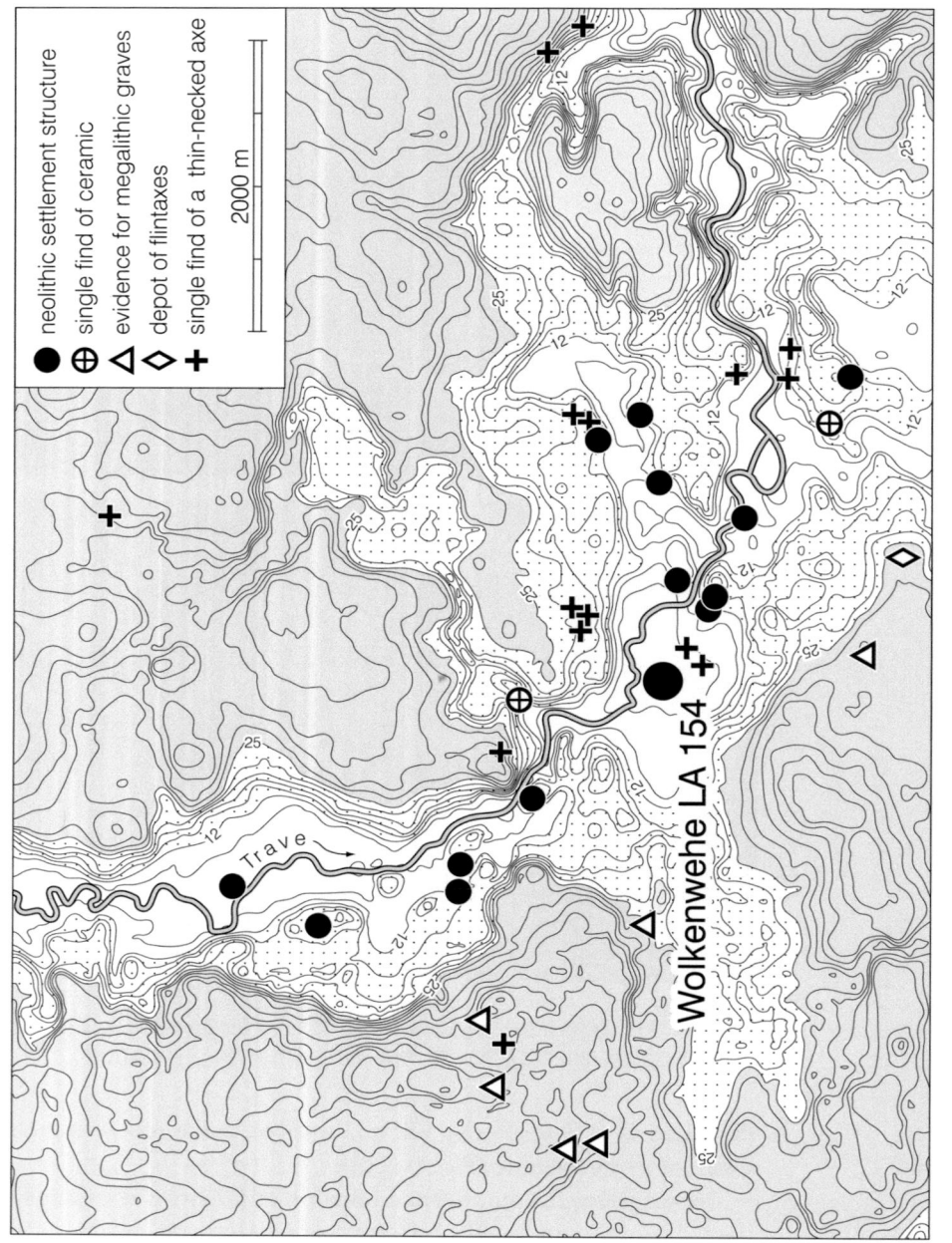

Figure 3.15 Distribution of settlements, single finds, votive deposits and burial places in the Mittlere Travetal, East Holstein (Hartz et al. 2007, 9, Fig. 2); the alignment of sites along the river Trave is obvious.

This includes fishing; no real signs of fishing were found. What took place on the site, beside the periodical use of the houses?

There are irregular artificial ditch systems, which were already excavated by Schwabedissen and whose presence was reconfirmed by the new excavations (Figures 3.13 and 3.14). These ditches might be compared with similar structures, which are known from different salt production places. In spite of the fact that no briqetтages were found on the site, different methods of salt extraction without any clear archaeological leftovers are documented ethno-historically for northern Europe. This is of more interest, as saline wells are present in the vicinity of the site. In combination with the high amount of charcoal on the site, and ashes visible in the pollen analyses, and with the many posts beside the houses which might belong to some kind of wooden construction for water evaporation, we developed the hypothesis that salt production was practised at Wolkenwehe. Despite this, about two and a half tons of flint, brought into the peaty area, support the idea that production of flint tools and adzes took place here (Mischka 2006).

All in all, problems of site interpretation remain and field activities continue in the area. Nevertheless, the presence of middle Neolithic domestic sites in the Mittlere Trave valley shows a more or less linear distribution along the river (Figure 3.15). As other sites are situated on the promontory-like locations which I described above, the special location of Wolkenwehe LA 154 probably reflects its specific functions within the economic and settlement system.

Beside the problems with the sites and the combinations of dry and waterlogged conditions, East Holstein yields many waterlogged features from the Neolithic, which allow the reconstruction of both sites and their economic and ritual background. The results are underlined, among other things, by laminated pollen profiles, which give a clear indication of human impact and agriculture; open fields with barley and emmer and wild rose, the presence of apple orchards and the annual pattern of animals driven over the fields for manuring, existed in the area between 3600-3100 BC (Wiethold 1998; Kirleis et al. 2011a; Kirleis et al. b, accepted; Müller et al. in print). The decrease in population around 3200 BC, which is also linked to the end of the construction of megalithic monuments, is still without an explanation. Nevertheless, the increase in activities at around 2800 cal BC, linked to Store Valby or the Single Grave culture, is visible on the sites mentioned here as well as on others (Hinz et al. 2012).

Bronze Age research: Bruszczewo

As already noted, the only excavated site with a large amount of waterlogged features is the site of Bruszczewo 5 in Greater Poland, about 60km south of Poznań (Czebreszuk and Müller 2004a, Müller et al. 2010, Kneisel et al. 2008; Figure 3.1). The site was discovered already in the first half of the twentieth century and excavated during the 1960s by Pienzenski of the Poznań museum. During that time it

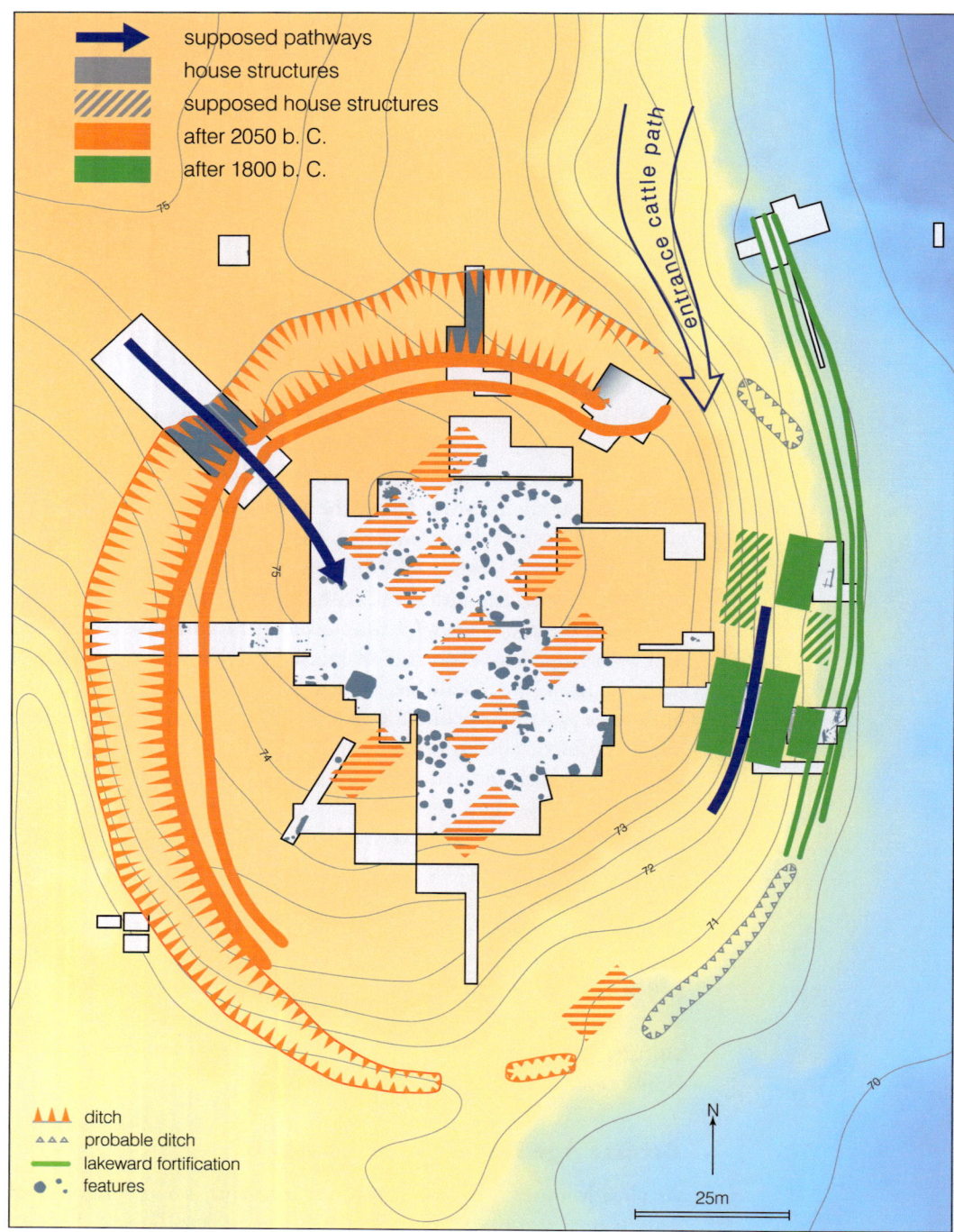

Figure 3.16 The excavation of the Early Bronze Age site Bruszczewo 5: interpretation of settlement development, house locations and entrances. The structures postdating 1800 BC are preserved under wet conditions in the Samica lowlands (Müller and Kneisel 2010, 763, Fig. 5).

Figure 3.17 Aerial photograph of the excavation on the promontory (yellow vegetation) and in the Samica lowlands (green vegetation) (Kneisel 2010b, 95, Fig. 3-4).

became clear that, on the promontory which leads into the Samica lake lowlands, an Unetice settlement existed; it was fortified and there was evidence of metal processing. It was after 1999 that the potential of the site in respect of the wetland archive was discovered. The new joint Polish and German project extended the excavation areas to the Samica lake lowlands (Figures 3.16 and 3.17). Different waterlogged constructions were discovered. In this respect we are still dealing with the first and only waterlogged site of the Early

Bronze Age on the north European plain; later on in the Bronze Age the site of Biskupin, for example, clearly defines the further potential of wetland areas for the whole of the Bronze Age.

Bruscezwo 5 is situated in the Kościan basin of Greater Poland, which is a *Siedlungskammer* of the Unetice societies (Müller and Kneisel 2010). The area is well known for the rich burials of Łęki Małe which, beside Leubingen and Helmsdorf, are still the only surviving Early Bronze Age burial mounds in Central Europe. Due to the rich grave items and the alignment of four burial mounds along the river terrace, they indicate not only a high-ranked group of people within the stratified Bronze Age society, but also a continuity and stability in the political system over at least some centuries. Łęki Małe, at a distance of 14 km, is contemporary with Bruszczewo 5. As Bruszczewo is the only fortified site in the Kościan area, it seems also appropriate to associate this domestic site with Łęki Małe and the political organisation of this Early Bronze Age settlement area. In this respect Bruszczewo stays in clear contrast to single farmsteads or small hamlets, which are indicated by find scatters all over the Kościan area.

Bruszczewo 5 and its economic, social and cultural position in the Kościan basin have been described extensively in the final publication. Here I would only like to summarize the main results briefly and to focus on some aspects of the wet area (Figure 3.16). Environmental reconstructions indicate that during the Early Bronze Age the ridge of Bruszczewo was a kind of peninsula of the Samica lake, which extended to the east of the site and disappeared during the Iron Age. In the twenty-first century BC, about 0.5 ha of a ridge, which at its highest point originally towered above the Samica low ground by about 8m and above the bordering moraine by about 3m, was separated from the hinterland by a ditch of up to 20m wide and about 4m deep. At the inner edge of the ditch a double palisade, on average 2m wide, was erected. This was built as a wood and earth construction, using the material excavated from the ditch (Hildebrandt-Radke 2010). In the centre of the settlement area, houses, workshops, open spaces and silo pits were planned and built. In the eastern, lakeside area, an extension of the site was created at the beginning of the eighteenth century BC with new houses and a further lakeside fortification (Kneisel 2010b, Kneisel 2010a, Kneisel et al. 2008).

Access to the site lay in the north-west, leading directly to the most elevated area, and in the north-east, at the lower part of the site on the edge of the Samica lake. Settled areas in front of the fortification did not exist, but open areas are proven to the west and north, while the south and east are bordered by the Samica lake. Colluvial sediments of the main ditch, which most probably date to the seventeenth century BC (Hildebrandt-Radke 2010, 35), mark the end of settlement activities. Equally, the palynologically-detected decline of human impact falls within the same timescale and confirms the cessation of domestic activities (Diers 2010, Haas and Wahlmüller 2010), and soil scientists have reconstructed reforestation of the site (Bork 2010). A new utilisation of the area by the Lusatian settlement, which shifted more to the eastern area, started around 1000 BC.

Domestic structures

Due to erosion, the reconstruction of houses and house inventories is nearly impossible for the central settlement area of Bruszczewo 5. House structures were found mainly in the lowland adjoining the eastern ridge spur. Synopsis of the single construction elements is difficult because of their varying conservation state. In trench thirty-one, complex constructions consisting of stakes, posts, fallen wickerwork walls and superficially burned timber can be observed (Figure 3.18) whereas further to the west only stakes and wood shadows in the dry domain near the edge of the spur can be recognised (Kneisel 2010b 19, Fig. 33). From trench thirty stem numerous wedged stakes, which are grouped around great middle posts and belong to another construction (Figure 3.19). The dwelling structure consists of about twenty-six small posts that, unlike round wattle posts, have been halved.

In trench fifty-two, the excavators could unearth two house structures, separated from each other by a pathway, under up to three metres of slope colluvium. Here too only wood shadows could be recognised in the dry soil. In contrast to the wet area however, clay structures were also conserved. Thus, directly at the edge of the old hill, the remnants of a tumbled wall could be excavated. It was slightly burnt on the outside. Nearby, a large deposit of burnt grain was discovered.

The houses in the lower land are aligned north-south, in parallel to the edge of the hill. The length must be 8 metres or more, the width amounts to 4–5 meters approximately (Figure 3.18). The pathway amounts to about 2 metres in width; below the path, and only there, traces of ploughing were found. On the spur, postholes yield no evidence of houses. Only some pits join in linear and rectilinear rows, so that we might tentatively reconstruct the position of houses in intervening open areas (Kneisel 2010a; Müller and Kneisel 2010, 763 Fig. 5).

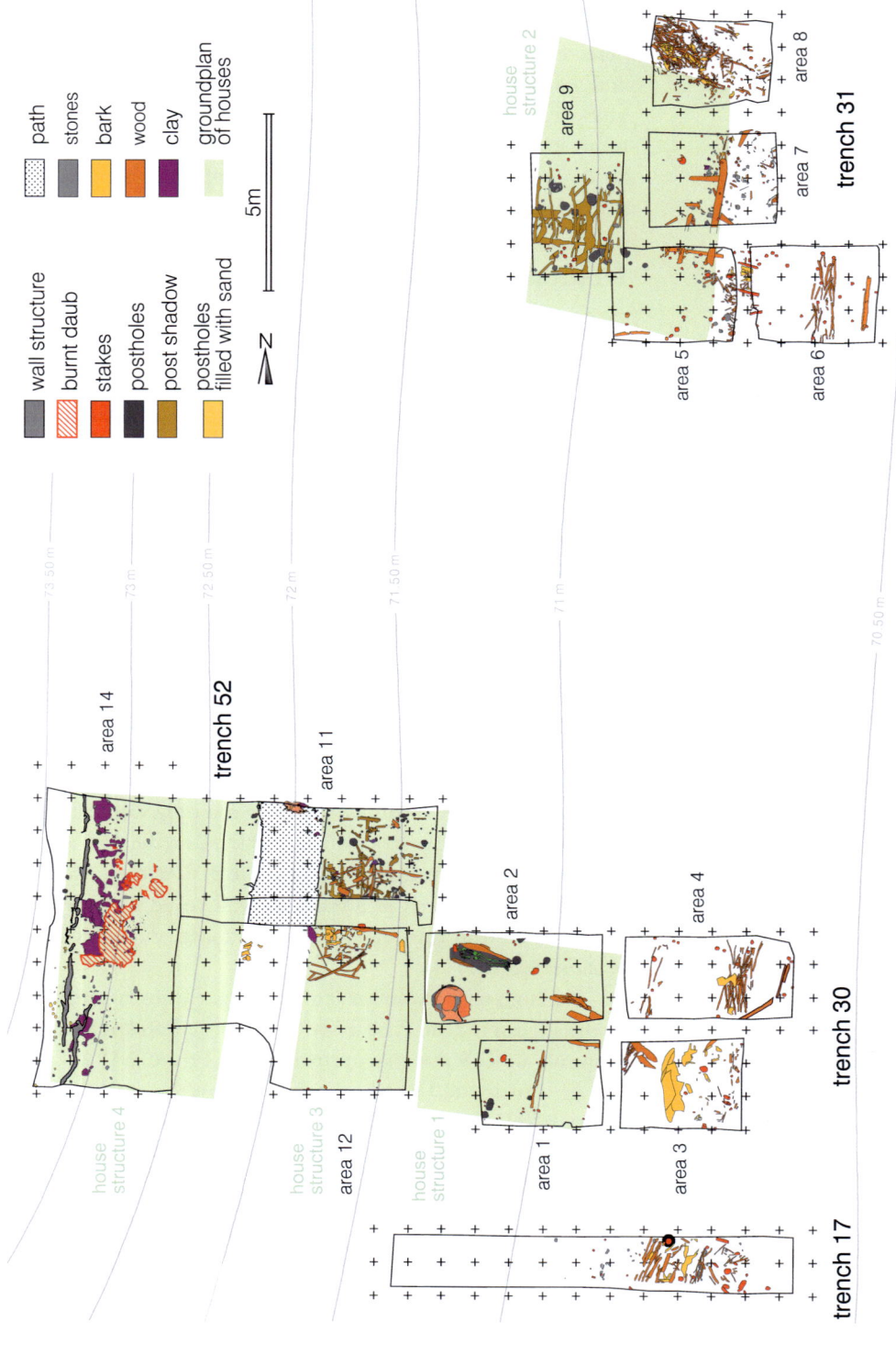

Figure 3.18 Houses in the eastern wet area. Mapped are the houses with collapsed walls (area 14), a settlement burial (area 2), difficult construction works (area 9), free spaces, a track (area 11) and the eastern shore fortification (area 4) (Müller and Kneisel 2010, 764, Fig. 6).

Figure 3.19 Details of wooden constructions in the eastern part of Bruszczewo 5. Remains of a wooden floor (left) and the construction of a house corner (right) (Kneisel 2010b, 123, Fig. 42-44).

In the wet area both the house structures as well as the open spaces are accompanied by a large number of finds. Beside ceramics, animal bones, flint artefacts and wooden tools have been preserved (Figure 3.20). There is a wooden nail, part of a wheel axle, wooden arrowheads and small birch bark bundles, which were used for lighting. The wooden posts show great expertise in woodworking and the timber flakes indicate timber workshops in front of the houses. The fascines of the fortification also indicate a clear knowledge of how to build a defensive system in such an area (Figure 3.21). Nevertheless, the character of the posts also indicates that no special care was given to the maintenance of forest so that, at a certain stage of the local development, posts with differences in ecological growing conditions had to be carried to the site from many areas (Figure 3.22). Despite the resulting difficulties arising for dendro-dating, several dates indicate the main phase of the wet area in the eighteenth century BC.

While in summary four house structures were found during the excavation in the waterlogged eastern part of the site, approximately eight houses might have existed on the ridge. With a margin of error, no more than between twenty and twenty-five houses were probably built during the 400 years of the settlement. Since the sequential calibration of the dendro- and AMS-data of house structure no. 4 points to a lifespan of 75-100 years for a single house (including archaeologically proven renewals), approximately ten houses existed contemporaneously (Kneisel and Kroll 2010, 573). Allowing for between five and ten inhabitants per house, this results in between fifty and a hundred inhabitants at Bruszczewo 5.

With reference to the graves in the immediate surroundings of the settlement, little is known to date. From the area of house structures, up to now a single settlement burial of a male individual,

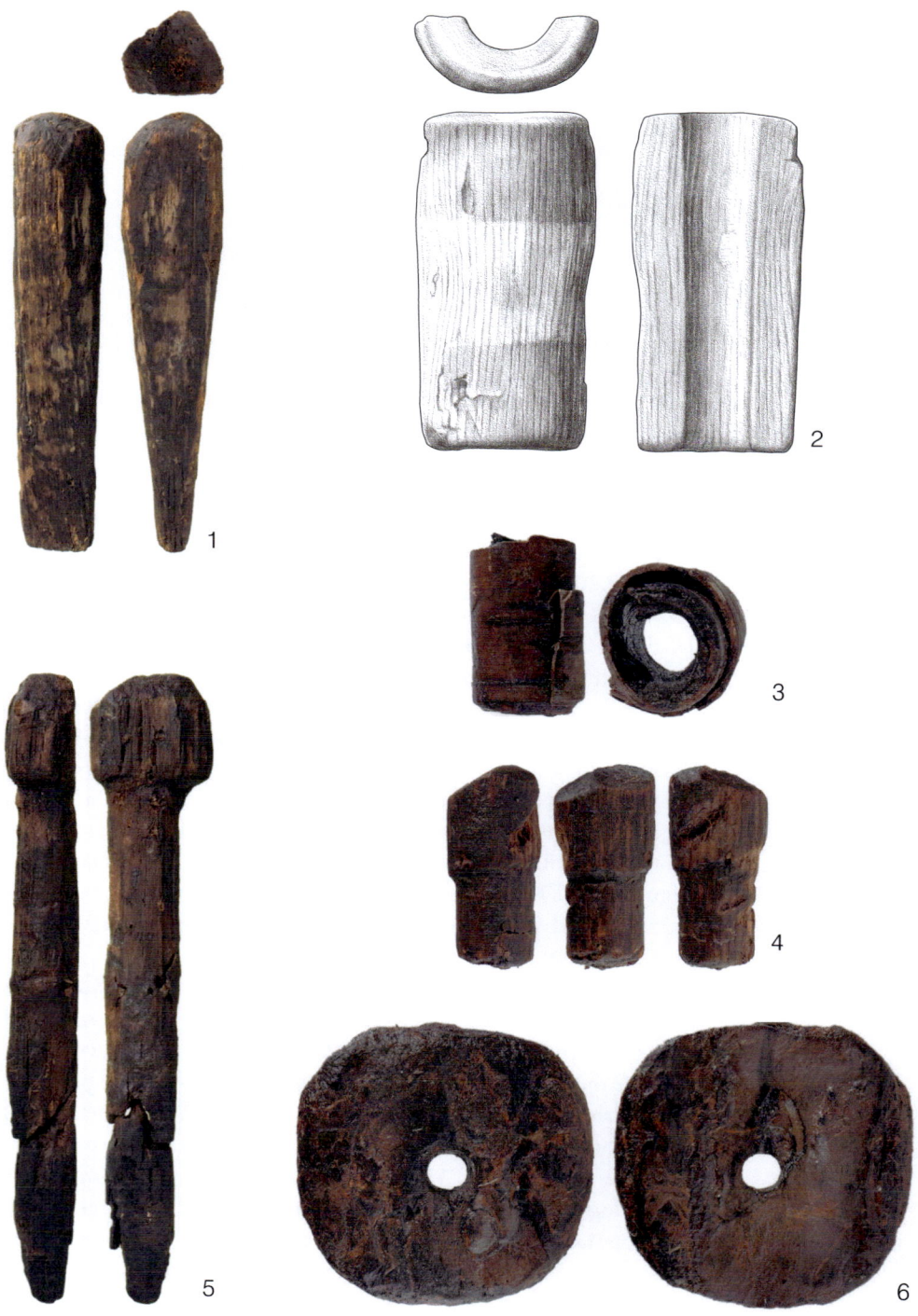

Figure 3.20 Early Bronze Age wooden artefacts from Bruszczewo (Kneisel and Kroll 2010, Fig. 52:2; Fig. 64: HA4304, HA4321; Fig. 65: HA5001; Fig. 71: HA6066, HA6063).

Figure 3.21 The eastern woodworking area with wooden flakes and other remains between a house and a part of the eastern fortification (Müller and Kneisel 2010, 771, Fig. 12).

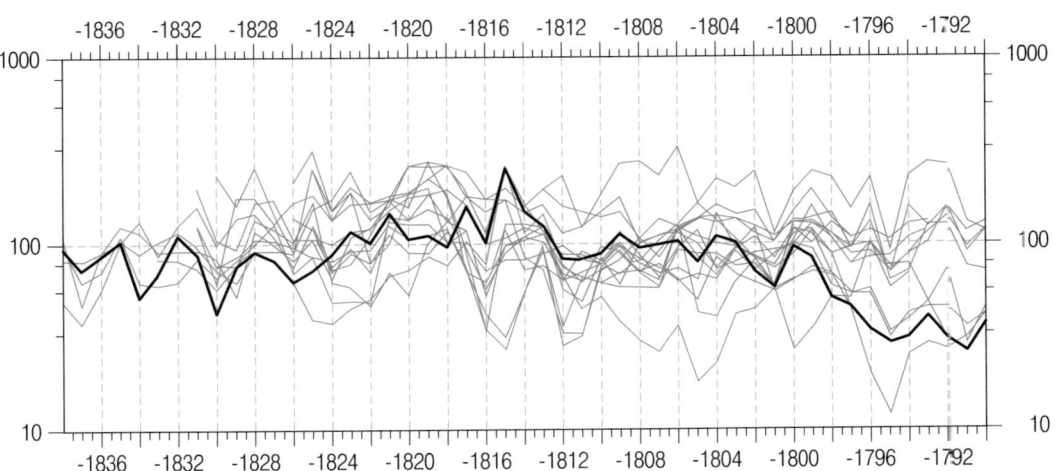

Figure 3.22 The local oak-dendro-curves and single oak-curves from Bruszczewo 5 define the huge variability of timber growing conditions (Heußner andWaszny 2010, 244, Fig. 1). Beside other economic problems a shortage of timber raw material is indicated by the lack of care of timber forest.

Figure 3.23 The settlement burial of a young, hard-working man, on top of a willow mat (Kneisel 2010c, 726, Fig.1).

wrapped in a mat made of willow rods, was found (Figure 3.23) (Iwanek et al. 2010, Kneisel 2010c). The 18- to 24-year-old male showed different pathological modifications of his skeleton, which were the result of hard physical work, probably carrying heavy loads during his work. With the exception of simple boulders no grave goods were present. Thus, the burials express the social span from ordinary community members to the rich individuals in the Łęki Małe mounds.

Fortification

The fortification consists of two different parts. A ditch is located on the spur, together with a double-row palisade. Their oak posts were stacked so deep in the ground that wooden posts were preserved in waterlogged conditions, even if the remaining upper structure was only preserved under dry conditions. This steep and wide ditch and palisade construction delimits the settlement to the West and North (Figure 3.16). At certain points, the ditch extends up to 20 metres in width and 4 metres in depth. Access to the settlement is gained at a narrow part in the northwest, as shown by the excavations in trench fifty-one (Kneisel 2010b, 94, Figures 2, 5¬7). To the east, towards the lake shore, the fortification structure is different. This entire structure, which stems from the same time as proven by dendrochronological data (Wazny 2010, Heußner and Wazny 2010), consists of two wickerwork walls of different thickness (Figure 3.24) and in some sections has a timber wall in front of it (Kneisel and Kroll 2010). This construction was found in all trenches in the wet ground (Müller 2004). It extends in the north far beyond the ditch on the spur. Evidently the settlement was extended to the east during the nineteenth century BC.

Taking architecture into consideration, the fortifications in particular set the time frame for the settlement. In the western area of the settlement the multiple renewal of a palisade, which covers the period between 2050 and 1650 BC (Czebreszuk and Müller 2004b, 297), was proved. In the north the segmented ditch was also dug up in the twenty-first century BC, and colluvial sedimentation within the ditch began in the seventeenth century BC. Principal settlement activities might have taken place between 2050 and 1650 BC.

In contrast, the duration of a house would not have exceeded 75 years (see above). Accordingly, ongoing building activities within the settlement have to be taken into account. Furthermore, main residential activities in the wet eastern area may have begun at about 1790 BC. The enlargement is marked by an additional fortification. The newly enclosed area was used for work activities as well as for new houses. The settlement activities, as indicated by lake transgression, end here with sudden flood events possibly about 1650 BC.

Figure 3.24 Eastern shore fortification with three elements, dendrochronologically dated to 1787 BC: two fascine walls and one wooden wall (Kneisel, 2010b, 112, Fig. 20).

Subsistence economy and environment

The ecological data indicate that the climax of settlement development was reached by approximately 1800 BC. On-site pollen analyses prove cereal production, pasture, forest use and clearances beginning from the twenty-first century BC at the latest (Diers 2010, 353ff.). At approximately 1800 BC an extensively used environment is evident with only a few forest areas left over that resemble park landscapes. These, in turn, appear under pressure from agriculture and an extensive cattle economy. The Samica lake, in particular, shows a high pollution level. The dendrochronological results suggest difficulties in the provision of timber (Wazny 2010, 237); wood was chopped unsystematically, from the few still available locations, and no cultivated timber is present. Beginning at about 1750 BC forest regeneration is already noticeable, with the remaining open spots pointing to the reduction of economic activities on the site.

The subsistence economy can presently be described from a snapshot overview of Bruszczewo phase three. Summer cereal fields, with separate cultivation of emmer and einkorn, are ploughed with cattle as draught animals; legumes, fennel and poppy are grown in garden-style manner, and fruits were collected in the park-like woods. The separate storage methods for emmer and einkorn, as well as their separate and different processing procedures, refer - similarly to the use of fruit - to private ownership of the surrounding fields. Nevertheless, the field system would have demanded a common political institution which, for example, regulated the grazing of stubble pasture by animals. Cereal processing did not take place everywhere but rather in certain areas of the settlement, whereas certain households were specialising in cereal processing. The processing, as well as the consumption of domestic livestock and wild animals, were concentrated in quite different areas of the settlement. Livestock farming with cattle, pigs and sheep/goat played a substantial role. Access to meat from area to area was rather diverse throughout the settlement. The extreme environmental effects of unregulated, free cattle grazing probably led, from 1750 BC, to the described environmental problems and the reduction of settlement activities as a whole.

Due to limited calculation possibilities it can just be assumed that between 50-100 persons lived in Bruszczewo. Participation in the subsistence economy varied among the inhabitants. A certain portion of the population laboured strenuously on agricultural tasks, for example carrying extremely heavy loads to the point of physical impairment, while other segments of the population had access to craft products and exotic commodities.

Specialisation, consumption and networks

On the one hand, these were activities which were based on local resources but, on the other hand, some of the production processes required not only raw material imports, but also a supra-regional knowledge transfer (Figure 3.25). Metallurgical activities, in particular, were concentrated in the central area of the settlement which is marked in itself by certain aspects of a more exclusive access to subsistence commodities.

Cereals are used everywhere, but they are processed only in certain areas of the settlement. Pork and wild animals are over-represented in the highest ridge area, where butchering did not take place. In the southern ridge areas, and the eastern wet zone, sheep/goat are more important. While in the northern ridge area beside pins and flanged axes daggers are also seen, in the wet area only pins were found. Assuming that the few metal objects and their depositional processes permit an interpretation, a different distribution is obvious.

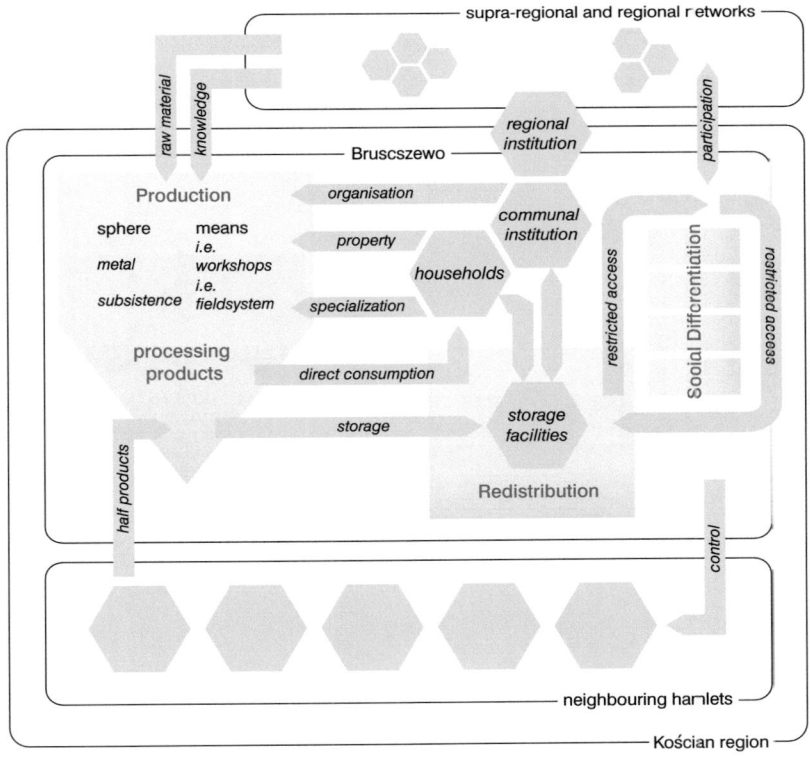

Figure 3.25 Reconstruction of socio-economic activities and political institutions, in which Bruszczewo 5 and its single households are bound together (Müller and Kneisel 2010, 780, Fig. 20).

Finally, the higher portion of storage jars in the central area of the settlement might suggest a certain monopolization of commodity distribution.

Thus, the control of the supra-regional networks, with the possibility of metal production and centralised storage, were the main aspects of political power in Bruszczewo. In addition, the contribution of Bruszczewo to such supra-regional networks has also been taken into consideration: for example, on the one hand the rather early development of new casting technologies (over-casting and hollow casting) and, on the other hand, the guarantee of stable amber supply for southern regions.

Ceramic production rates, vessel and decoration variations increase continuously throughout the periods of Bruszczewo 1 to 3, followed by a sudden decrease. At the same time the innovation potential increases without any break. This might be explained by the presence of a contradiction between the terms of production and social development - while creative production in the village is still formidable and a creative atmosphere in the village community still prevails, the economic system collapses (Figure 3.26). Environmental

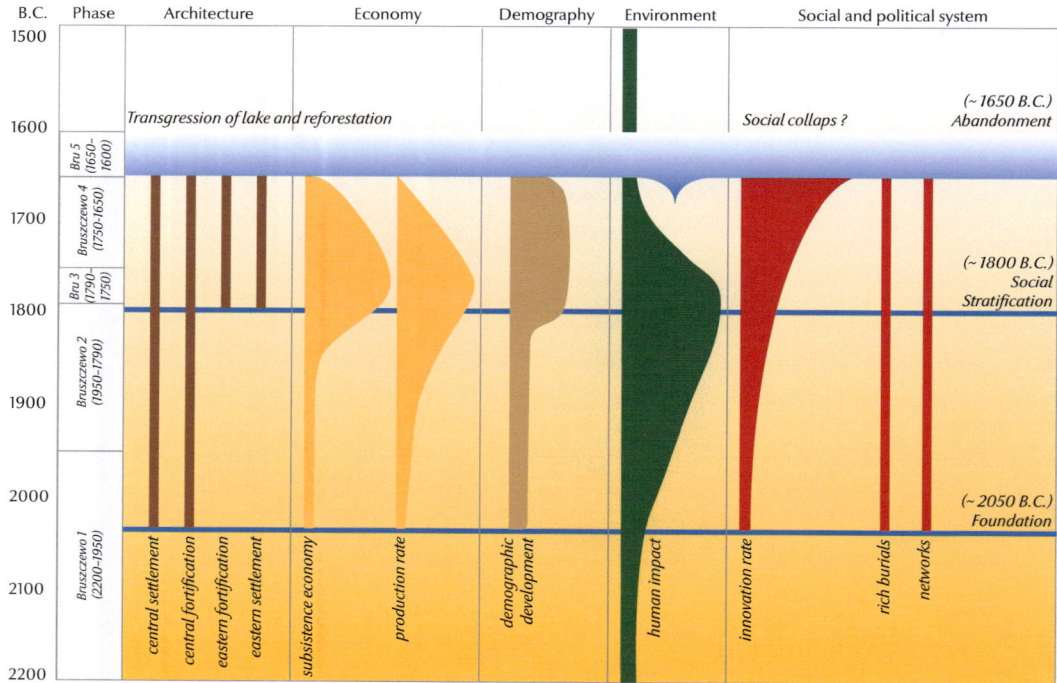

Figure 3.26 Diagram of the overall development in Bruszczewo 5 (Müller and Kneisel 2010, 781, Fig. 21). The evidence of different waterlogged archives allowed the reconstruction of different processes which mark the end of domestic activities around 1650 cal BC.

problems, such as shortage of timber, the strongly eutrophic Samica lake, the strain on the villagers active in the subsistence sphere, as well as a possible increase in conflict potential within the society, lead to a destabilisation. When, on account of changed relations, the amber exchange with Carpathian societies which was important for Bruszczewo had subsided, the central role of the settlement was lost. The destruction of the eastern settlement, after considerable flood events at about 1650 BC, is just one episode which further contributes to the end of the settlement. Reforestation marks the end of a political system and its central site in this small region.

The distribution of goods, and their consumption both as daily supplies and as elements of a consumptive representation, vary within the settlement (Müller and Kneisel, 2010).

Conclusion

So far, research in wetland areas on the north European plain has not produced a record of Neolithic or Early Bronze Age domestic sites that is comparable to that of the circum-Alpine region. This is probably due to different accessibilities of the areas along the lake shores and their value for prehistoric settlement. Without exception, settlements were placed on top of former islands or peninsulas, which are now under dry conditions. Nevertheless, as the examples from Neolithic sites in East Holstein and from the Early Bronze Age in Greater Poland suggest, the information from such sites is still very informative for the reconstruction of past societies.

References

Becker, D. and Benecke, N. 2002, *Die neolithische Inselsiedlung am Löddigsee bei Parchim. Archäologische und archäozoologische Untersuchungen*, Lübsdorf.

Behre, K.-E. 2004, Coastal Development, Sea-Level Change and Settlement History during the Later Holocene in the Clay District of Lower Saxony (Niedersachsen), Northern Germany. *Quaternary International,* 112: 37-53.

Behre, K.-E. and Kucan, D. 1994, *Die Geschichte der Kulturlandschaft und des Ackerbaus in der Siedlungskammer Flögeln, Niedersachsen, seit der Jungsteinzeit.* Oldenburg.

Billamboz, A. 2005, 20 Jahre Dendroarchäologie in den Pfahlbausiedlungen Südwestdeutschlands - Bilanz und Perspektiven. In: P. D. Casa and M. Trachsel, (eds.) *WES'04 Wetland Economies And Societies. Proceedings Of The International Conference Zurich, 10-13 March 2004.* Zürich: Museum, 47-56.

Bork, H.-R. 2010, Archäologische und umweltgeschichtliche Untersuchung eines markanten Sporns am westlichen Talrand der Samica. In: J. Müller, J. Czebreszuk and J. Kneisel (eds.) *Bruszczewo II. Ausgrabungen und Forschungen in einer prähistorischen Siedlungskammer Großpolens.* Bonn: Habelt, 16-37.

Brozio, J. P. 2010, Neue Untersuchungen zu trichterbecherzeitlichen Organisationsformen in Ostholstein. *Archäologischen Nachrichten aus Schleswig-Holstein* 16: 30-33.

Brozio, J. P. 2011, Neolithische Gemeinschaft im westlichen Oldenburger Graben - Wasserversorgung und Totenbehandlung vor über 5000 Jahren. *Archäologischen Nachrichten aus Schleswig-Holstein* 17: 26-29.

Burmeister, S. 2004, Neolithische und bronzezeitliche Moorfunde aus den Niederlanden, Nordwestdeutschland und Dänemark. In: M. Fansa and S. Burmeister (eds.) *Rad und Wagen. Der Ursprung einer Innovation. Wagen im Vorderen Orient und Europa.* Mainz: Iwensee, 321-340.

Czebreszuk, J. and Müller, J. (eds.) 2004a, *Bruszczewo I. Forschungsstand - Erste Ergebnisse - Das östliche Feuchtbodenareal,* Poznan/Kiel/Rahden: Leidorf.

Czebreszuk, J. and Müller, J. 2004b, Zur absolutchronologischen Datierung des Siedlungsgeschehen. In: J. Czebreszuk and J. Müller (eds.) *Bruszczewo I. Forschungsstand - Erste Ergebnisse - Das östliche Feuchtbodenareal,* Poznan/Kiel/Rahden: Leidorf, 211-220.

Diers, S. 2010, Feinstratigrafie und Chronologie: Archäologische und palynologische Analysen. Eine Fallstudie zum Fundplatz Bruszczewo 5 in Großpolen. In: J. Müller, J. Czebreszuk and J. Kneisel (eds.) *Bruszczewo II. Ausgrabungen und Forschungen in einer prähistorischen Siedlungskammer Großpolens.* Bonn: Habelt, 344-469.

Dörfler, W. and Müller, J. (eds.) 2008, *Umwelt - Wirtschaft - Siedlungen im dritten vorchristlichen Jahrtausend Mitteleuropas und Südskandinaviens [Tagung Kiel 2005],* Neumünster: Wachholtz.

Ebersbach, R. 2003, Paleoecological Reconstruction and Calculation of Calorie Requirements at Lake Zurich. In: J. Kunow and J. Müller (eds.) *Landschaftsarchäologie und geographische Informationssysteme. Prognosekarten, Besiedlungsdynamik und prähistorische Raumordnungen.* Wünsdorf: Landesamt, 69-88.

Haas, J. N. and Wahlmüller, N. 2010, Floren-, Vegetations- und Milieuveränderungen im Zuge der bronzezeitlichen Besiedlung von Bruszczewo (Polen) und der landwirtschaftlichen Nutzung der umliegenden Gebiete. In: J. Müller, J. Czebreszuk and J. Kneisel (eds.) *Bruszczewo II. Ausgrabungen und Forschungen in einer prähistorischen Siedlungskammer Großpolens.* Bonn: Habelt, 38-49.

Hartz, S., Heinrich, D. and Lübke, H. 2000, Frühe Bauern an der Küste. Neue 14C-Daten und aktuelle Aspekte zum Neolithisierungsprozeß im norddeutschen Ostseeküstengebiet. *Prähistorische Zeitschrift* 75: 129-152.

Hartz, S., Jakobsen, O. and Hoffmann-Wieck, G. 2004, Geoarchäologie im Oldenburger Graben. Genese und steinzeitliche Besiedlung einer ehemaligen Fjordlandschaft der westlichen Ostsee. *Offa* 82: 15-29.

Hartz, S., Mischka, D. and Müller, J. 2004/2005 (2007), Die neolithische Feuchtbodensiedlung Bad Oldesloe-Wolkenwehe LA 154. Resultate der Untersuchungen 1950-1952. *Offa* 61/62: 7-24.

Heußner, K.-U. and Wazny, T. 2010, Synchronisation der Dendrodaten für Bruszczewo nach der ostdeutschen Kurve. In: J. Müller, J. Czebreszuk and J. Kneisel (eds.) *Bruszczewo II. Ausgrabungen und Forschungen in einer prähistorischen Siedlungskammer Großpolens.* Bonn: Habelt, 244-249.

Hildebrandt-Radke, I. 2010, Das geologische Alter und die Hauptphasen der Denudations- und Akkumulationsprozesse vor dem Hintergrund der topografischen Verhältnisse des archäologischen Fundplatzes Bruszczewo. In: J. Müller, J. Czebreszuk and J. Kneisel (eds.) *Bruszczewo II. Ausgrabungen und Forschungen in einer prähistorischen Siedlungskammer Großpolens.* Bonn: Habelt, 16-37.

Hinz, M., Feeser, I., Sjögren, K.-G. and Müller, J. 2012, Demography and the intensity of cultural activities: an evaluation of Funnel Beaker Societies (4200-2800 cal BC). *Journal of Archaeological Science* 39, 3331-3340.

Hulthen, B. 1998, *The Alvastra pile dwelling pottery: an attempt to trace the society behind the sherds,* Stockholm/Lund: Historiska museet; Keramiska forskningslaboratoriet.

Iwanek, B., Piontek, J. and Nowak, O. 2010, Anthropologische Analyse des Skelettes aus Bruszczewo. In: J. Müller, J. Czebreszuk and J. Kneisel (eds.) *Bruszczewo II. Ausgrabungen und Forschungen in einer prähistorischen Siedlungskammer Großpolens.* Bonn: Habelt, 730-755.

Kirleis, W., Feeser, I. and Klooß, S. 2011a, Umwelt und Ökonomie. *Archäologie in Deutschland,* 2: 34-37.

Kirleis, W., Klooß, S., Kroll, H. and Müller, J. 2011b, New results on crop growing and gathering in the northern German Neolithic. *Vegetation History and Archaeobotany* DOI: 10.1007/s00334-011-0328-9.

Kirleis, W. and Klooß, S. (*accepted*), More than simply fallback food? Social context of plant use in the northern German Neolithic. In: A. Chevalier, E. Marinova and L Peña-Chocarro (eds.) *Plants and people. Choices and diversity through time. Earth Series 1.* Oxford: Oxbow Books.

Kneisel, J. 2010a, Das östliche Feuchtbodenareal: Stratigrafie des Schnitt 30, Fläche 1-4. In: J. Müller, J. Czebreszuk and J. Kneisel (eds.) *Bruszczewo II. Ausgrabungen und Forschungen in einer prähistorischen Siedlungskammer Großpolens.* Bonn: Habelt, 166-231.

Kneisel, J. 2010b, Die Grabungskampagnen Bruszczewo 2004-2006. In: J. Müller, J. Czebreszuk and J. Kneisel (eds.) *Bruszczewo II. Ausgrabungen und Forschungen in einer prähistorischen Siedlungskammer Großpolens.* Bonn: Habelt, 92-165.

Kneisel, J. 2010c, Eine Siedlungsbestattung der Frühbronzezeit. In: J. Müller, J. Czebreszuk and J. Kneisel (eds.) *Bruszczewo II. Ausgrabungen und Forschungen in einer prähistorischen Siedlungskammer Großpolens.* Bonn: Habelt, 724-729.

Kneisel, J., Bork, H.-R., Czebreszuk, J., Dörfler, W., Grootes, P., Haas, J. N., Heußner, K.-U., Hildebrandt-Radke, I., Kroll, H., Müller, J., Wahlmüller, N. and Wazny, T. 2008, Bruszczewo - Early Bronze Defensive Settlement in Wielkopolska. Metallurgy, peat zone finds and chnages in the environment. In: J. Czebreszuk, S. Kadrow and J. Müller (eds.) *Defensive Structures from Central Europe to the Aegean in the 3rd and 2nd millennia BC.* Poznan/Bonn: Habelt, 155-169.

Kneisel, J. and Kroll, H. 2010, Die Holzanalysen aus dem östlichen Feuchtbodenareal. In: J. Müller, J. Czebreszuk and J. Kneisel (eds.) *Bruszczewo II. Ausgrabungen und Forschungen in einer prähistorischen Siedlungskammer Großpolens.* Bonn: Habelt, 576-661.

Kossian, R. 2007, *Hunte 1: Ein mittel- bis spätneolithischer und frühbronzezeitlicher Siedlungsplatz am Dümmer, Ldkr. Diepholz (Niedersachsen). Die Ergebnisse der Ausgrabungen des Reichsamtes für Vorgeschichte in den Jahren 1938 bis 1940.* Hannover, Niedersächsisches Landesmuseum.

Magny, M., Bégeot, C., Peyron, O., Richoz, I., Marguet, A. and Billaud, Y. 2005, Habitats littoraux et histoire des premières communautés agricoles au Néolithique et à l'Âge du Bronze: une mise en perspective paléoclimatique. In: P. D. Casa and M. Trachsel (eds.) *WES'04 Wetland Economies And Societies. Proceedings Of The International Conference In Zurich, 10-13 March 2004.* Zürich, 133-142.

Mischka, D. 2006, Die Steinartefakte von Bad Oldesloe LA 154, Wolkenwehe: Ein Praktikum zum Umgang mit den Funden der Grabungen von 1950-1952. *Starigard* 7: 81-89.

Mischka, D., Dörfler, W., Grootes, P., Heinrich, D., Müller, J. and Nelle, O. 2003/2004 (2007), Die neolithische Feuchtbodensiedlung Bad Oldesloe-Wolkenwehe: Vorbericht zu den Untersuchungen 2006. *Offa* 59/60: 25-64.

Müller, J. 2004, Die östlichen Feuchtbodenareale. In: J. Czebreszuk and J. Müller (eds.) 2004a, *Bruszczewo I. Forschungsstand - Erste Ergebnisse - Das östliche Feuchtbodenareal,* Poznan/Kiel/Rahden: Leidorf, 99-134.

Müller, J. 2011, *Megaliths and Funnel Beakers: Societies in Change 4100-2700 BC,* Amsterdam: Amsterdams Archaeologisch Centrum van der Universiteit Amsterdam.

Müller, J., Czebreszuk, J. and Kneisel, J. (eds.) 2010, *Bruszczewo II. Ausgrabungen und Forschungen in einer prähistorischen Siedlungskammer Großpolens,* Bonn: Habelt.

Müller, J., Bork, H. R., Brozio, J. P., Demnick, D., Diers, S., Dibbern, H., Dörfler, W., Feeser, I., Fritsch, B., Furholt, M., Hage, F., Hinz, M., Kirleis, W., Klooß, S., Kroll, H., Lorenz, M. L. L., Mischka, D. and Rinne, C. in print, Landscapes as Social Spaces and Ritual Meaning: Some New Results on TRB in Northern Germany. *Borger-Conference.*

Müller, J. and Kneisel, J. 2010, Bruszczewo 5: Production, distribution, consumption, and the formation of social differences. In: J. Müller, J. Czebreszuk, and J. Kneisel (eds.) *Bruszczewo II. Ausgrabungen und Forschungen in einer prähistorischen Siedlungskammer Großpolens.* Bonn: Habelt, 756-783.

Reinerth, H. 1939, Ein Dorf der Großsteingräberleute - Die Ausgrabungen des Reichsamtes für Vorgeschichte am Dümmer. *Germanenerbe* 4: 226-242.

Schlichtherle, H. (ed.) 1997, *Pfahlbauten rund um die Alpen.* Stuttgart: Theiss.

Schwabedissen, H. 1940, Aufdeckung eines Wohnplatzes der Großsteingräberkultur im Heidmoor, Gem. Berlin, Kr. Segeberg. *Nachrichtenblatt für deutsche Vorzeit.* 16: 83-85.

Schwabedissen, H. 1951, Probegrabungen auf Moorsiedlungen der jüngeren Steinzeit. *Germania* 29: 310.

Schwabedissen, H. 1953, Probegrabungen auf Moorsiedlungen der jüngeren Steinzeit. *Germania* 31: 310.

Schwabedissen, H. 1959, Die jungsteinzeitlichen Wohnplätze der Trichterbecherkultur aus Sachsenwaldau und Wolkenwehe. In: H. Hingst (ed.) *Vorgeschichte Kreis Storman.* Neumünster: Wacholtz, 24-27.

Wazny, T. 2010, Bericht zur dendrochronologischen Datierung von Bruszczewo, Grabungen 2004-2005. In: J. Müller, J. Czebreszuk and J. Kneisel (eds.) *Bruszczewo II. Ausgrabungen und Forschungen in einer prähistorischen Siedlungskammer Großpolens.* Bonn: Habelt, 232-237.

Wiethold, J. 1998. *Studien zur jüngeren postglazialen Vegetations- und Siedlungsgeschichte im östlichen Schleswig-Holstein,* Bonn, Habelt.

Chapter 4

ALL IN GOOD TRADITION? SOME THOUGHTS ON CULTURAL MARKERS IN A LATE NEOLITHIC LAKESIDE DWELLING FROM SWITZERLAND

*Thomas Doppler, Sandra Pichler,
Brigitte Röder, Jörg Schibler[1]*

Abstract

With its Neolithic and Bronze Age wetland sites, Switzerland offers an incomparable source of information on prehistoric dwellings. The exceptional preservation of wooden construction elements, along with the advances in dendrochronology allow not only identification and dating of individual houses to the year, but also understanding of a settlement's evolution and comparison of material assemblages between individual houses. Such an approach was taken on the late Neolithic lakeside dwelling Arbon Bleiche 3, where coexistence of a local and an immigrant population group is attested. The hypothesis put forward is that animal food remains are more stable and lasting indicators of cultural traditions than ceramics.

Keywords: Neolithic, Switzerland, wetland archaeology, social archaeology, archaeozoology, ceramics

---

1 IPAS, Institute for Prehistory and Archaeological Science, Basel University, Spalenring 145, 4055 Basel (Switzerland), thomas.doppler@unibas.ch; sandra.pichler@unibas.ch; brigitte.roeder@unibas.ch; joerg.schibler@unibas.ch

Introduction

Archaeological sites around moors, coastlines and lake sides, which already fascinated Robert Munro, are of particular importance due to their exceptional preservation. Indeed, wooden construction elements are generally preserved well enough to be dated to the year based on tree rings. As a result, the layout of individual houses and their exact year of construction can be determined. This, in turn, enables archaeologists to reconstruct the development of the entire settlements, permitting detailed insights otherwise unattainable. This potential of information, described as a "treasurehouse of knowledge" by Andrew Sherratt (2004, 269), is characteristic of Switzerland, with its numerous Neolithic and Bronze Age lakeside dwellings. The wetland site discussed here dates from the 34th century BC. In the Swiss chronology, this corresponds to the early Late Neolithic, where a generalized and continuous transition from the Pfyn to the Horgen culture took place. Not only does this site lie at a transition period, but it also represents a timespan for which few sites are known. Further, it is a period which is marked by an increasing influence from the East (e.g. Köninger et al. 2001).

Arbon Bleiche 3: glimpse into a sparsely known period

The settlement of Arbon Bleiche 3 is located on the southern shore of Lake Constance (Figure 4.1). It was excavated from 1993 to 1995 by the Archaeological Service of Thurgau (Amt für Archäologie Thurgau). Due to the waterlogged, hermetically sealed archaeological sediments, organic remains as well as finds and features were very well preserved. Over a surface of about 1100 m^2 a total of 27 house plans were identified (Figure 4.2). It is thought to represent a third, or even half, of the original settlement surface (Leuzinger 2000, 15-17, 173). Compared to other lakeside dwellings, the excavated area is remarkable and the results of its analysis can be considered representative. The uncovered houses are quite uniform, with an average size of 4 x 8 metres. Only two small buildings appear square in plan measuring 2 x 2 metres (house 17 and 25) and are exceptions to this regularity. The houses are lined up in rows which are separated by narrow lanes. Dendrochronological analyses enabled the establishment of the year of construction for every house, thus allowing the reconstruction of the settlement history and its dynamics in the excavated area. It has been shown that the settlement came into existence in 3384 BC and had to be abandoned, due to a devastating fire, in 3370 BC (Leuzinger 2000, 51-87). The fact that no other settlement phase was found before or after the

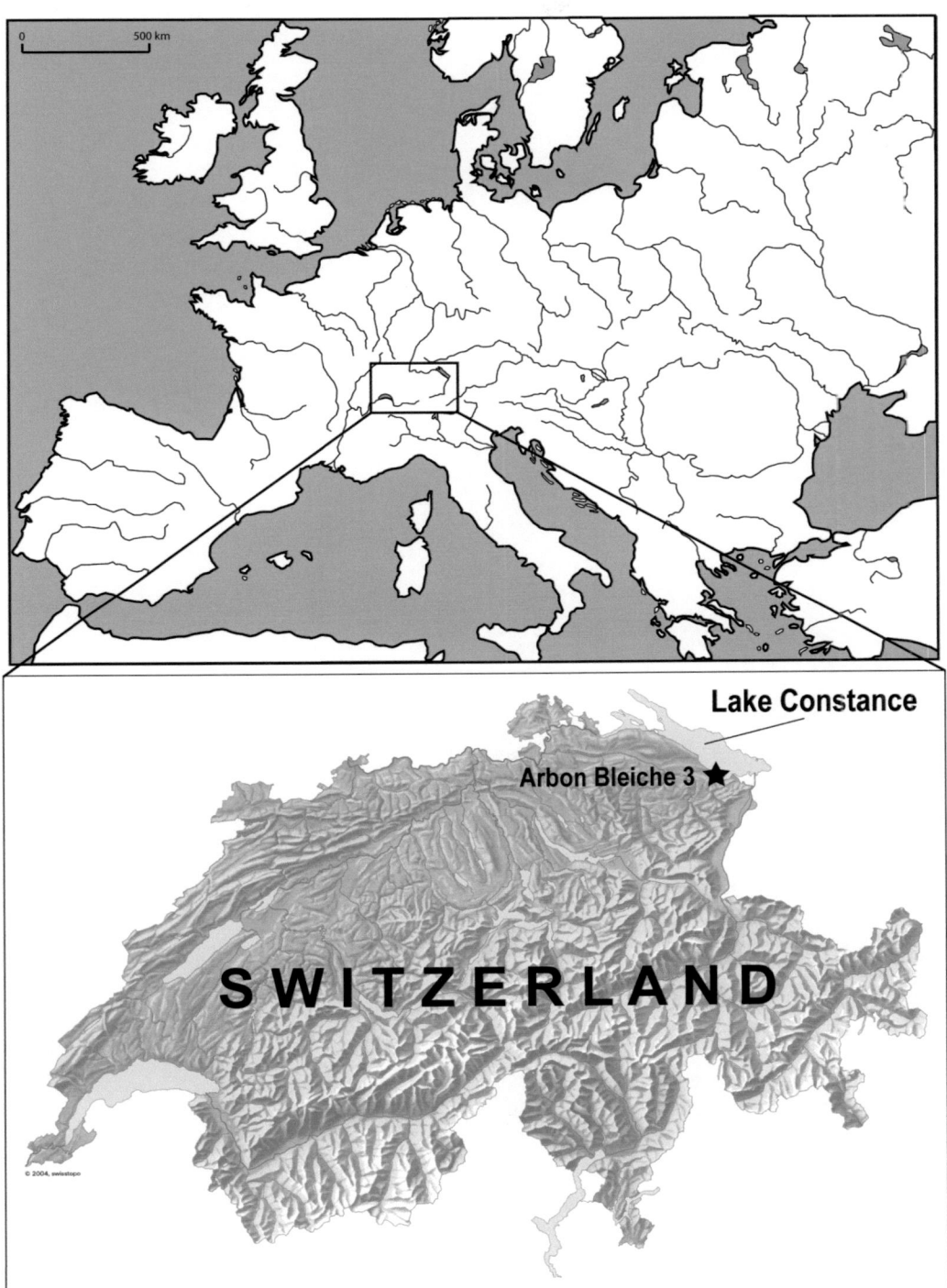

Figure 4.1 Location of the Neolithic lakeside settlement of Arbon Bleiche 3.

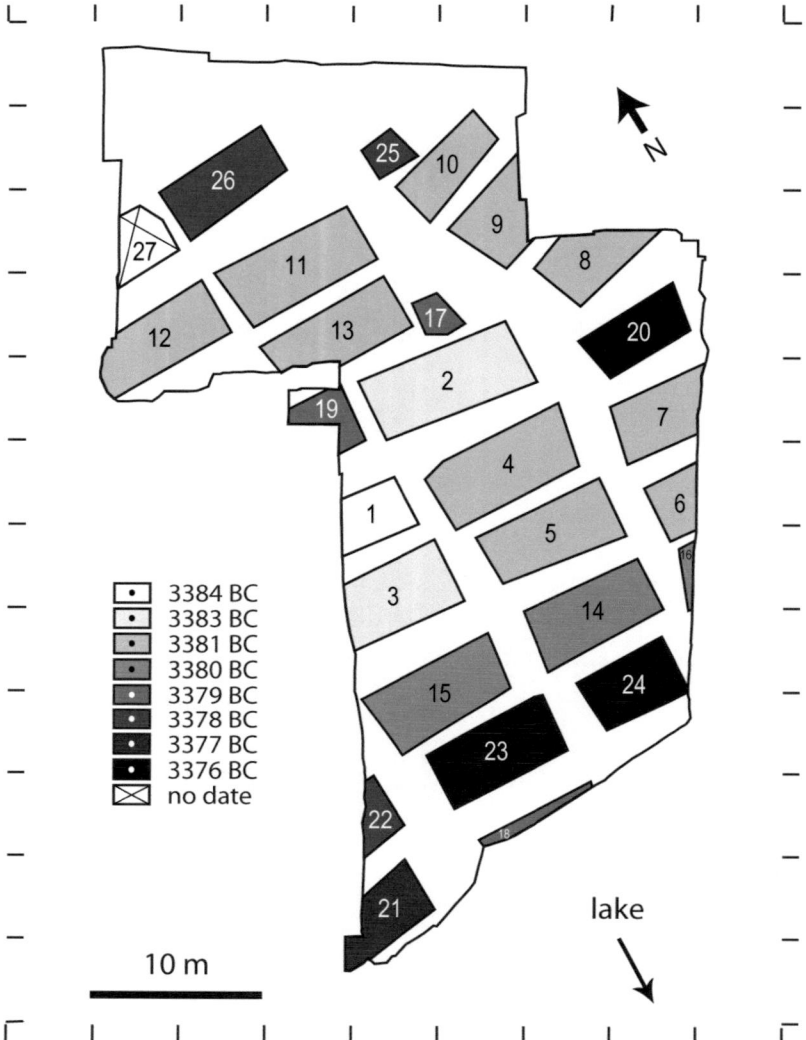

Figure 4.2 Dendrochronologically dated house plans with year of construction (modified after de Capitani et al. 2002, 21, Fig. 10).

documented occupation excludes a mixing up of different layers and periods. Even within the short and single-phased occupation, hardly any horizontal and vertical mixing took place which was revealed by several interdisciplinary analyses of the layer formation processes (Brombacher and Hadorn 2004, Deschler-Erb and Marti-Grädel 2004a, Haas and Magny 2004, Ismail-Meyer and Rentzel 2004, Thew 2004). The settlement is therefore particularly well suited to studying spatial patterns of material remains, both in individual houses and in the settlement as a whole. It is the most intensively analyzed Neolithic wetland site in Switzerland and all results have been published in three volumes (Leuzinger 2000, de Capitani et al. 2002, Jacomet et al. 2004a).

Different ceramic traditions within one settlement

Besides local ceramics which – as the settlement is positioned in a chronological transition phase – show characteristics of both Pfyn and Horgen traditions, there is evidence of vessels attributed to the Baden culture and, to a lesser extent, to the Altheim culture

Figure 4.3 The ceramic found in Arbon Bleiche 3 could be attributed to different cultures. Above: pottery with characteristics of both Pfyn and Horgen traditions. Below, left: Baden pottery. Below, right: Altheim pottery (modified after de Capitani 2002, 146, Fig. 198; 210, Fig. 311; 218, Fig. 319 – all photographs by Amt für Archäologie Thurgau, D. Steiner).

(de Capitani 2002, 222; Figure 4.3). The ceramics found in Arbon Bleiche 3 belonging to the Baden Culture correspond mostly to the early Baden period, also called the Boleráz group. Its core lies in east Austria, west Hungary, southwestern Slovakia and Moravia. Bohemia, Silesia, Little Poland and the northeastern part of old Yugoslavia form the periphery of the Boleráz group (de Capitani 2002, 210). Concerning the pottery belonging to the Altheim culture, parallels could be drawn with Bavaria (de Capitani 2002, 219). Since this foreign pottery is not just represented by single finds but appears on a regular basis (34 vessels attributed to the Baden culture and 11 vessels attributed to the Altheim culture; de Capitani 2002, 216, 219), it is thought that they are not imported objects. This is supported by the fact that the foreign pottery has been manufactured with clay found around the site and which therefore is of local origin (Bonzon 2004, 312). As a result, it is believed that, since the ceramic objects were not exchange goods, people from the Baden and Altheim culture areas came to Lake Constance, bringing with them their technological know-how, and integrated with already established local inhabitants. This would explain the coexistence of distinct ceramic traditions present at Arbon Bleiche 3. In accordance with the pottery, there are other elements pointing towards an eastern influence. This is the case with plant remains where flax and emmer increase in frequency. The same is true for clay spindle whorls, and the increasing amount of cattle remains, which could be linked to the advent of draught animals (Jacomet et al. 2004b, 410-411), although the latter may also be due to specific subsistence strategies and dietary habits.

Archaeozoological data as valuable information source

Arbon Bleiche 3 is characterized by rich and diverse material remains comprising not only archaeological artefacts but also a wealth of archaeobiological remains. Animal bones represent an especially valuable information source because they are found in almost every site and are closely connected to dietary habits – an essential element of everyday life.

The basic animal bone identification for the Arbon Bleiche 3 site was undertaken by Sabine Deschler-Erb and Elisabeth Marti-Grädel, while fish remains were studied by Heide Hüster Plogmann (Deschler-Erb and Marti-Grädel 2004b, Hüster Plogmann 2004). Their subsequent distribution analyses yielded truly remarkable results. The analysis of the rich faunal remains – about 70,000 bone fragments in total – revealed an interesting internal division of the settlement. In the northern part evidence of intense beef consumption was found, whereas in the southern part more pork was consumed (Deschler-Erb and Marti-Grädel 2004b, 221-223; Marti-Grädel et al. 2004). Less conspicuous, but likewise significant, was the concentration of ovicaprid bones in the northern houses nos. 2, 11 and 13. This was quite clearly confirmed by our analyses (Doppler *in preparation*).

Remarkably, the difference between the two settlement halves was also visible in the fish remains; while larger amounts of fish caught near the shore were found in the northern part of the settlement, open water species prevailed in the southern half (Hüster Plogmann 2004, 272-274; Figure 4.4). Although the database for the fish – as well as for the botanical remains, which will not be discussed here (see Hosch and Jacomet 2004, Röder et al. *in preparation* a) – is somewhat limited by the restricted sampling area (Leuzinger and Jacomet 2004, 35-39), the findings nonetheless support the results obtained for the large animal bones. These are certainly valid because they were recorded, with numerous specimens recovered,

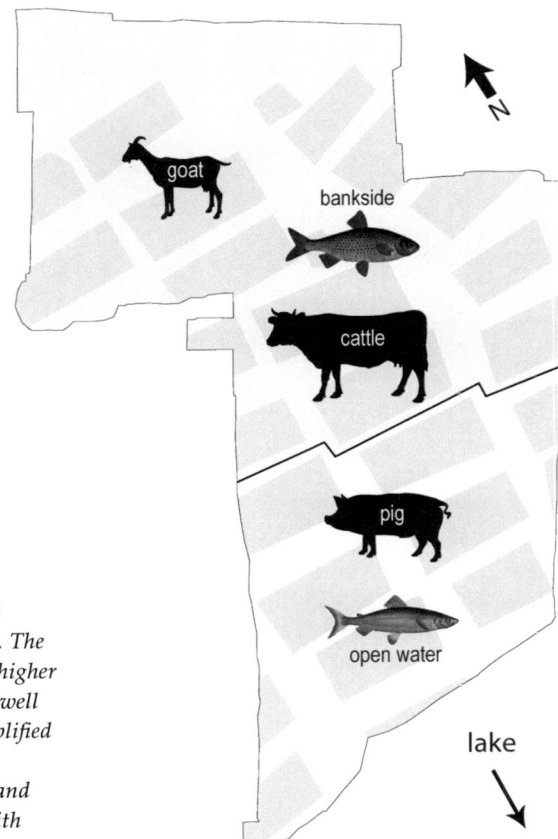

Figure 4.4 Simplified sketch of the internal division of Arbon Bleiche 3 according to archaeozoological data. The northern part is characterized by a higher amount of cattle and goat bones, as well as fish caught near the shore (exemplified here with a carp). In the southern part, a higher amount of pig bones and open water fish (exemplified here with whitefish) is to be noted.

Figure 4.5 Horizontal distribution of all animal bones in the cultural layer according to fragment number (modified after Deschler-Erb and Marti Grädel 2004b, 159, Fig. 140). The northwestern part is poor in finds due to preservation issues. The grey stripes in the northern part of the settlement represent test trenches examined in 1983 which are not mapped here (Leuzinger and Jacomet 2004, 29-30).

over the whole settlement area. The only grey area remains the northwestern part of the settlement which showed poor preservation (Deschler-Erb and Marti Grädel 2004a, 93-94; Figure 4.5). Based on the marked contrast in the distribution pattern of the animal remains, the question of differences in subsistence and dietary habits arises. Indeed, this pattern may reflect, at least partially, a difference in cultural tradition, or the presence of culturally distinct groups (Marti-Grädel et al. 2004, 175).

Hybridisation of ceramic traditions? Animal bones as cultural markers?

There are only a few archaeozoological studies which have been carried out on Altheim or Baden sites and the current state of knowledge in that domain is far from satisfying. The existing data points towards cattle and small ruminants being central to the economy in both of these cultures, whereas pig seems to have been less favoured (Murray 1973, 182-184; Milisauskas and Kruk 1989, 436-437; Benecke 1994, 79, 89-90; Pucher and Schmitzberger 1999, 623; Deschler-Erb and Marti-Grädel 2004b, 251). In east Switzerland, however, pig is more ubiquitous in archaeozoological assemblages, making the high number of pig fragments in Arbon Bleiche 3 unsurprising (Schibler 2004, 2006). Thus, it would seem that the high amount of cattle and goat bones in the northern part of the dwelling reflects an actual dietary preference linked to an external cultural influence.

In light of the formulated hypothesis, based on animal remains, that cultural preferences can be observed spatially in Arbon Bleiche 3, ceramic as a cultural indicator was also considered. A first step was to concentrate on the foreign pottery (Figure 4.6). Although there are some general tendencies as to their distribution in space, there are no particular concentration spots showing a marked difference between the northern and southern parts of the settlement. The poor preservation in the northernmost part of the site, however, has to be taken into account (de Capitani 2002, 139-140). Even if the given picture is not uniformly representative, the pottery does not seem to point towards any cultural discrepancy between the northern and the southern halves of the settlement. At first sight, this may come as a disappointment when considering the promising results revealed by the archaeozoological analysis. A closer investigation of the ceramic analyses does, however, uncover some interesting aspects.

Archaeometry and archaeology indicate that an exchange of technological know-how took place. This is shown by the presence of foreign vessels manufactured using local technology (granite temper) and local vessels manufactured using foreign technology

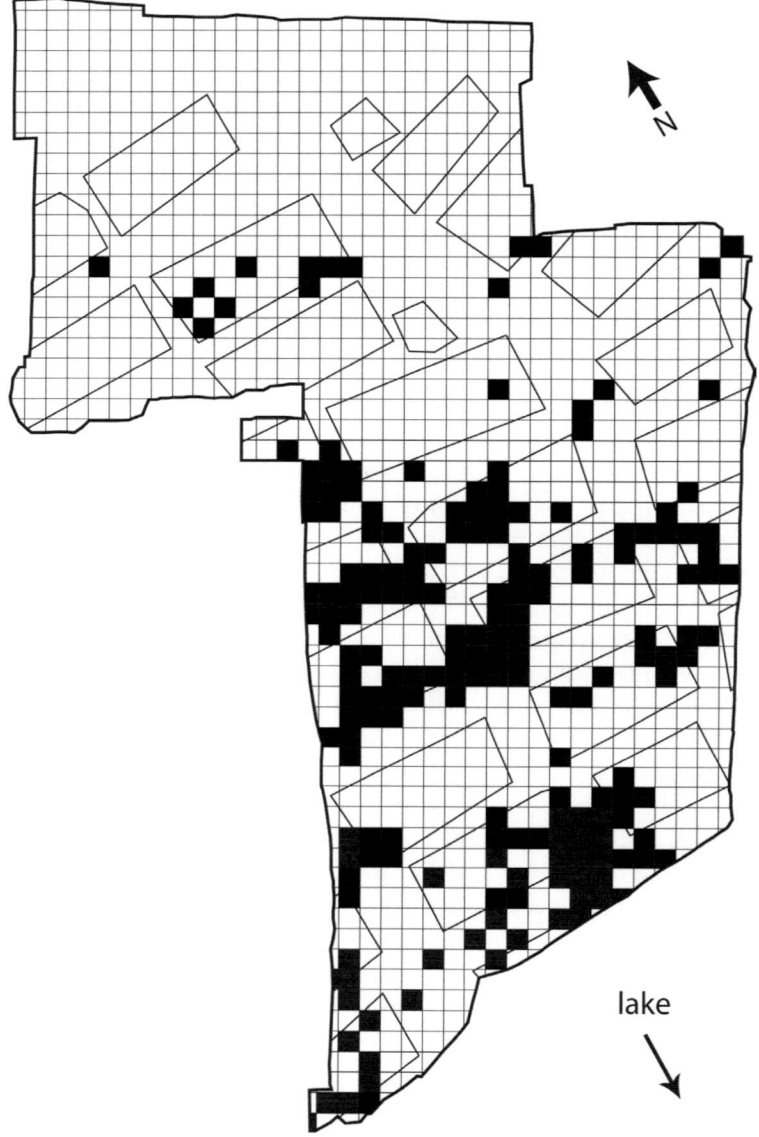

Figure 4.6 Horizontal distribution of foreign ceramic (culture and burnt layers shown together; Baden fragments: n = 626, Altheim fragments: n = 351). Evidence for foreign ceramic is shown per square meter (black: presence, white: absence) regardless of fragmentation (modified after de Capitani 2002, 217, Fig. 317, 219, Fig. 321).

(grog temper; de Capitani 2002, 215-216; Bonzon 2004, 294). This type of evidence points towards active interchange between the inhabitants of Arbon Bleiche 3. This would possibly include the exchange of both knowledge and artefacts, leading to a uniform spatial distribution of the different types of pottery; hence the absence of any visible spatial division of cultural groups within the settlement. Also, linked to this inter-mixture of pottery forms, are the observations made by de Capitani (2002, 169) that pottery manufactured according to the Baden technology is more common in Arbon Bleiche 3 at the beginning of the settlement. If we presume that these "foreigners" didn't simply emigrate, then the only explanation is that they adopted local technology as well as, in time, form.

In order to develop the cultural differences hypothesis, a correspondence analysis on the available data was carried out. Correspondence analysis is widely used in archaeology but its application is mostly limited to chronological issues, particularly in connection with the seriation of grave inventories. Its potential for the detection of associations beyond chronological questions – in the sense of exploratory data analysis – has hardly been realized so far. The method offers great potential for the analysis of archaeobiological data with regard to socio-historical issues as demonstrated in first attempts by Moreno-García et al. (1996), Hüster-Plogmann et al. (1999), Valamoti (2005), Jacomet and Schibler (2006) and van der Veen (2007).

In the case of the cultural differences hypothesis specific to Arbon Bleiche 3, the potential of canonical correspondence analysis is of special interest. The methodological approach, the underlying data, and the exhaustive statistical interpretation will be explained in a forthcoming publication (Doppler *in preparation*). We will therefore not go into much detail here. It should just be noted that this variant of correspondence analysis works with ordination variables, which makes it possible to include pre-existing findings or knowledge in the analysis and to predefine the analytical structure (e.g. ter Braak 1986, Greenacre 2007). The data – the target variables – are arranged according to the specifications. From the resulting diagram, the distribution of the target variables in relation to each ordination variable, which appear as arrows on the illustration, can be deduced and interpreted. In our analysis, we chose ordination variables which are believed to be connected with the Baden culture and which can therefore be interpreted as markers for a cultural influence from the Baden culture area (Jacomet et al. 2004b, 410-411). The potential influence from the Altheim culture will not be discussed due to the paucity of the evidence. Besides the pottery, we included spindle whorls, indications for the use of draught animals and the evidence of emmer and flax as ordination variables (Figure 4.7). The result of these analyses shows that the blending of cultural traditions is especially apparent in artefacts and tool technologies (Doppler *in*

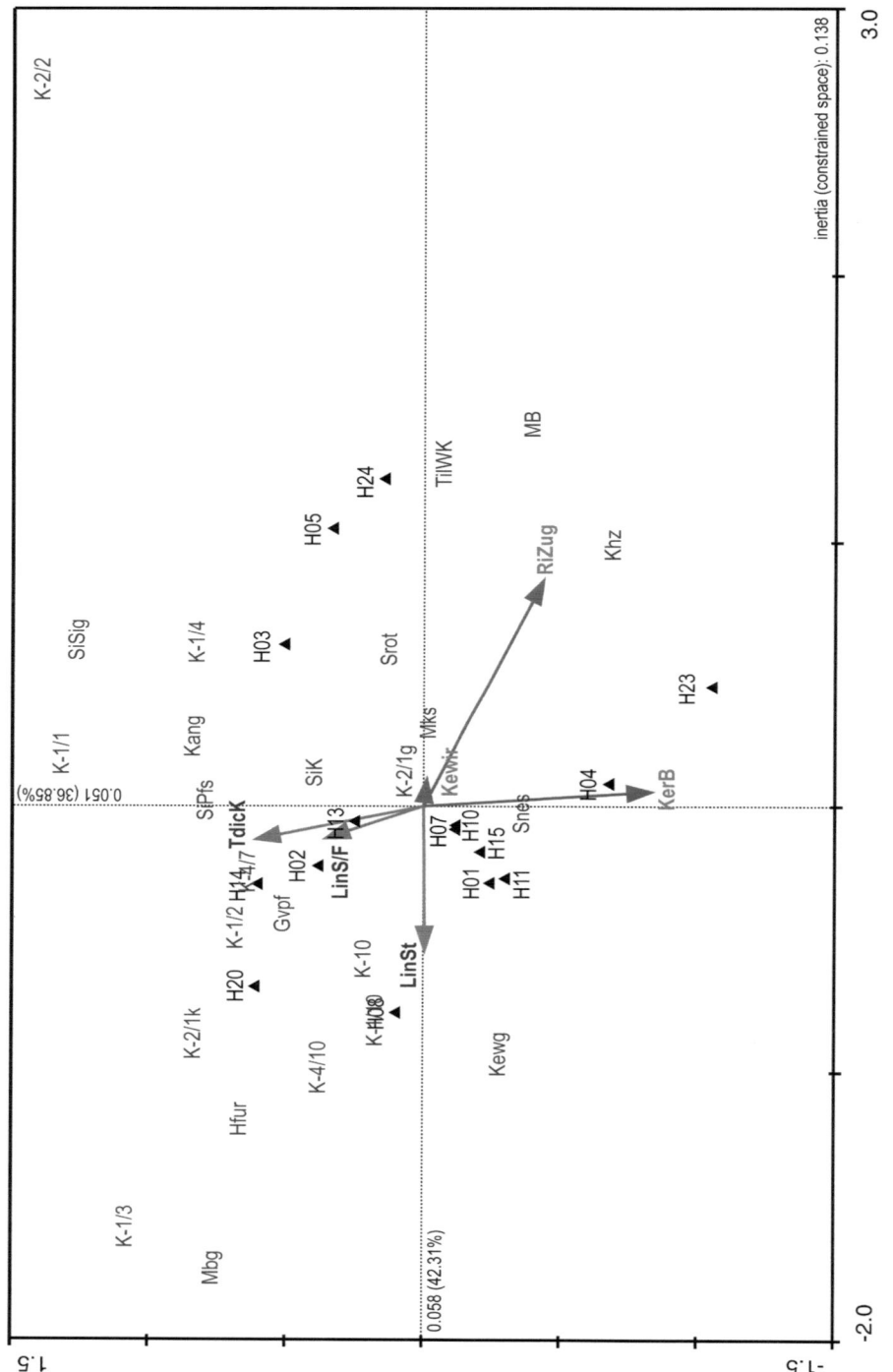

Figure 4.7 Example of a canonical correspondence analysis based on the number of selected artefact types in the Arbon Bleiche 3 cultural layer. The arrows represent the ordination variables ceramics (KerB), spindle whorls (Kewir), indications for the use of draught animals (RiZug), emmer (TdicK) and flax (LinS/F and LinSt). Total inertia: 0.630; inertia of the constrained space: 0.138 (= 21.9%). The diagram illustrates the first and second dimension of the constrained space, which explain 79.2% of the data variance.

preparation). This corroborates our hypothesis that blending, or reciprocal influence, results in producing distribution patterns which can no longer be interpreted with regard to identifying cultural differences in the archaeological record. In spite of the blending, the presence of different cultural traditions was still fairly easy to detect in Arbon Bleiche 3 because of the conspicuous Baden and Altheim vessels. Yet, our findings clearly show that ceramics are not necessarily a strong marker of cultural identity – a statement which certainly is not entirely easy to accept in archaeology.

However, differences between the northern and southern halves of the settlement do emerge from the analysis of the animal bones. This leads us to conclude that, in our case, the animal bones, or rather the dietary habits they represent, might possibly be better cultural markers than the ceramics. In our opinion, it is therefore quite feasible to link the differences in the distribution of animal bones in Arbon Bleiche 3 to different cultural traditions. The literature clearly shows that dietary habits are determined to a high degree by cultural factors and that they represent a very stable cultural element (e.g. Messer 1984). Even if alternative interpretations for the observed differences might be considered, for instance the existence of unequal religious dietary rules or the existence of social groups based on gender or alliances, we think it likely that the increased portions of cattle and goats – and possibly the high amount of fish caught close to shore – in the northern part of the settlement are linked to eastern cultural traditions.

Conclusions

Our findings illustrate varying forms of intercultural contacts within Arbon Bleiche 3. We can state that this settlement allows the detection of dynamic processes that highlight coexistence and interaction of different cultural groups which led to reciprocal influences and hybridisation seen in the material remains. Such processes may result in the blending of distinct characteristics in material culture so that they are no longer detectable with conventional analyses. These observations are of socio-historical importance. They highlight the need to go beyond our all too often static perspectives of archaeological finds and features (e.g. Bleicher 2009, Ebersbach 2010). In our case, this is certainly made possible by the rich number of houses excavated within a large surface and dated to precise years, as well as the possibility to contrast the cultural layer with a conflagration layer (Leuzinger 2000, Doppler *in preparation*). Our conclusions indicate that we must anticipate finding developments and changes which may have occurred in a short time even though the temporality of such processes depends on different factors (Fokkens 2008) and may not be conclusively determined. However, our results suggest that such processes occurred much faster in the case of tools and technologies than of dietary habits and the use of animal resources. The latter appear to be much more stable and lasting. This, in turn, leads us to conclude that, in our case study, the animal bones might be a more reliable indicator of cultural identity than the ceramics. It remains to be seen whether future studies will corroborate this observation.

Furthermore, the clear settlement division as shown by animal bone distribution is a remarkable contradiction to a latent premise in wetland archaeology which suggests that the commonly uniform houses in lakeside dwellings reflect cultural, social and economic uniformity. Such an assumption rules out the possible coexistence of social groups with different traditions and subsistence strategies. All houses are supposed to follow the same subsistence strategy using identical means of production and having the same dietary habits. Due to the presupposed uniform resource use and dietary habits, there should not be any substantial differences in refuse composition and inventories among the houses (Doppler et al. 2011). The fact that we see such differences between the houses in Arbon Bleiche 3 leads us to take another look at archaeological households (most fundamentally Wilk and Rathje 1982) and shows that untested research premises have to be challenged. Instead of the autarky of houses and homogenous behaviour in Neolithic lakeside settlements we must rather assume heterogeneity and the existence of complex networks of interaction and cooperation within settlements (Doppler *in preparation*). Such networking may, for example, have constituted an advantage in handling difficult situations or crises (Doppler et al. *in preparation*, Röder et al. *in preparation* b).

The fact that animal remains are the focus of this study is by no means a coincidence. Firstly, they are generally abundant on archaeological sites and secondly, the last twenty years of research have increasingly shown their potential in answering socio-historical questions (e.g. Crabtree 1990, Gifford-Gonzalez 1991, Scott 1996, Gumerman 1997, Rowley-Conwy 2000, Miracle and Milner 2002, Jones O'Day et al. 2004, Marciniak 2005, Vigne et al. 2005, deFrance 2009). We therefore strongly advocate a more diverse utilization of the socio-historical potential of archaeozoological data in order to establish social archaeozoology as a valuable and accepted tool in archaeological research. Using the proposed approach on the wealth of data available from Europe's numerous wetland sites will contribute significantly to our understanding of the past, and refine the picture drawn by Robert Munro more than 100 years ago.

Acknowledgements

We owe our thanks to Stefanie Jacomet and many collaborators at the Institute for Prehistory and Archaeological Science at Basel University for fruitful discussions and many useful hints. We also thank the Archaeological Service of Thurgau for help and further information on Arbon Bleiche 3. We are furthermore grateful to Géraldine D'Eyrames and Ben Jennings for their support during translation. This paper was realized as part of the research project "New foundations for research in prehistoric archaeology", funded by the Swiss National Science Foundation.

References

Benecke, N. 1994, *Archäozoologische Studien zur Entwicklung der Haustierhaltung in Mitteleuropa und Südskandinavien von den Anfängen bis zum ausgehenden Mittelalter.* Schriften zur Ur- und Frühgeschichte 46. Berlin: Akademie Verlag.

Bleicher, N. 2009, *Altes Holz in neuem Licht - Archäologische und dendrochronologische Untersuchungen an spätneolithischen Feuchtbodensiedlungen Oberschwabens.* Materialhefte zur Archäologie in Baden-Württemberg 83. Stuttgart: Konrad Theiss Verlag.

Bonzon, J. 2004, Archaeometrical study (petrography, mineralogy and chemistry) of the ceramics. In: S. Jacomet, U. Leuzinger and J. Schibler (eds.) *Die jungsteinzeitliche Seeufersiedlung Arbon-Bleiche 3: Umwelt und Wirtschaft.* Archäologie im Thurgau 12. Frauenfeld: Departement für Erziehung und Kultur des Kantons Thurgau, 294-312.

Brombacher, C. and Hadorn, P. 2004, Untersuchungen der Pollen und Makroreste aus den Profilsäulen. In: S. Jacomet, U. Leuzinger and J. Schibler (eds.) *Die jungsteinzeitliche Seeufersiedlung Arbon Bleiche 3: Umwelt und Wirtschaft.* Archäologie im Thurgau 12. Frauenfeld: Departement für Erziehung und Kultur des Kantons Thurgau, 50-65.

Crabtree, P.J. 1990, Zooarchaeology and Complex Societies: Some Uses of Faunal Analysis for the Study of Trade, Social Status, and Ethnicity. In: M.B. Schiffer (ed.) *Archaeological Method and Theory.* Tucson: The University of Arizona Press, 155-205.

de Capitani, A. 2002, Gefässkeramik. In: A. de Capitani, S. Deschler-Erb, U. Leuzinger, E. Marti-Grädel and J. Schibler (eds.) *Die jungsteinzeitliche Seeufersiedlung Arbon Bleiche 3: Funde.* Archäologie im Thurgau 11. Frauenfeld: Departement für Erziehung und Kultur des Kantons Thurgau, 135-276.

de Capitani, A., Deschler-Erb, S., Leuzinger, U., Marti-Grädel, E. and Schibler, J. (eds.) 2002, *Die jungsteinzeitliche Seeufersiedlung Arbon Bleiche 3: Funde.* Archäologie im Thurgau 11. Frauenfeld: Departement für Erziehung und Kultur des Kantons Thurgau.

deFrance, S.D. 2009, Zooarchaeology in Complex Societies: Political Economy, Status, and Ideology. *Journal of Archaeological Research* 17: 105-168.

Deschler-Erb, S. and Marti-Grädel, E. 2004a, Hinweise zur Schichterhaltung aufgrund der Tierknochen. In: S. Jacomet, U. Leuzinger and J. Schibler (eds.) *Die jungsteinzeitliche Seeufersiedlung Arbon-Bleiche 3: Umwelt und Wirtschaft*. Archäologie im Thurgau 12. Frauenfeld: Departement für Erziehung und Kultur des Kantons Thurgau, 90-100.

Deschler-Erb, S. and Marti-Grädel, E. 2004b, Viehhaltung und Jagd. Ergebnisse der Untersuchung der handaufgelesenen Tierknochen. In: S. Jacomet, U. Leuzinger and J. Schibler (eds.) *Die jungsteinzeitliche Seeufersiedlung Arbon-Bleiche 3: Umwelt und Wirtschaft*. Archäologie im Thurgau 12. Frauenfeld: Departement für Erziehung und Kultur des Kantons Thurgau, 158-252.

Doppler, T. in preparation, *Archäozoologie als Zugang zur Sozialgeschichte in der Feuchtbodenarchäologie. Forschungsperspektiven am Fallbeispiel der neolithischen Seeufersiedlung Arbon Bleiche 3 (Schweiz)*. PhD Thesis 2009, Basel University.

Doppler, T., Pollmann, B., Pichler, S., Jacomet, S., Schibler, J. and Röder, B. 2011, Bauern, Fischerinnen und Jäger: Unterschiedliche Ressourcen- und Landschaftsnutzung in der neolithischen Siedlung Arbon Bleiche 3 (Thurgau, Schweiz)? In: J. Studer, M. David-Elbiali and M. Besse (eds.) *Paysage…Landschaft…Paesaggio… L'impact des activités humaines sur l'environnement du Paléolithique à la période romaine*. Cahiers d'archéologie romande 120. Lausanne: Musée d'archéologie et d'histoire, 143-158.

Doppler, T., Pichler, S., Röder, B. and Schibler, J. in preparation, Coping with crises: Subsistence variety and resilience in the Neolithic lakeshore settlement Arbon Bleiche 3 (Switzerland).

Ebersbach, R. 2010, Vom Entstehen und Vergehen – Überlegungen zur Dynamik von Feuchtbodenhäusern und –siedlungen. In: I. Matuschik, C. Strahm, B. Eberschweiler, G. Fingerlin, A. Hafner, M. Kinsky, M. Mainberger and G. Schöbel (eds.) *Vernetzungen. Aspekte siedlungsarchäologischer Forschung*. Festschrift für Helmut Schlichtherle zum 60. Geburtstag. Freiburg im Breisgau: Lavori Verlag, 41-50.

Fokkens, H. 2008, The temporality of culture change. In: H. Fokkens, B.J. Coles, A.L. van Gijn, J.P. Kleijne, H.H. Ponjee, C.G. Slappendel (eds.) *Between Foraging and Farming – an extended broad spectrum of papers presented to Leendert Louwe Kooijmans*. Analecta Praehistorica Leidensia 40. Leiden: Faculty of Archaeology, Leiden University, 15-24.

Gifford-Gonzalez, D. 1991, Bones are not enough: analogues, knowledge, and interpretive strategies in zooarchaeology. *Journal of Anthropological Archaeology* 10: 215-254.

Greenacre, M. 2007, *Correspondence Analysis in Practice*. Boca Raton: Chapman & Hall/CRC.

Gumerman, G. 1997, Food and Complex Societies. *Journal of Archaeological Method and Theory* 4(2): 105-139.

Haas, J.N. and Magny, M. 2004, Schichtgenese und Vegetationsgeschichte. In: S. Jacomet, U. Leuzinger and J. Schibler (eds.) *Die jungsteinzeitliche Seeufersiedlung Arbon Bleiche 3: Umwelt und Wirtschaft*. Archäologie im Thurgau 12. Frauenfeld: Departement für Erziehung und Kultur des Kantons Thurgau, 43-49.

Hosch, S. and Jacomet, S. 2004, Ackerbau und Sammelwirtschaft. Ergebnisse der Untersuchung von Samen und Früchten. In: S. Jacomet, U. Leuzinger and J. Schibler (eds.) *Die jungsteinzeitliche Seeufersiedlung Arbon Bleiche 3: Umwelt und Wirtschaft*. Archäologie im Thurgau 12. Frauenfeld: Departement für Erziehung und Kultur des Kantons Thurgau, 112-157.

Hüster Plogmann, H. 2004, Fischfang und Kleintierbeute. Ergebnisse der Untersuchung von Tierresten aus den Schlämmproben. In: S. Jacomet, U. Leuzinger and J. Schibler (eds.) *Die jungsteinzeitliche Seeufersiedlung Arbon-Bleiche 3: Umwelt und Wirtschaft*. Archäologie im Thurgau 12. Frauenfeld: Departement für Erziehung und Kultur des Kantons Thurgau, 253-276.

Hüster-Plogmann, H., Jordan, P., Rehazek, A., Schibler, J. and Veszeli, M. 1999, Mittelalterliche Ernährungswirtschaft, Haustierhaltung und Jagd. Eine archäozoologische Untersuchung ausgewählter Fundensembles aus der Schweiz und dem angrenzenden Ausland. *Beiträge zur Mittelalterarchäologie in Österreich* 15: 223-240.

Ismail-Meyer, K. and Rentzel, P. 2004, Mikromorphologische Untersuchung der Schichtabfolge. In: S. Jacomet, U. Leuzinger and J. Schibler (eds.) *Die jungsteinzeitliche Seeufersiedlung Arbon Bleiche 3: Umwelt und Wirtschaft*. Archäologie im Thurgau 12. Frauenfeld: Departement für Erziehung und Kultur des Kantons Thurgau, 66-80.

Jacomet, S. and Schibler, J. 2006, Traction animale et données paléoenvironnementales au Néolithique dans le nord des Alpes. In: P. Pétrequin, R.-M. Arbogast, A.-M. Pétrequin, S. van Willigen, and M. Bailly (eds.) *Premiers chariots, premiers araires - La diffusion de la traction animale en Europe pendant les IVe et IIIe millénaires avant notre ère*. Paris: CNRS éditions, 141-155.

Jacomet, S., Leuzinger, U. and Schibler, J. (eds.) 2004a: *Die jungsteinzeitliche Seeufersiedlung Arbon Bleiche 3: Umwelt und Wirtschaft*. Archäologie im Thurgau 12. Frauenfeld: Departement für Erziehung und Kultur des Kantons Thurgau.

Jacomet, S., Leuzinger, U. and Schibler, J. 2004b, Synthesis. In: S. Jacomet, U. Leuzinger and J. Schibler (eds.) *Die jungsteinzeitliche Seeufersiedlung Arbon Bleiche 3: Umwelt und Wirtschaft.* Archäologie im Thurgau 12. Frauenfeld: Departement für Erziehung und Kultur des Kantons Thurgau, 379-416.

Jones O'Day, S., van Neer, W. and Ervynck, A. (eds.) 2004, *Behaviour Behind Bones. The zooarchaeology of ritual, religion, status and identity.* Proceedings of the 9th ICAZ Conference, Durham 2002. Oxford: Oxbow Books.

Köninger, J., Kolb, M. and Schlichtherle, H. 2001, Elemente von Boleráz und Baden in den Feuchtbodensiedlungen des südwestdeutschen Alpenvorlandes und ihre mögliche Rolle im Transformationsprozess des lokalen Endneolithikums. In: P. Roman and S. Diamandi (eds.) *Cernavodă III – Boleráz. Ein vorgeschichtliches Phänomen zwischen dem Oberrhein und der unteren Donau.* Studia Danubiana, Series Symposia 2. București: Institutul Român de Tracologie, 641-673.

Leuzinger, U. 2000, *Die jungsteinzeitliche Seeufersiedlung Arbon-Bleiche 3: Befunde.* Archäologie im Thurgau 9. Frauenfeld: Departement für Erziehung und Kultur des Kantons Thurgau.

Leuzinger, U. and Jacomet, S. 2004, Einleitung. In: S. Jacomet, U. Leuzinger and J. Schibler (eds.) *Die jungsteinzeitliche Seeufersiedlung Arbon Bleiche 3: Umwelt und Wirtschaft.* Archäologie im Thurgau 12. Frauenfeld: Departement für Erziehung und Kultur des Kantons Thurgau, 25-39.

Marciniak, A. 2005, *Placing Animals in the Neolithic: Social Zooarchaeology of Prehistoric Farming Communities.* London: University College London Press.

Marti-Grädel, E., Deschler-Erb, S., Hüster-Plogmann, H. and Schibler, J. 2004, Early evidence of economic specialization or social differentiation: a case study from the Neolithic lake shore settlement 'Arbon-Bleiche 3' (Switzerland). In: S. Jones O'Day, W. van Neer and A. Ervynck (eds.) *Behaviour Behind Bones. The zooarchaeology of ritual, religion, status and identity.* Proceedings of the 9th ICAZ Conference, Durham 2002. Oxford: Oxbow Books, 164-176.

Messer, E. 1984, Anthropological Perspectives on Diet. *Annual Review of Anthropology* 13: 205-249.

Milisauskas, S. and Kruk, J. 1989, Neolithic Economy in Central Europe. *Journal of World Prehistory* 3(4): 403-446.

Miracle, P. and Milner, N. (eds.) 2002, *Consuming passions and patterns of consumption.* McDonald Institute Monographs. Cambridge: McDonald Institute for Archaeological Research, University of Cambridge.

Moreno-García, M., Orton, C. and Rackham, J. 1996, A New Statistical Tool for Comparing Animal Bone Assemblages. *Journal of Archaeological Science* 23: 437-453.

Murray, J. 1973, Einige Gesichtspunkte über die Beziehung zwischen Viehzucht und archäologischen Kulturen im Spätneolithikum in Europa. In: J. Matolcsi (ed.) *Domestikationsforschung und Geschichte der Haustiere*. Budapest: Akadémiai Kiadó, 177-186.

Pucher, E. and Schmitzberger, M. 1999, Einige Bemerkungen zu den bisher in Österreich geborgenen Tierknochenfunden der Boleráz-Gruppe. *Fundberichte aus Österreich* 38: 623-625.

Röder, B., Doppler, T., Pichler, S., Pollmann, B., Jacomet, S. and Schibler, J. in preparation a, Beyond the settlement grid: investigating social differences through archaeobiology in waterlogged sites.

Röder, B., Pichler, S. and Doppler, T. in preparation b, Coping with crises: The impact of social aspects on vulnerability and resilience.

Rowley-Conwy, P. (ed.) 2000, *Animal Bones, Human Societies*. Oxford: Oxbow Books.

Schibler, J. 2004, Bones as a key for reconstructing the environment, nutrition and economy of the lake-dwelling societies. In: F. Menotti (ed.) *Living on the lake in prehistoric Europe. 150 years of lake-dwelling research*. London: Routledge, 144-161.

Schibler, J. 2006, The economy and environment of the 4th and 3rd millennia BC in the northern Alpine foreland based on studies of animal bones. *Environmental Archaeology* 11(1): 49-64.

Scott, E.M. 1996, Who ate what? Archaeological Food Remains and Cultural Diversity. In: E.J. Reitz, L.A. Newsom and S.J. Scudder (eds.) *Case Studies in Environmental Archaeology*. New York: Plenum, 339-356.

Sherratt, A. 2004, The importance of lake-dwellings in European prehistory. In: F. Menotti (ed.) *Living on the lake in prehistoric Europe. 150 years of lake-dwelling research*. London: Routledge, 267-275.

ter Braak, C.J.F. 1986, Canonical Correspondence Analysis: A new eigenvector technique for multivariate direct gradient analysis. *Ecology* 67(5): 1167-1179.

Thew, N. 2004, The Aquatic and Terrestrial Molluscs from the Profile Columns. In: S. Jacomet, U. Leuzinger and J. Schibler (eds.) *Die jungsteinzeitliche Seeufersiedlung Arbon Bleiche 3: Umwelt und Wirtschaft*. Archäologie im Thurgau 12. Frauenfeld: Departement für Erziehung und Kultur des Kantons Thurgau, 81-89.

Valamoti, S.M. 2005, Grain versus chaff: identifying a contrast between grain-rich and chaff-rich sites in the Neolithic of Northern Greece. *Vegetation History and Archaeobotany* 14: 259-267.

van der Veen, M. 2007, Formation processes of desiccated and carbonized plant remains. The identification of routine practice. *Journal of Archaeological Science* 34: 968-990.

Vigne, J.-D., Arbogast, R.-M., Horard-Herbin, M.-P., Méniel, P. and Lepetz, S. 2005, Animaux, sociétés et cultures. In: M.-P. Horard-Herbin and J.-D. Vigne (eds.) *Animaux, environnements et sociétés*. Collection "Archéologiques". Paris: Editions Errance, 151-181.

Wilk, R.R. and Rathje, W.L. 1982, Household Archaeology. *American Behavioral Scientist* 25(6): 617-639.

Chapter 5

COPPER ARTEFACTS OF THE MONDSEE GROUP AND THEIR POSSIBLE SOURCES

Carolin Frank and Ernst Pernicka[1]

Abstract

The Copper Age Mondsee group is known from a number of lake settlements in Upper Austria and this material has been studied since the later nineteenth century. The present paper concentrates on the chemical analyses of copper artefacts, including impurities such as silver, nickel, arsenic and antimony, as well as lead isotopes. Possible sources of copper ores, from Alpine as well as the SE European sources, which may have been used in the manufacture of the Mondsee artefacts are also discussed.

Key words: Mondsee group, copper artefacts, copper impurities, lead isotope, Ai Bunar, Majdanpek

Introduction

The Mondsee group is a Copper Age cultural group with a relatively narrow regional distribution mainly in Upper Austria. Chronologically and geographically the Mondsee group is placed at the periphery of the Funnel Beaker Culture (Ruttkay et al. 2004, 54). Other contemporary related cultures are Remedello in Northern Italy, Cham in Bavaria, Cortaillod in Switzerland and France, Altheim in southern Germany, the Moravian group in the Czech Republic and the (Balaton)-Lasinja- and Baden cultures of Austria and Hungary.

---

[1] Institut für Ur- und Frühgeschichte und Archäologie des Mittelalters, Universität Tübingen, Germany

Most settlements of the Mondsee group are to be found along the shores of the Salzkammergut lakes, primarily at Mondsee, Attersee and Traunsee. Today there are twenty-three settlements known around these lakes (Figure 5.1). The best-known are See at the Mondsee, and the Weyregg and Seewalchen sites at the Attersee. There are also a few settlements on dry land (some of them hilltop settlements) where the characteristic Mondsee pottery has been found, for example at Götschenberg-Bischofshofen and Obergrünburg. Based on these locations, the distribution of the Mondsee group can be roughly defined as the area south of the Danube between the rivers Salzach in the west and Enns in the east (Ruttkay 1981, 269); it is shown as such in the *Archaeological Atlas of Prehistoric Europe* (Buchvaldek 2007, Map 14a, 15a).

The Mondsee group is characterised mainly by its ceramic assemblage recovered principally from the lake dwelling sites along the shores of the Upper Austrian lakes. They feature incised ornaments made with the *Furchenstich* technique, and designs which comprise line and chevron bands, triangles, sun discs and arcs in

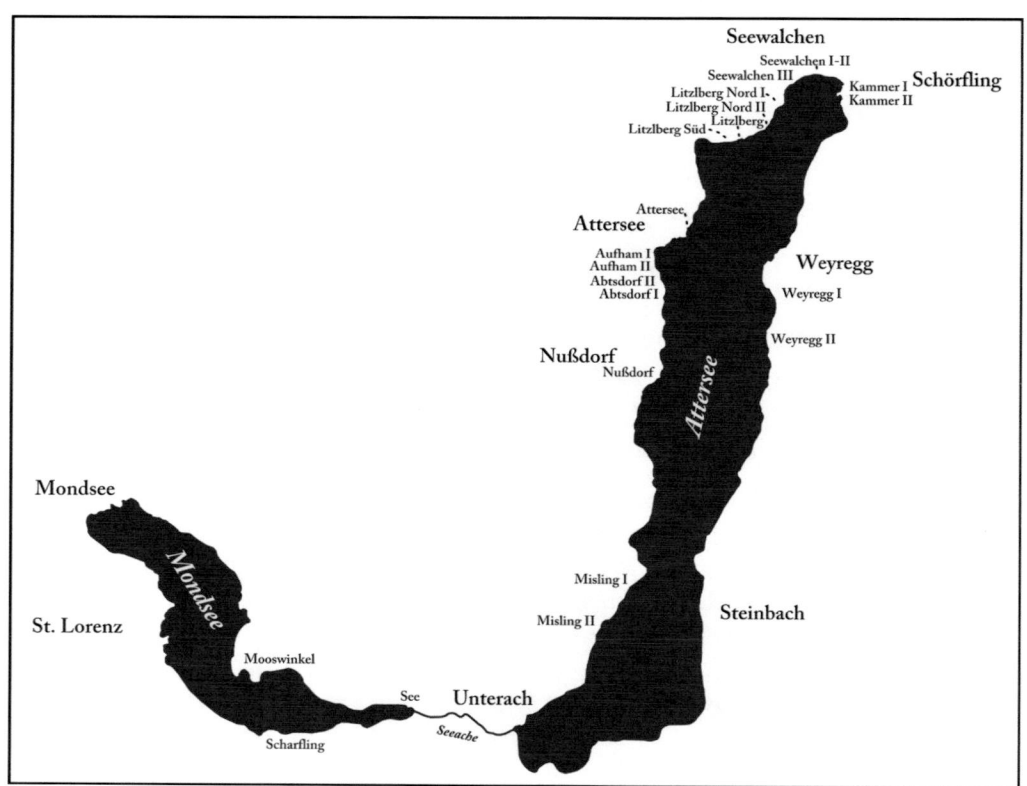

Figure 5.1 Sites of the Mondsee group around the lakes of Mondsee and Attersee (after Dworsky and Reitmaier 2004, 4, Fig. 1).

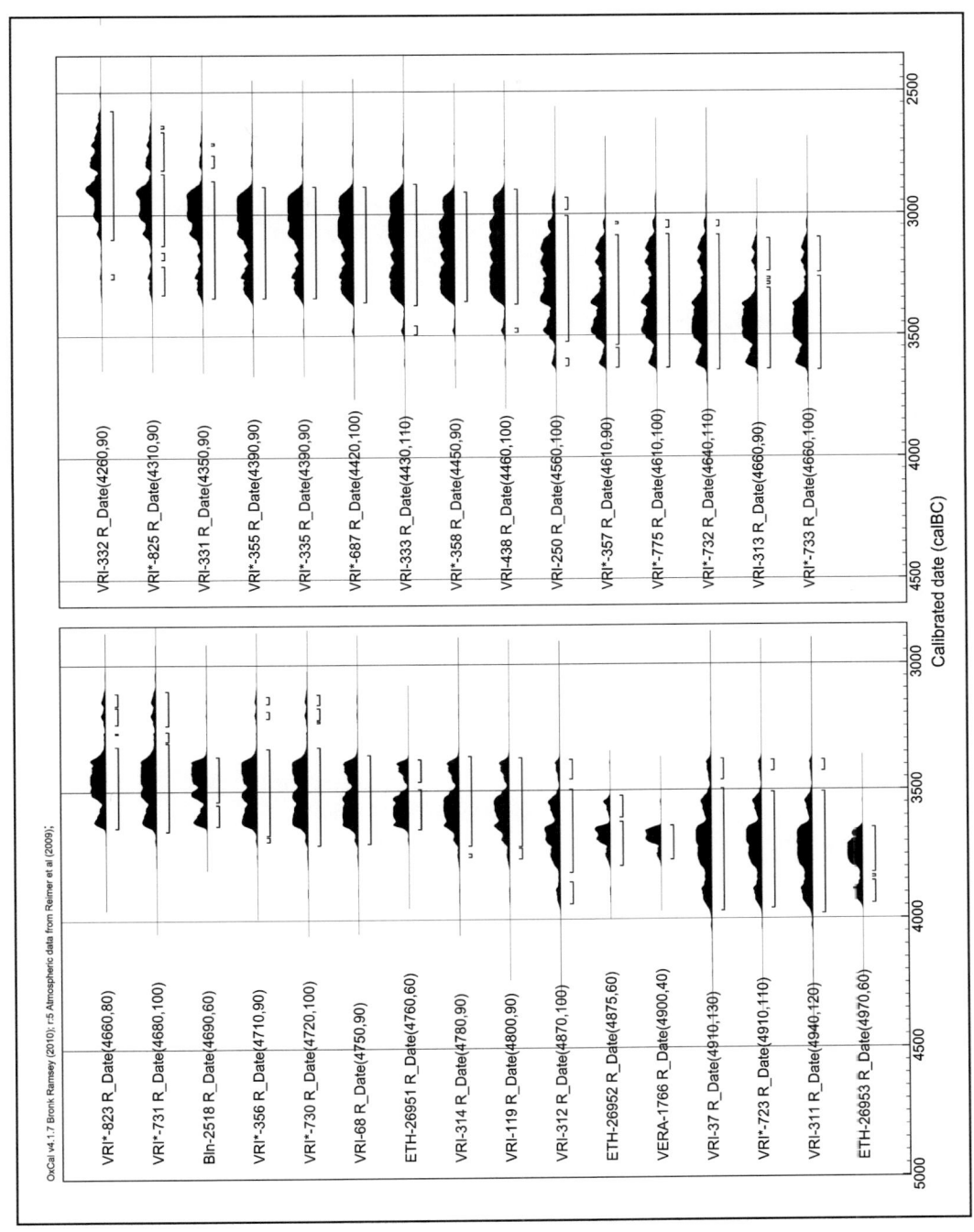

Figure 5.2 C-14 dates for the sites of Mondsee group compiled from Reiter (2008, 36), Dworsky and Reitmaier (2004, 13) and Breitwieser and Stradal (2001, 94), calibrated with Oxcal 4.1.7.

different combinations. Some vessels were decorated with a white incrustation mass after firing. Franz and Weninger published, in 1927, a description of the ceramic finds in the collection of the Institute for Prehistory at the University of Vienna, and several more studies on the ceramics were published later [for example Kunze (1981) and Lochner (1997)].

The most relevant study of the Mondsee pottery was published in 1981 by Elisabeth Ruttkay, when she classified it into three groups which serve as the basis for the subdivision of Mondsee into three horizons (Ruttkay 1981). This subdivision is still used today as can be seen in the chronological chart for the Neolithic period of eastern Austria published in 2006 (Krenn-Leeb 2006).

Along with the ceramic finds there are many artefacts made of stone and flint, including flat axes, perforated stone axes and arrowheads, that were examined by Morgan (1983), Antl-Weiser (2006) and Binsteiner and Ruprechtsberger (2006); for information on stone axes of the Mondsee group see Götzinger (2008).

The animal bones found at the sites around the Mondsee lake were studied by Pucher and Engl (1997), palaeoecological investigations using drill cores to reconstruct the prehistoric environment in the Mondsee region were undertaken by Chondrogianni et al. (1986), and Schmidt (1986) published palynological and sedimentological investigations from the site of Aufham I at the Attersee and site See at the Mondsee.

Due to good preservation conditions on the lake shores many organic remains were also recovered during excavations. Waterlogged conditions led to the discovery of textiles (Grömer 2006), including fragments from fishing nets, seed remains and, of course, wooden framework and substructures of the lakeshore-huts that provide insight into their construction techniques (Offenberger 1981, 320–337).

The absolute chronology of the Mondsee group is based mainly on more than thirty radiocarbon and dendrochronological dates published in the literature, with extensive listings of dates available in Stadler (1995, 218) and the RADON database by Rinne (2011). Figure 5.2 contains thirty dates calibrated with Oxcal 4.1 compiled from the aforementioned and other publications.

In a recently published chronological chart, showing Neolithic cultural groups of eastern Austria based upon radiocarbon dates and stratigraphical considerations (Krenn-Leeb 2006), the first two horizons of the Mondsee culture (I and II) have been placed between around 3800 cal BC and 3000 cal BC, with Mondsee III, the latest horizon, being considered as a regional manifestation of the Cham culture and dating from around 3000 cal BC to 2900 cal BC.

History of research

Matthäus Much discovered the prehistoric remains along the shores of Mondsee at See in 1872, and, after a first publication in the same year, two more followed (Much 1874, 1876). The first stratigraphic information on the Mondsee sites was obtained in 1938, during investigations of a profile of the lake and the nature of the bedrock conducted by Leonhard Franz (Offenberger 1995, 6). Both before and after the First World War, fishermen Theodor Wang and Albert Wendl discovered new sites of lakeshore dwellings. They salvaged many objects by digging them up with nets and poles, to sell to the private collector M. Schmidt, as well as to the Heimathaus Vöcklabruck and to the Museum of Natural History in Vienna. However, Schmidt's large collection was stored in Hungary and was lost during the Second World War (Offenberger 1981, 303).

The first successful measurements of pile dwellings were undertaken in the years 1951/1952 when Gertrud Moßler, from the Office of Monument Protection, led a campaign in the Keutschacher See (Moßler 1954). In 1968 Kurt Willvonseder published a detailed report on the Mondsee group as a whole, with the translated title *The late Neolithic and Bronze Age lake dwellings of the Attersee in Upper Austria*. In this seminal work he also discussed the provenance and possible sources of the Mondsee copper finds (Willvonseder 1963/1968).

Due to the ongoing destruction of the settlement sites along the shores of the Salzkammergut lakes, it was considered necessary to carry out a systematic survey of the sites and to document their state of preservation. This program was directed by Johann Offenberger for the Federal Office of Monument Protection from 1969 to 1986, and eventually all Salzkammergut lakes were surveyed to a depth of 10 m (Offenberger 1995, 8–9). A great asset in this endeavour was the divers' club, UNION-Tauchclub Wels, founded in 1977 by Karl Czech. These divers resumed the task of topographical surveys and also developed new methods and equipment for measuring archaeological structures underwater (Offenberger 1995, 10). By 1989, Czech had published twelve reports on the survey and the documentation of pile dwellings (Czech 1989).

The last extensive research project on the Mondsee group, namely the *Interdisciplinary lake dwellings project*, was organised by Elisabeth Ruttkay between 1989 and 1995 (Ruttkay 1995, 18). Her own research on Mondsee began much earlier and was centered around the Mondsee ceramics (see above). The most recent research on a larger scale was the inventory of the known lakeshore settlements around Mondsee and Attersee by Cyril Dworsky and Thomas Reitmaier (Dworsky and Reitmaier 2003; 2004) and more detailed accounts of the history of research on Mondsee can be found in publications by Ruprechtsberger (2006) and also Offenberger (1981, 295–312; 1995).

Copper finds of the Mondsee group

Together with other cultural groups, including Altheim and Cortaillod, the Mondsee group belongs to the earliest copper-using horizon in central Europe as it was defined by Ottaway (1982, 23). Copper finds are abundant, as are other tools for copper working such as casting moulds and crucibles. The typological spectrum of the metal finds includes flat axes, daggers, awls, curved blades, copper spirals and fragments of metal sheets.

The metal finds of the Mondsee group have always been of considerable interest and, accordingly, a number of studies are available. A comprehensive analytical program, examining ore deposits in the eastern Alps and prehistoric copper artefacts from central Europe, was undertaken by a group in Vienna led by Richard Pittioni and Heinz Neuninger. Mondsee artefacts were included in this program and appear in three tables of the published analyses (Neuninger and Pittioni 1960, 58, Table 1; Pittioni 1957, 54, Table 26; 1966, 93, Table 1). From a contemporary point of view the major flaw of this ambitious project was the fact that only semi-quantitative analyses were carried out. This made it impossible to compare their data with the results of other laboratories, and it is now known that the quantitative trace element pattern carries important information. Accordingly, these analyses are mostly neglected in discussions of the composition and provenance of the Mondsee copper artefacts today. However, the advantage of the Vienna program was the awareness of the importance of complementary analyses of copper ores, and these may still be useful despite their limited analytical quality. A summary of the analyses from the east Alpine ore deposits, and some ore deposits in surrounding regions, was provided by Pittioni (1980, 85–87).

An extensive research program, roughly contemporary with that at Vienna, was conducted at the Württembergisches Landesmuseum in Stuttgart led by Siegfried Junghans under the name of *Studien zu den Anfängen der Metallurgie* (usually abbreviated as "SAM"; Junghans et al. 1954; 1960; 1968; 1974). This project aimed to analyse copper and copper-based artefacts of the Early Bronze Age and earlier periods from all over Europe; it took care to provide quantitative analyses but did not include any copper ore samples. In total, some 22 000 samples were analyzed by optical emission spectroscopy. The analyses were grouped according to the concentrations of five elements, and the distribution of such groups in time and space was discussed from an archaeological viewpoint.

This corpus still serves as the basis for many studies of early copper and bronze artefacts, although additional information included in new studies is now acquired with the help of modern methods such as neutron activation analysis or atomic mass spectrometry [see Härke (1978) for an explanation of the optical emission spectroscopy and its problems, and Pernicka (1990, 66–67) for a short summary of the SAM project and comments on criticism of the SAM database].

Some sets of new data were added to the database of the SAM project, the most important of which were those acquired during the FMZM project and the analyses performed in Heidelberg for the North-Alpine neolithic period (tagged HDM in the database; Krause 2003, 11–13). Today this extended database is held at the Curt-Engelhorn-Zentrum Archäometrie (CEZA) in Mannheim. It also served as the basis for a new study revising the SAM database and the information obtained on the development of early metallurgy: the so-called *Stuttgarter Metallanalysenprojekt* (SMAP) which used multivariate techniques for the grouping of metal analyses. Some results of this work were published by Krause (2003).

Artefacts in this study

The artefacts which form the basis of this paper are those from four collections that hold Mondsee finds: those at the Institute for Prehistory at the University of Vienna, the Museum of Natural History (NHM) in Vienna, the Museum in Mondsee and Heimathaus Vöcklabruck.

In the most recent compilation around 70 metal artefacts were ascribed to the Mondsee group and over 160 casting devices or fragments (Obereder et al. 1993). All metal objects are unstratified and most were found at the end of the nineteenth century.

Artefacts from these four collections have been examined by Nicole Witte in her diploma thesis at the University of Freiberg in 2004 (Witte 2004). Witte used data published by Junghans et al. in the *Studien zu den Anfängen der Metallurgie* (published between 1960 and 1974), and added lead isotope and x-ray fluorescence analyses. She excluded some artefacts from the Salzkammergut lakes, in the aforementioned four collections, because of their high nickel and tin contents. Most probably this group of items is to be associated with the Attersee group, dating to the Early Bronze Age. Today there are sixty-four chemical analyses of artefacts assigned to the Mondsee group available and, of those, thirty-one contain lead isotope data.

Classification of chemical analyses of copper objects

Characterisations of different copper types are obtained by using measurements of chemical element concentrations and isotope abundance ratios. Grouping of copper artefacts, by their chemical composition, goes back to the middle of the twentieth century when Otto and Witter (1952) undertook the first study based on a large number of analysed artefacts. Since then, much progress has been made with analytical methods and also in the creation of groups using statistical techniques.

Lutz and Pernicka (1996) explain the x-ray fluorescence analytical methods used in this study, and Pernicka (1984) explains the neutron activation analysis; an introduction to the grouping of copper artefacts according to their chemical composition is given by Pernicka (1999; 1990, 67–85). Questions concerning changes in element composition during the smelting process of ore into metal, and during remelting (e.g. for refining) of copper objects, are also addressed in these studies. For a short explanation on the use of metal analyses for research on early metallurgy and, especially, for information on the SAM/SMAP database and criticism on the use of analytical data, see Krause (2003,14–27) and Pernicka (1990, 89–99).

Pernicka et al. (1993, 14; Figure 5.4) visualise copper types with the help of chemical "fingerprints" in their work on copper artefacts from the Balkans, and a slight variation can be found in their later work on Bulgarian copper artefacts (Pernicka et al. 1997, 92, Fig. 16). This approach was also used by Krause (2003, 91, Fig. 41) and recently by Lutz et al. (2010), while discussing ores from the Eastern Alpine Mitterberg area.

An introduction to the principles of lead isotope analysis, for provenance studies of archaeological copper and copper alloys, is provided by Gale and Stos-Gale (1982 and 2000). Their more recent publication also includes a description of the measurement techniques and a short explanation of the use of three-isotope diagrams. This highlights specific isotope ratios as the basis for the characterisation of groups of metal objects and ore deposits.

Geochemical characteristics of the copper-based artefacts of the Mondsee group

The chemical characteristics of any copper type can be visualised by using a diagram showing two elements on logarithmic axes. For the discussion of the copper used by the Mondsee group, the element-combinations of silver to nickel, and arsenic to antimony, are presented (Figure 5. 3). The data scatter for most elements over two orders of magnitude, but silver covers only a little more than one magnitude. Silver and nickel are the two most significant trace elements that allow the finished copper to be related to the original ore. Accordingly, one would initially conclude that the three samples with very low nickel concentrations should not belong to the main group. However, one has to take into account that, in a relatively large number of artefacts, only upper limits can be determined for

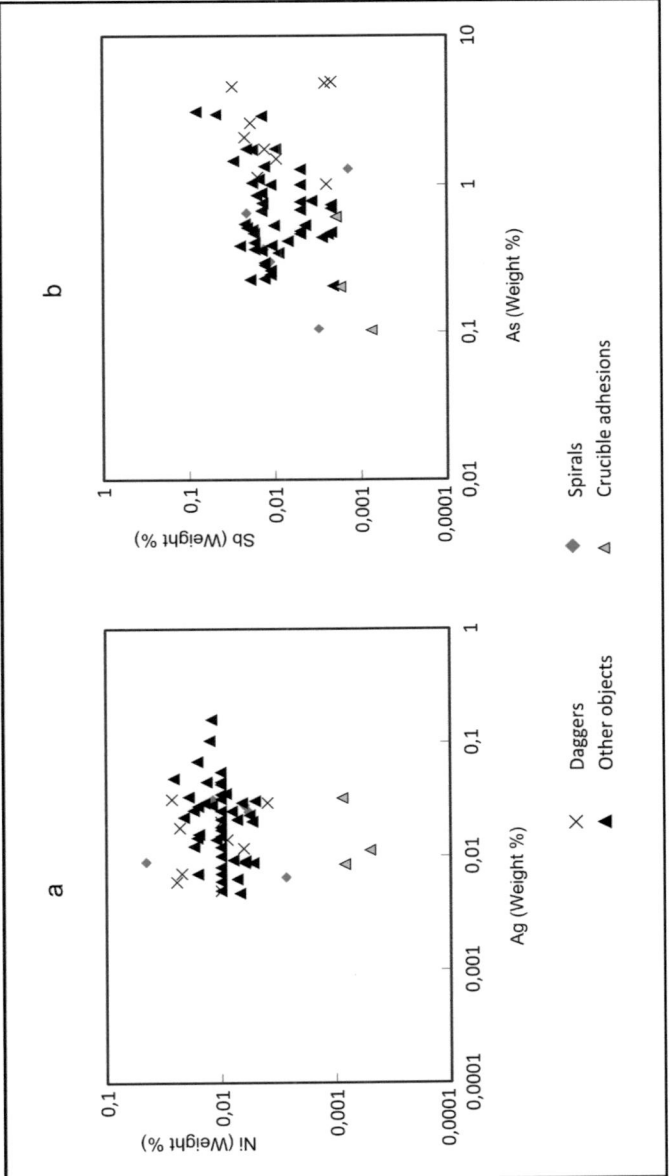

Figure 5.3 Chemical characteristics of the copper used in Mondsee artefacts. The two element diagrams Ag vs. Ni and As vs. Sb each show a rather homogenous material.

the nickel concentrations. These artefacts plot along a horizontal line at 0.01% Ni, which is the detection limit of the EDXRF method that was used for these samples (Figure 5.3a). Nevertheless, it is interesting that the three samples with low nickel concentrations are copper-rich adhesions from crucibles, although the concentrations were normalised to copper in order to be comparable with the metal samples. It remains to be seen whether they truly represent a different type of copper or just the lower end of a continuous nickel distribution.

Arsenic and antimony can also be used for relating finished artefacts to ores, but only if it can be assumed that no loss by volatilisation has occurred. This is usually the case when oxidised copper ores are reduced to the metal. However, it has been shown (Tylecote et al. 1977, Pernicka 1999) that when smelting sulfide ores which require roasting before reduction, arsenic in particular can be lost to a great extent. In the arsenic versus antimony diagram (Figure 5.3b) the samples from crucibles are also at the outer edges of the distribution. This may mean that different metal was melted in the crucibles than that which was used in the finished artefacts. Furthermore, it is noteworthy that the daggers contain systematically more arsenic (but not more antimony) than most of the other artefacts. This has already been observed by Obereder et al. (1993) and may suggest that arsenic was somehow added to produce a material better suited to use for a dagger (see below).

An alternative way to illustrate a copper type is to use the medians of the measured values (Table 1) and to plot them using a bar chart (Figure 5.4).

As	Sb	Au	Ni	Ag
0.66	0.012	0.00055	0.01	0.018

Table 1: Median values of some element concentrations that are typical of the copper artefacts of the Mondsee culture group.

Arsenic clearly stands out as the dominant impurity; other characteristics are the very low gold contents, and the nickel content with its median at 0.01 %. Even more descriptive is a boxplot showing 80% of all measured values, the so-called interdecile range, with the remaining measurements shown by the protruding whiskers (Figure 5.5; for a short introduction to the use of boxplots in structuring statistical data see Baxter and Buck 2000, 698). By connecting and shading the concentration ranges in this boxplot, one obtains a visual "fingerprint" of the copper type. This chart also makes it easy to compare different copper types or groups of artefacts.

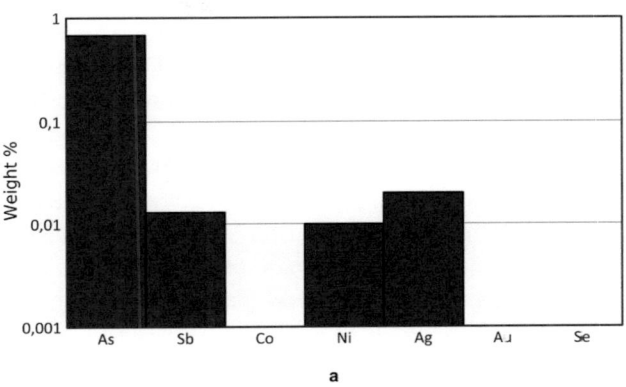

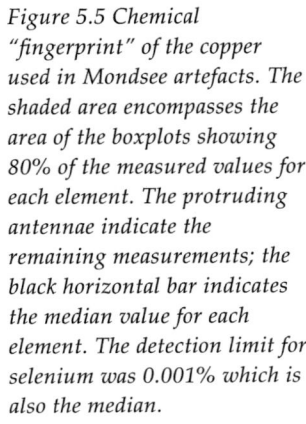

Figure 5.4 Chemical characteristics of the copper used in Mondsee artefacts. Linear (top) and logarithmic (bottom) bar chart showing the median values of the copper used in Mondsee artefacts.

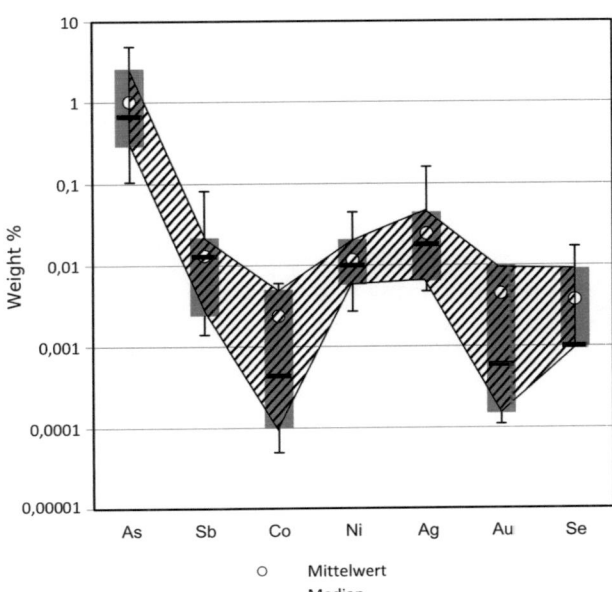

Figure 5.5 Chemical "fingerprint" of the copper used in Mondsee artefacts. The shaded area encompasses the area of the boxplots showing 80% of the measured values for each element. The protruding antennae indicate the remaining measurements; the black horizontal bar indicates the median value for each element. The detection limit for selenium was 0.001% which is also the median.

COPPER ARTEFACTS OF THE MONDSEE GROUP AND THEIR POSSIBLE SOURCES | 123

The chemical characteristics of the copper used for the Mondsee artefacts can thus be summarised as having high arsenic content (between roughly 0.5 and 5%), while antimony, silver and nickel are only present in very low concentrations. To produce copper with such high arsenic concentrations one has to avoid an oxidising step, such as roasting of sulphide ores, because this leads to substantial losses of arsenic by volatilisation. Accordingly, this type of copper may derive from smelting oxide copper ores with a high arsenical content. Alternatively, relatively pure copper may have been treated with speiss, a material consisting of copper, iron and arsenic, which may have been produced separately from ores with arsenic as a major component, such as arsenopyrite (FeAsS). This process was known and practised on a relatively large scale in Iran (Thornton et al. 2009, Rehren et al. 2012).

Of all the copper artefacts available from the Mondsee group, a representative selection was analysed in 2003 for their lead isotope compositions. The selection was based on typology, so at least one sample of each artefact type was analysed. In addition, items with unusual chemical compositions, as compared to Mondsee copper proper, were also analysed. The data (Figure 5.6) are presented in the so-called three-isotope diagram. The Mondsee copper artefacts show a relatively small scatter, between 0.835 and 0.845 for the ratio $^{207}Pb/^{206}Pb$, and between 2.075 and 2.079 for $^{208}Pb/^{206}Pb$. Only one sample, an awl, plots at some distance from the main group (in the upper right corner). But since its chemical composition is entirely consistent with the rest, it is still considered as part of the group. As a result, one can note that the chemical as well as the lead isotopic composition of the copper artefacts of the Mondsee group is comparatively homogeneous.

Possible copper sources of the Mondsee group

The geological unit in which the most important copper deposits are located is the Northern Greywacke Zone but it is mostly referred to just as the Greywacke Zone (or GWZ). It consists mainly of palaeozoic rocks, and stretches roughly from Schwaz/Tirol in the west to Ternitz in the east, where it sinks under the Vienna Basin (Ebner 1997, 173). The GWZ is subdivided into a western and eastern part, with most non-ferrous ore deposits in the west (Schulz 1997, 338). This can clearly be seen on a map showing traces of prehistoric mining in the Eastern Alps (Figure 5.7).

The most important copper ore deposits are located in the ore districts of Mitterberg and Kitzbühel, from which there is also plenty of evidence of prehistoric mining and copper processing (Rieser and Schrattenthaler 1998-1999; 2004). Another well-known copper ore

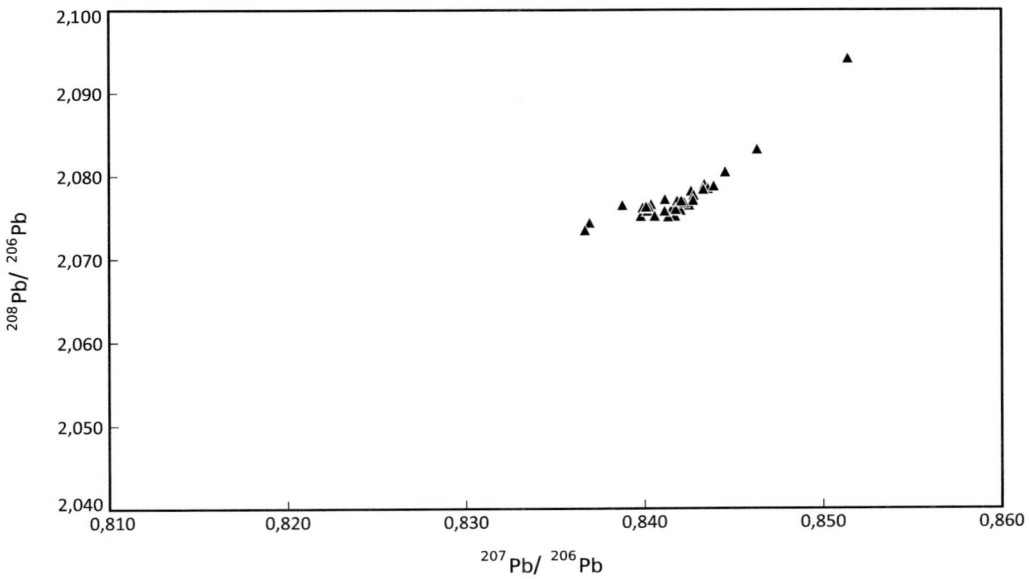

Figure 5.6 Lead isotope ratios of artefacts of the Mondsee group in the three-istope diagram ^{208}Pb, ^{207}Pb and ^{206}Pb.

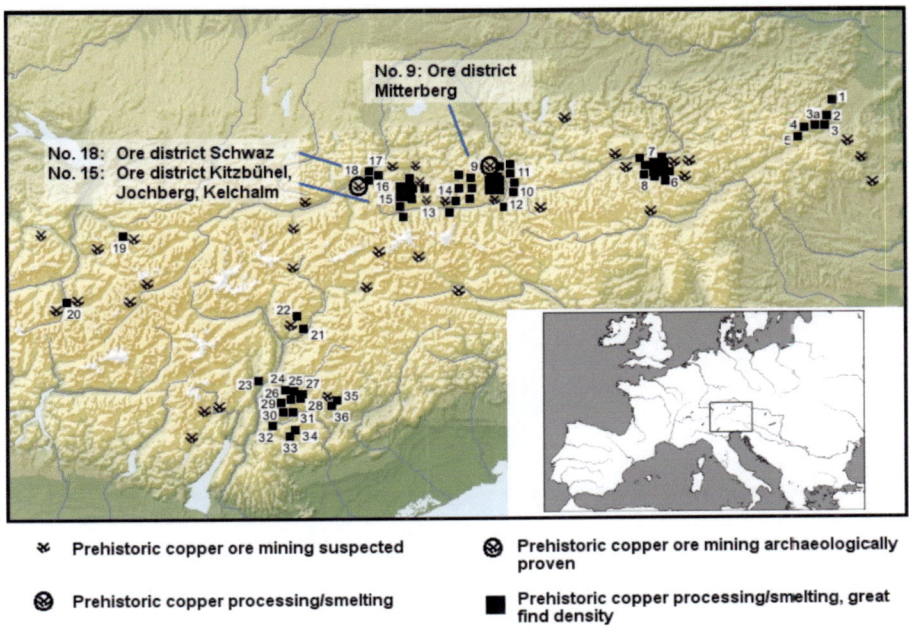

Figure 5.7 Ore districts in the east Alpine area (after Bartelheim 2007, catalog IV).

district is Schwaz-Brixlegg (Gstrein 1981; Goldenberg and Rieser 2004; Martinek and Sydow 2004) with fahlores (mainly antimony fahlores) as the main ore minerals (Höppner et al. 2005). These ores can be safely excluded as possible raw material for the Mondsee copper artefacts, since fahlores are complex copper sulfides characterised by high concentrations of impurities, mainly of antimony, arsenic, bismuth and other elements (Martinek and Sydow 2004, 200).

A visual characterisation of the analytical data, obtained from chalcopyrite and fahlores of the East Alpine region, particularly from the ore districts Kitzbühel, Mitterberg and Schwaz, has been published by Christoforidis et al. (1988, 535, Fig. 2) and, with much better resolution of the mining districts, by Lutz et al. (2010). In summarising the chemical characteristics of the Alpine copper ores, one can state that Alpine copper ores do contain arsenic but always in combination with antimony, silver and nickel. In contrast to this, the Mondsee copper is characterised by high arsenic contents only (Figure 5. 4).

The next step is to look at the available lead isotope data of Alpine copper ores (Figure 5.8). It is obvious that there is also little isotopic correlation between the Alpine ore isotope fields from the Mitterberg region, the fahlores from Tirol and the Mondsee group artefacts. In this case the variation of lead isotope ratios in the artefacts should

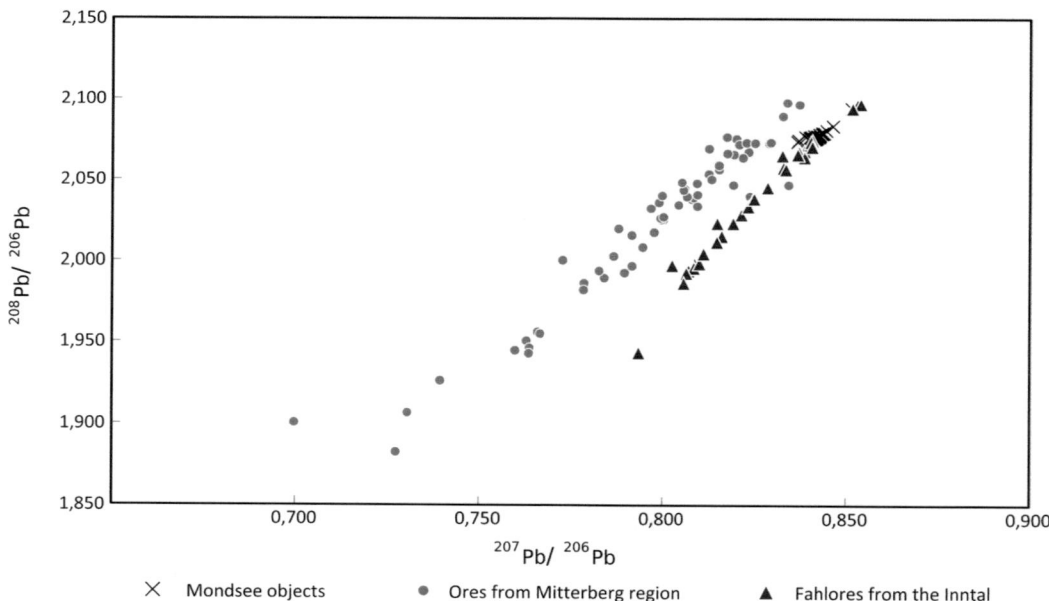

Figure 5. 8 Lead isotope ratios of eastern Alpine copper ore samples and measured isotope ratios of the Mondsee artefacts. Fahlores from the Inntal after Höppner et al. (2005, p. 305). Ore samples from the Mitterberg area as in Lutz et al. (2010).

also show a scatter much more along the lines defined by the East Alpine copper ores. This corroborates the conclusion drawn from the general chemical characteristics of East Alpine copper deposits. As a result, the East Alpine copper ores can for now be safely excluded as possible sources for the Mondsee copper.

Southeastern copper sources and the Mondsee group

It has always been suggested that metallurgy spread into central Europe from the southeast and this is also implied by the distribution of typologically similar artefacts (see, for example, the articles about early daggers or 'spectacle spirals' by Matuschik 1998, 1996). It is therefore important to examine the geochemical characteristics of southeastern copper sources, such as the data published by Pernicka et al. (1993, 1997) on copper deposits in Serbia and Bulgaria, and by Schreiner (2007) on copper deposits in the Slovakian Hron valley.

Pernicka et al. (1993) attempted to answer the question of whether the chalcolithic mine at Rudna Glava could have been the source of contemporary copper artefacts in Serbia. In order to do this, eighty-nine chalcolithic copper artefacts from Serbia, and ore samples from Serbian copper ore deposits, were analysed for their chemical compositions and lead isotope ratios. It was convincingly shown that most of the Serbian artefacts could be related to the large deposit of Majdanpek and not, as had been expected, to the chalcolithic mine at Rudna Glava. On the basis of typological dating the copper artefacts were assigned to three chronological horizons termed "early" (corresponding to Vinča-Pločnik IIA or earlier), "intermediate" (corresponding to Bodrogkeresztúr/Bubanj-Hum I a) and "late" (corresponding to Baden-Kostolac or later; Pernicka et al. 1993, 15, Table 4). The trace element patterns of these artefacts could be classified into seven groups, which were very consistent with their chronological assignment in that almost all artefacts belonging to the same chemical cluster were also assigned to the same chronological horizon (Pernicka et al. 1993, 16). Two of these clusters (nos. 4 and 7) comprise items with very high arsenical contents and differ mainly in their nickel concentrations. All artefacts in those clusters are dated to the Baden-Kostolac horizon, which is roughly contemporary with the Mondsee culture group. It is noteworthy that the chemical cluster no. 4 matches very closely the copper found in the Mondsee artefacts. However, it was not possible to assign this chemical group to any of the analysed copper deposits.

This study was later extended to Bulgaria (Pernicka et al. 1997) where the second known chalcolithic copper mine is located at Ai Bunar. Altogether, 335 artefacts for which chemical and isotope data was available were again grouped by cluster analysis into nine major chemical clusters, and the lead isotope ratios were used to define eleven "isotope grouplets". These were then compared with lead isotope ratios of Bulgarian copper ore deposits (Amov and Văkova 1994). The most important result was the assignment of two "isotope grouplets", that also formed a chemically homogenous group or chemical cluster, to the large copper deposit of Majdanpek in Serbia and to Ai Bunar in Bulgaria. While the exploitation of Ai Bunar was already known from archaeological excavations (Černych 1978), mining activity from at least six thousand years ago at Majdanpek was thus indirectly confirmed. A further chalcolithic mining centre was also postulated in the region of Medni Rid, south of Burgas, at the Bulgarian Black Sea coast.

In Figure 5.9, a three-isotope diagram of the most relevant ore fields in Serbia and Bulgaria is indicated by ellipses, with the ore isotope fields of Majdanpek and Ai Bunar slightly overlapping. The lead isotope ratios of the copper artefacts from Mondsee are not consistent with Ai Bunar and show only a slight overlapping with the Majdanpek ore isotope field. The chemical characteristics of both deposits are also clearly different from the Mondsee artefacts (Figure 5.10) so that the combined evidence, of chemical and lead isotope data, excludes both occurrences as sources for the Mondsee copper. Incidentally, the same line of argument also applies to the Slovakian copper deposits in the Hron valley (Schreiner 2007).

Although at present there is no copper deposit known in southeastern Europe that matches the Mondsee artefacts in their chemical and lead isotope characteristics, there is a group of analysed artefacts from the Balkans which show the same chemical composition as the Mondsee copper items. Figure 5.11 shows the combined artefacts of chemical cluster no. 4 and no. 7 which were part of the study by Pernicka et al. (1993). These two clusters are also copper types with unusually high arsenic content. Unfortunately, as mentioned above, it was not possible to link this chemical group to any specific deposit in southeastern Europe, so the provenance of this specific metal type remains unknown.

The geographical distribution of arsenical copper in the fourth millennium BC coincides with the distribution of the metal types as shown in Figure 5.12. The distribution of the copper spirals, the so-called "hooked spirals of the Hlinsko type" (Matuschik 1996, 21, Fig. 10) to which the Mondsee copper spirals belong, forms an area stretching from Hungary in the east to the Bodensee in the west.

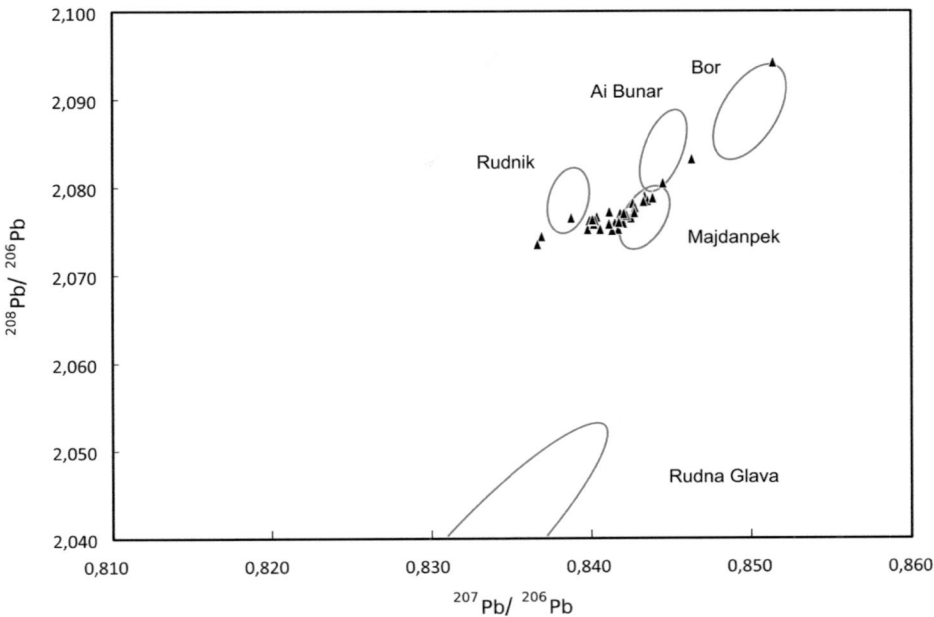

Figure 5.9 Lead isotope ratios of artefacts of the Mondsee group in three-isotope diagram ^{208}Pb, ^{207}Pb and ^{206}Pb in comparison with ore fields from southeastern copper sources according to Pernicka et al. (1993) and (1997).

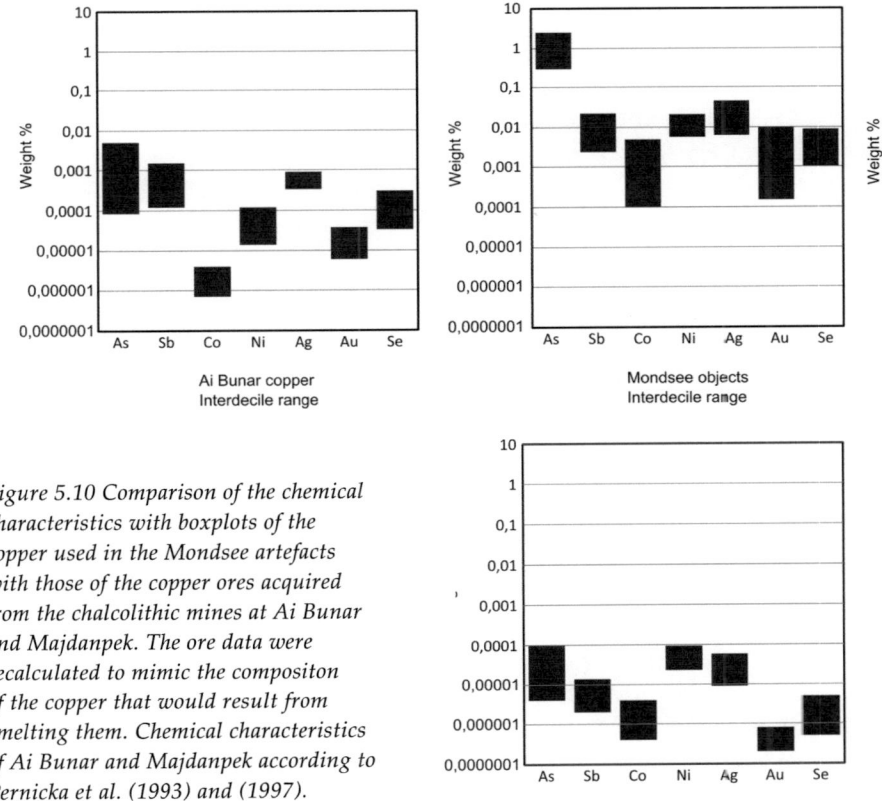

Figure 5.10 Comparison of the chemical characteristics with boxplots of the copper used in the Mondsee artefacts with those of the copper ores acquired from the chalcolithic mines at Ai Bunar and Majdanpek. The ore data were recalculated to mimic the compositon of the copper that would result from smelting them. Chemical characteristics of Ai Bunar and Majdanpek according to Pernicka et al. (1993) and (1997).

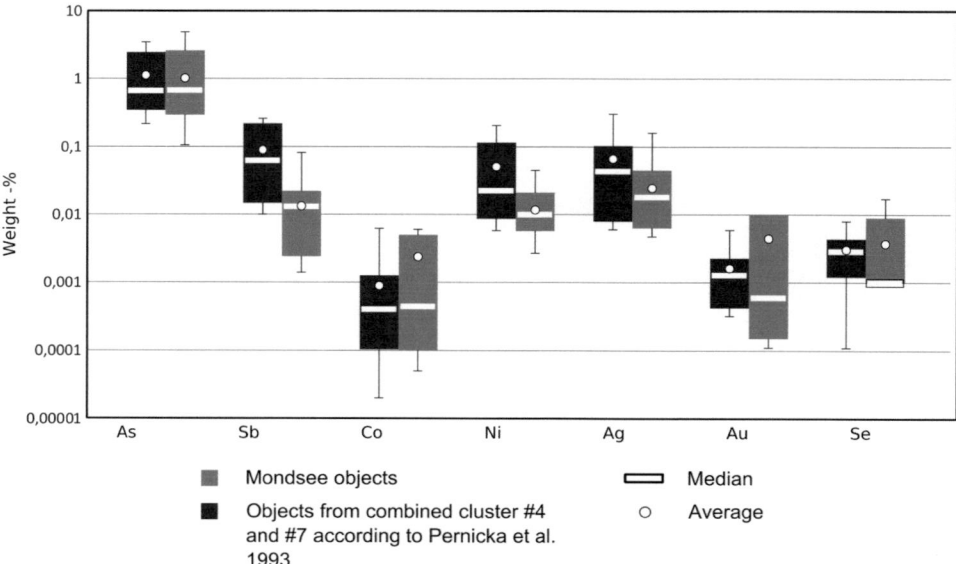

Figure 5.11 Serbian artefacts from combined clusters no. 4 and no.7 according to Pernicka et al. (1993) compared with copper from Mondsee artefacts.

The map also shows the distribution of Copper Age daggers (after Matuschik 1998, 223, Fig. 224). Matuschik classified all but one of the daggers of the Mondsee group as daggers of the Lovas variant of the Cucuteni type. The remaining dagger was classified as a Mondsee variant of the Cucuteni type. All Cucuteni daggers date to the developed southeastern Copper Age (Matuschik 1998, 235–238). According to Matuschik, the rivetted daggers are a development of the Carpatho-Balkan Metallurgical Province as defined by Chernykh (Matuschik 1998, 243). Daggers of the Mondsee variant are not as abundant as those of the Lovas type. They are concentrated along the northern Piedmont of the Alps, extending to the east in the direction of the Carpathian Mountains, while the distribution of the Lovas type follows the course of the Danube and serves again to suggest an origin in southeast Europe.

There are two possible explanations for the Mondsee-type copper being mainly distributed over central and southeastern Europe, and for being quite chemically and isotopically homogenous: either the copper source that produced such metal has not yet been identified, or a new technology had been introduced - namely the intentional addition of arsenic to the already available copper. Although such a process has presently only been identified in Iran at the end of the fourth millennium BC, it is not inconceivable that it was invented earlier and may have given rise to the phenomenon of arsenical copper being the dominant metal type of the fourth millennium BC

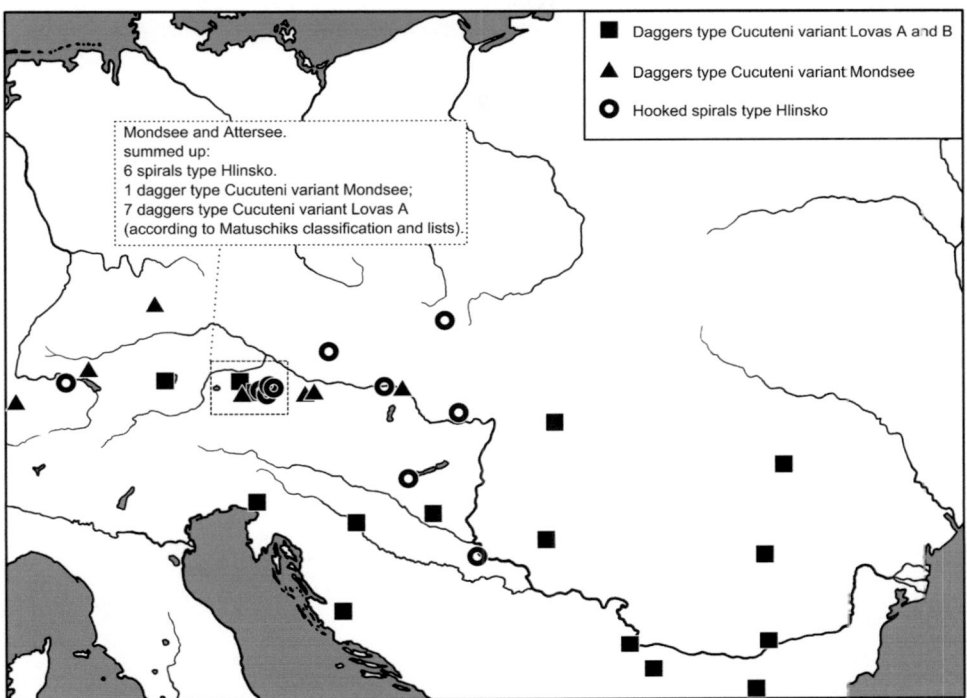

Figure 5.12 Daggers of Cucuteni type - variant Lovas A and B, variant Mondsee and hooked spirals of Hlinsko type as classified by Matuschik (1998) and (1996). Plotted artefacts: for hooked spirals of Hlinsko type see Matuschik 1996, 34-35, nos. 23-33; Daggers listed in Matuschik 1998, 247-249; artefacts shown here: Daggers of Cucuteni type - variant Lovas A: No. 6A, 7A, 25, 31, 32, 36, 42, 43, 45, 46; variant Lovas B: No. 29, 35, 39, 40; variant Mondsee: No. 1,2, 4, 6A, 9, 10, 11, 13.

from Iran to Europe. In this case, it could also be explained by the fact that, except for arsenic, the Mondsee-type copper is relatively pure and chemically homogenous. The addition of arsenic, e.g. by co-melting with speiss, would not alter the trace element pattern significantly, except for arsenic, but could change the lead isotope ratios because of the low lead concentrations of the already available copper. If one follows this suggestion then at least Majdanpek may still represent a possible source because of the high-purity copper it provided, and also because its lead isotope ratios, at least partially, overlap with the copper objects of the Mondsee group from our sample suite.

Conclusions

The chemical and lead isotopic characteristics of the copper used by the Mondsee group are relatively homogeneous. The dominant element is arsenic so that the term "arsenical copper" is most appropriate. Comparison of chemical and isotope data from Eastern Alpine ores with the "Mondsee copper" shows that there is no correlation, and that East Alpine copper ores must be excluded as possible sources, at least those that have been analysed so far.

Although the distribution of arsenical copper in the fourth millennium BC, and the distribution of the metal types that are characteristic of the Mondsee group, have a distinct tendency towards southeastern Europe there is as yet no good correlation of isotope data with known copper deposits from there. Hopefully, future research in the region, and new and detailed work on the identifying and mapping artefacts made of arsenical copper similar to those used by the Mondsee group, will shed further light on the question of origin.

References

Amov, B.G. and Vákova, V. N. 1994, A summary of lead isotope data for ore deposits in Bulgaria. In: H. Todorova and P. Popov (eds.) *Problemi na naj-rannata metalurgija.* Sofia, 122-138.

Antl-Weiser, W. 2006, Silexplatten als Grundform für Geräte in der Station See/Mondsee. In: A. Krenn-Leeb, K. Grömer, and P. Stadler (eds.) *Ein Lächeln für die Jungsteinzeit: Ausgewählte Beiträge zum Neolithikum Ostösterreichs. Festschrift für Elisabeth Ruttkay.* Wien: Österreichische Gesellschaft für Ur- und Frühgeschichte, 96–103.

Bartelheim, M. 2007, *Die Rolle der Metallurgie in vorgeschichtlichen Gesellschaften: Sozioökonomische und kulturhistorische Aspekte der Ressourcennutzung; ein Vergleich zwischen Andalusien, Zypern und dem Nordalpenraum.* Rahden/Westf.: Marie Leidorf.

Baxter, M. and Buck, C. 2000, Data Handling and Statistical Analysis. In: E. Ciliberto and G. Spoto (eds.) *Modern analytical methods in art and archaeology.* New York: Wiley, 681–746.

Binsteiner, A. and Ruprechtsberger, E.M. (eds.) 2006, *Mondsee-Kultur und Analyse der Silexartefakte von See am Mondsee.* Linz: Magistrat der Landeshauptstadt Linz.

Buchvaldek, M. 2007, *Archeologický atlas pravěké Evropy: Atlas zur Prähistorischen Archäologie Europas.* Prague: Universita Karlova.

Chondrogianni, C., Schmidt, R. and Schneider, J. 1986, Palynologische und sedimentologische Untersuchungen an Bohrprofilen der neolithischen Station Aufham I am Attersee (Oberösterreich). *Archaeologia Austriaca* 70: 237–246.

Christoforidis, A., Pernicka, E. and Schickler, H. 1988, Ostalpine Kupferlagerstätten und ihre Bedeutung für die prähistorische Metallgewinnung in Mitteleuropa. *Jahrbuch des Römisch-Germanischen Zentralmuseums Mainz*, 35(2): 533–536.

Černych, N.E. 1978, Gornoje delo i metallurgija v drevnejšej Bolgarii. Sofia.

Czech, K. 1989, Bestandsaufnahme des Unterwasserkulturerbes in den Salzkammergutseen. *Fundberichte aus Österreich* 28: 27–32.

Dworsky, C. and Reitmaier, T. 2003, "Salzkammergut reloaded" Ein Arbeitsbericht zur Kurzinventarisation der prähistorischen Seeufersiedlungen in Mond- und Attersee. *Nachrichtenblatt Arbeitskreis Unterwasserarchäologie* 10: 51–56.

Dworsky, C. and Reitmaier, T. 2004, Moment, da war doch noch was! Neues zur Pfahlbauarchäologie im Mond- und Attersee 1854-2004: 150 Jahre Entdeckung der Pfahlbauten. *Archäologie Österreichs* 15(2): 4–15.

Ebner, F. 1997, Die geologischen Einheiten Österreichs und ihre Rohstoffe. In: L. Weber, I. Cerny, and W.E. Petrascheck (eds.) *Handbuch der Lagerstätten der Erze, Industrieminerale und Energierohstoffe Österreichs: Erläuterungen zur metallogenetischen Karte von Österreich 1 : 500 000 unter Einbeziehung der Industrieminerale und Energierohstoffe [in memoriam Walther Emil Petrascheck]*. Wien: Geologische Bundesanstalt, 49–229.

Franz, L. and Weninger, J. 1927, *Die Funde aus den prähistorischen Pfahlbauten im Mondsee*. Wien: Anthropologische Gesellschaft.

Gale, N.H. and Stos-Gale, Z.A. 1982, Bronze Age copper sources in the Mediterranean. *Science* 216: 11-19.

Gale, N.H. and Stos-Gale, Z.A. 2000, Lead Isotope Analysis applied to Provenance Studies. In: E. Ciliberto and G. Spoto (eds.) *Modern analytical methods in art and archaeology*. New York: Wiley, 503–584.

Goldenberg, G. and Rieser, B. 2004, Die Fahlerzlagerstätten von Schwaz/Brixlegg (Nordtirol) - Ein weiteres Zentrum urgeschichtlicher Kupferproduktion in den österreichischen Alpen. Alpenkupfer Rame delle Alpi. *Der Anschnitt* 17, 35-52.

Götzinger, M. 2008, Die Steinrohstoffe der Mondseebelle in der Studiensammlung des Institutes für Ur- und Frühgeschichte an der Universität Wien. *Archäologie Österreichs, Mitteilungen der Österreichischen Gesellschaft für Ur- und Frühgeschichte* 19 (2): 39–42.

Grömer, K. 2006, Vom Spinnen und Weben, Flechten und Zwirnen: Hinweise zur neolithischen Textiltechnik an österreichischen Fundstellen. In: A. Krenn-Leeb, K. Grömer, and P. Stadler (eds.) *Ein Lächeln für die Jungsteinzeit: Ausgewählte Beiträge zum Neolithikum Ostösterreichs. Festschrift für Elisabeth Ruttkay*. Wien: Österreichische Gesellschaft für Ur- und Frühgeschichte, 177–192.

Gstrein, P. 1981, Prähistorischer Bergbau am Burgstall bei Schwaz (Tirol). *Veröffentlichungen des Tiroler Landesmuseums Ferdinandeum* 61: 25–46.

Härke, H. 1978, Probleme der optischen Emissionsspektralanalyse in der Urgeschichtsforschung. *Prähistorische Zeitschrift* 53: 165–276.

Höppner, B., Bartelheim, M., Huijsmans, M., Krauss, R., Martinek, K.-P., Pernicka, E., Schwab, R. 2005, Prehistoric copper production in the Inn valley, Austria, and the earliest copper in central Europe. *Archaeometry* 47: 293-315.

Junghans, S., Klein, H., Scheufele, E. 1954, Untersuchungen zur Kupfer- und Frühbronzezeit Süddeutschlands. *Bericht der Römisch-Germanischen Kommission* 34: 77-114.

Junghans, S., Sangmeister, E., and Schroeder, M. 1960, *Metallanalysen kupferzeitlicher und fruehbronzezeitlicher Bodenfunde aus Europa*. Berlin: Mann.

Junghans, S., Sangmeister, E., and Schroeder, M. 1968a, *Kupfer und Bronze in der frühen Metallzeit Europas. Band 1: Die Materialgruppen beim Stand von 12000 Analysen.* Berlin: Mann.

Junghans, S., Sangmeister, E., and Schroeder, M. 1968b, *Kupfer und Bronze in der frühen Metallzeit Europas. Band 2: Tafeln, Tabellen, Diagramme, Karten*. Berlin: Mann.

Junghans, S., Sangmeister, E., and Schroeder, M. 1968c, *Kupfer und Bronze in der frühen Metallzeit Europas. Band 3: Katalog der Analysen Nr. 985-10040*. Berlin: Mann.

Junghans, S., Sangmeister, E., Schroeder, M. 1974. *Kupfer und Bronze in der frühen Metallzeit Europas. Bd. 4: Katalog der Analysen Nr. 10041-22000 (mit Nachuntersuchungen der Analysen Nr. 1-10040)*. Berlin: Mann.

Krause, R. 2003, *Studien zur kupfer- und frühbronzezeitlichen Metallurgie zwischen Karpatenbecken und Ostsee*. Rahden, Westf: Marie Leidorf.

Krenn-Leeb, A. 2006, Chronologietabelle des Neolithikums in Ostösterreich. In: A. Krenn-Leeb, K. Grömer and P. Stadler (eds.) *Ein Lächeln für die Jungsteinzeit: Ausgewählte Beiträge zum Neolithikum Ostösterreichs. Festschrift für Elisabeth Ruttkay*. Wien: Österreichische Gesellschaft für Ur- und Frühgeschichte, 195.

Kunze, W. 1981, *Keramik der Pfahlbauern: Berichte über Untersuchungen der jungsteinzeitlichen Töpferei am Mondsee*. Linz: Verlag Oberösterreichischer Musealverein.

Lochner, M. 1997, *Studien zur Pfahlbauforschung in Österreich. Materialien 1. Die Pfahlbaustationen des Mondsees. Keramik*. Wien: Österreichische Akademie der Wissenschaften.

Lutz, J. and Pernicka, E. 1996, Energy dispersive X-ray fluorescence analysis of ancient copper alloys: empirical values for precision and accuracy. *Archaeometry* 38(2): 313-323.

Lutz, J., Pernicka, E., Pils, R. 2010, Geochemische Charakterisierung der Erzvorkommen am Mitterberg und in Kitzbühel. In: K. Oeggl (ed.) *Die Geschichte des Bergbaus in Tirol und seinen angrenzenden Gebieten: Proceedings zum 3. Milestone-Meeting des SFB-HiMAT vom 23. - 26.10.2008 in Silbertal*. Innsbruck: Innsbruck University Press, 175–181.

Martinek K. P. and Sydow, W. 2004, Frühbronzezeitliche Kupfermetallurgie im Unterinntal (Nordtirol). Rohstoffbasis, archäologische und archäometallurgische Befunde. In: G. Weisgerber and G. Goldenberg (eds.) *Alpenkupfer - Rame delle Alpi: Tagung "Urgeschichtliche Kupfergewinnung im Alpenraum", an der Universität Innsbruck, vom 4. - 8. Oktober 1995*. Bochum: Dt. Bergbau-Museum, 199–211.

Matuschik, I. 1996, Brillen- und Hakenspiralen der frühen Metallzeit Europas. *Germania* 74 (1): 1–43.

Matuschik, I. 1998, Kupferfunde und Metallurgie-Belege, zugleich ein Beitrag zur Geschichte der kupferzeitlichen Dolche Mittel-, Ost- und Südosteuropas. In: M. Mainberger and A. Billamboz (eds.) *Das Moordorf von Reute: Archäologische Untersuchungen in der jungneolithischen Siedlung Reute-Schorrenried*. Staufen: Teraqua CAP, 207–312.

Morgan, A. 1983, Die Silexpfeilspitzen von Mondsee. *Archaeologia Austriaca* 67: 1–95.

Moßler, G. 1954, Neues zum vorgeschichtlichen Pfahlbau im Keutschacher See. *Carinthia I* 144: 76–109.

Much, M. 1872, Erster Bericht über die Auffindung eines Pfahlbaus im Mondsee. *Mitteilungen der Anthropologischen Gesellschaft in Wien* 2: 203–206.

Much, M. 1874, Zweiter Bericht über Pfahlbauforschungen in den Oberösterreichischen Seen. *Mitteilungen der Anthropologischen Gesellschaft in Wien* 4: 293–308.

Much, M. 1876, Dritter Bericht über Pfahlbauforschungen im Mondsee (1875-76). *Mitteilungen der Anthropologischen Gesellschaft in Wien* 6: 161–194.

Neuninger, H. and Pittioni, R. 1960, Zur Herkunft des frühen Kupfers in Oberösterreich. *Archaeologia Austriaca* 28: 58–60.

Obereder, J., Pernicka, E., Ruttkay, E. 1993, Die Metallfunde und die Metallurgie der kupferzeitlichen Mondseegruppe. *Archäologie Österreichs* 4(2): 5–9.

Offenberger, J. 1981, Die Pfahlbauten der Salzkammergutseen. In: D. Straub (ed.) *Das Mondsee-Land.: Geschichte und Kultur. Ausstellung des Landes Oberösterreich, 8. Mai - 26. Oktober 1981, Kirche und ehemaliges Stift Mondsee (Heimatmuseum Mondsee)*. Linz: Oberösterreichischer Landesverlag, 295–357.

Offenberger, J. 1995, 5000 Jahre Kulturgut unter Wasser. Pfahlbauforschung - der österreichische Weg. *Zeitschrift für Geschichte und Archäologie in Oberösterreich* 10: 4–15.

Ottaway, B.S. 1982, *Earliest copper artefacts of the northalpine region: their analysis and evaluation.* Bern: Seminar für Urgeschichte.

Otto, H. and Witter, W. 1952, *Handbuch der ältesten vorgeschichtlichen Metallurgie in Mitteleuropa.* Leipzig: Barth.

Pernicka, E. 1984, Instrumentelle Multi-Elementanalyse archäologischer Kupfer- und Bronzeartefakte: Ein Methodenvergleich. *Jahrbuch des Römisch-Germanischen Zentralmuseums Mainz* 31: 517-531.

Pernicka, E. 1990, Gewinnung und Verbreitung der Metalle in prähistorischer Zeit. *Jahrbuch des Römisch-Germanischen Zentralmuseums Mainz* 37: 21–129.

Pernicka, E. 1999, Trace Element Fingerprinting of Ancient Copper: A Guide to technology or Provenance? In: S. M. M. Young, A. M. Pollard, P. Budd and R.A. Ixer (eds.) *Metals in Antiquity.* BAR International Series 792, Oxford: Archaeopress, 163-171.

Pernicka, E., Begemann, F., Schmitt-Strecker, S., Wagner, G.A. 1993, Eneolithic and Early Bronze Age Copper Artefacts from the Balkans and their Relation to Serbian Copper Ores. *Prähistorische Zeitschrift* 68: 1-54.

Pernicka, E., Begemann, F. Schmitt-Strecker, S., Todorova, H., Kuleff, I. 1997, Prehistoric copper in Bulgaria: Its composition and provenance. *Eurasia Antiqua* 3: 41-180.

Pittioni, R. 1957, *Urzeitlicher Bergbau auf Kupfererz und Spurenanalyse: Beiträge zum Problem der Relation Lagerstätte-Fertigobjekt.* Wien: Deuticke.

Pittioni, R. 1966, Weitere Spektralanalysen von Funden aus dem Attersee, Oberösterreich. *Archaeologia Austriaca* 39: 93.

Pittioni, R. 1980. *Urzeit 1.* Wien: Österreichische Akademie der Wissenschaften.

Pohl, W. 2011, *Economic geology: Principles and practice: metals, minerals, coal and hydrocarbons - introduction to formation and sustainable exploitation of mineral deposits.* Chichester: Wiley-Blackwell.

Pucher, E. and Engl, K. 1997, *Die Pfahlbaustationen des Mondsees: Tierknochenfunde.* Wien: Österreichische Akademie der Wissenschaften.

Rehren, Th., Boscher, L., Pernicka, E. 2012, Large scale smelting of speiss and arsenical copper at Early Bronze Age Arisman, North-West Iran. *Journal of Archaeological Science* 39(6), 1717-1727.

Rieser B. and Schrattenthaler H. 2004, Prähistorischer Kupferbergbau im Raum Schwaz/Brixlegg (Nordtirol). Geländebefunde und experimentelle Untersuchungen zur Schlägelschäftung. In: G. Weisgerber and G. Goldenberg (eds.) *Alpenkupfer - Rame delle Alpi: Tagung "Urgeschichtliche Kupfergewinnung im Alpenraum", an der Universität Innsbruck, vom 4. - 8. Oktober 1995*. Bochum: Dt. Bergbau-Museum, 75–94.

Rieser, B. and Schrattenthaler, H. 1998-1999, Urgeschichtlicher Kupferbergbau im Raum Schwaz-Brixlegg, Tirol. *Archaeologia Austriaca* 82/83: 135–179.

Rinne, C. 2011, *RADON radiocarbon dates online* [online] www.jungsteinsite.de/radon/radon_neu.htm.

Ruprechtsberger, E.M. 2006, Die Mondseekultur und ihre Erforschung - Ein Überblick. In: A. Binsteiner and E.M. Ruprechtsberger (eds.) *Mondsee-Kultur und Analyse der Silexartefakte von See am Mondsee*. Linz: Magistrat der Landeshauptstadt, 7–22.

Ruttkay, E. 1981, Typologie und Chronologie der Mondsee-Gruppe. In: D. Straub (ed.) *Das Mondsee-Land : Geschichte u. Kultur; Ausstellung des Landes Oberösterreich, 8. Mai - 26. Oktober 1981, Kirche und ehemaliges Stift Mondsee (Heimatmuseum Mondsee)*. Linz: Oberösterreichischer Landesverlag, 269–294.

Ruttkay, E. 1995, Neue Hoffnungen. Das Pfahlbauprojekt vom Fonds zur Förderung der wissenschaftlichen Forschung und der Österreichischen Nationalbank. *Zeitschrift für Geschichte und Archäologie in Oberösterreich* 10: 18–19.

Ruttkay, E., Cichocki, O., Pernicka, E. and Pucher, E. 2004, Prehistoric lacustrine villages on the Austrian lakes: past and recent research developments. In: F. Menotti (ed.) *Living on the lake in prehistoric Europe : 150 years of lake-dwelling research*. London: Routledge, 50–68.

Schmidt, R. 1986, Palynologie, Stratigraphie und Großreste von Profilen der neolithischen Station See am Mondsee. *Archaeologia Austriaca* 70: 227–235.

Schreiner, M. 2007, *Erzlagerstätten im Hrontal, Slowakei: Genese und prähistorische Nutzung*. Rahden/Westf.: Marie Leidorf.

Schulz, O. 1997, Östliche Grauwackenzone - Buntmetalle (inkl. Kiesvererzungen). In: L. Weber, I. Cerny, and W.E. Petrascheck (eds.) *Handbuch der Lagerstätten der Erze, Industrieminerale und Energierohstoffe Österreichs: Erläuterungen zur metallogenetischen Karte von Österreich 1 : 500 000 unter Einbeziehung der Industrieminerale und Energierohstoffe ; [in memoriam Walther Emil Petrascheck]*. Wien: Geologische Bundesanstalt, 338.

Stadler, P. 1995, Ein Beitrag zur Absolutchronologie des Neolithikums in Ostösterreich aufgrund der 14C-Daten. In: E. Lenneis (ed.) *Jungsteinzeit im Osten Österreichs*. Wien: Niederösterreichiche Pressehaus, 210–224.

Thornton, C.P., Rehren, Th., Pigott, V.C. 2009, The production of speiss (iron arsenide) during the Early Bronze Age in Iran. *Journal of Archaeological Science* 36: 308–316.

Tylecote, R. E., Ghaznavi, H. A. and Boydell, P. J. 1977, Partitioning of Trace Elements Between the Ores, Fluxes, Slags and Metal During the Smelting of Copper. *Journal of Archaeological Science* 4: 305-333.

Wagner, G.A. 2000, Isotope Analysis, Dating and Provenance Methods. In: E. Ciliberto and G. Spoto (eds.) *Modern analytical methods in art and archaeology*. New York: Wiley, 445–464.

Willvonseder, K. 1963/1968, *Die jungsteinzeitlichen und bronzezeitlichen Pfahlbauten des Attersees in Oberösterreich*. Wien: Böhlau.

Witte, N. 2004, *Herkunftsuntersuchungen an Kupferartefakten der Mondseekultur*. Unpublizierte Diplomarbeit. TU Bergakademie Freiberg.

Chapter 6

FORGING A CHRONOLOGICAL FRAMEWORK FOR SCOTTISH CRANNOGS; THE RADIOCARBON AND DENDROCHRONOLOGICAL EVIDENCE

Anne Crone[1]

Abstract

The chronological evidence for Scottish crannogs is presented and evaluated. This consists of a substantial dataset of 159 radiocarbon dates, dendrochronological dates from three sites, and a wiggle-match date from another. Taken together, these sources of evidence indicate a periodicity in the use of crannogs. Over a scale of millennia there were particular centuries when crannog-building was popular. During the 1st millennium BC, when the majority of dated crannogs were built, there appear to be specific spikes in crannog-building activity in the 5th and 2nd centuries BC respectively. At the scale of decades dendrochronological data portrays more short-lived episodic settlement, where the episodes of occupation are of varying duration, and are separated by intervals, themselves of varying duration.

Keywords: Scotland, crannogs, Iron Age, Early Historic, dendrochronology, radiocarbon-dating, settlement dates, settlement durations, periodicity of use

---

1 AOC Archaeology Group, Edgefield Industrial Estate, Loanhead, EH20 9SY

Introduction

Crannogs are islands, made or significantly modified by human agency, which, with the exception of Llangorse in Wales (Redknap and Lane 1994), are found only in Scotland or Ireland. This paper will demonstrate that crannogs were used, albeit intermittently, over the course of two and half millennia. It is thus probable that widely divergent natural, social, economic and political circumstances provided the stimulus for their construction, use and re-use at different times. Unfortunately, the use of a single portmanteau term to describe these sites implies a commonality of form and function which has yet to be demonstrated. Perhaps more importantly, it tends to obscure their particular relationships with the settlement context within which they should be interpreted (Harding 2004, 103). A detailed chronological framework is essential if those relationships are to be fully understood and crannogs are to be integrated with their contemporary settlement histories. As a contribution to the creation of this chronological framework this paper seeks to summarise current understanding of crannog chronologies.

When Robert Munro undertook his seminal study of the crannogs of Scotland he had only the artefactual evidence to guide him in assessing their likely dates (1882, 275-84). Then, as indeed now (cf Cavers 2010, 106; Cavers et al. 2011), the only chronologically diagnostic artefacts found on these sites tended to be those of Roman or later date, and Munro concluded that the crannogs of south-west Scotland had been built by 'the Celtic inhabitants' in the years following the Roman withdrawal from Scotland. There are still many crannogs which can only be dated on the basis of artefacts retrieved during the nineteenth century (Oakley 1973, 97 – 111), but they will not be considered in this paper. Although diagnostic artefacts probably do provide a basic chronological structure for phases of crannog activity (MacSween 2000, 151), their interpretation is far from straightforward (Hunter 2007, 11-12). Indeed, the scientific dates presented in this paper may provide a framework within which the artefactual evidence can be more rigorously assessed.

Nearly two decades ago the present writer published a paper on the assemblage of radiocarbon dates then available for Scottish crannogs; this consisted of 23 radiocarbon dates from 12 crannogs (Crone 1993). There are now 159 radiocarbon dates from 52 sites (Table 6.1), and three crannogs have also been dated dendrochronologically. Most of the radiocarbon dates have already been published, but in many disparate sources, so the Munro Symposium in 2010 provided a much-needed stimulus to assemble the data and appraise this vastly-expanded dataset.

Name	Lab No.	Det. B.P.	St. Dev.	Cal 2-sigma	Context/material	Reference
Barean Loch	GU-2641	1280	50	AD 650 - 880	pile	Barber & Crone 1993
	GU-2642	2140	60	380 - 40 BC	pile	
Barhapple Loch	GU-10920	2130	50	360 - 40 BC	oak pile	Henderson et al 2006
Barlockhart	GU-11563	1975	45	90 BC - AD 130	hazel stake	Henderson et al 2006
	GU-11564	1980	40	AD 60 - 130	oak stake	
Black Loch of Myrton	SUERC-32597	2470	35	770 - 410 BC	alder pile	Unpublished
Black Loch of Sanquhar	GU-10918	1840	50	AD 60 - 340	oak pile	Henderson et al 2006
Buiston	GU-2635	2530	140	975 - 375 BC	oak plank	Crone 2000
	GU-2636	1430	50	AD 530 - 680	oak structural	
	GU-2637	1580	50	AD 385 - 615	oak pile	
	GU-2638	1380	50	AD 565 - 710	oak pile	
	GU-2688	1640	50	AD 250 - 540	charcoal mixed	
	GU-2999	2670	50	915 - 795 BC	oak plank	
	GU-3000	1950	50	100BC - AD 150	hazel brushwood	
	GU-3001	1660	50	AD 220 - 525	alder pile	
	GU-3002	1620	50	AD 315 - 600	alder pile	
	GU-3003	1610	50	AD 335 - 595	alder charcoal	
	GU-3004	1680	50	AD 230 - 520	charcoal mixed	
	GU-3005	1720	50	AD 143 - 427	charcoal mixed	
	GU-3006	1610	50	AD 335 - 595	charcoal mixed	
	GU-3007	1610	70	AD 260 - 615	alder	
	GU-3390	1570	60	AD 360 - 625	birch	
	GU-3391	1920	50	25 BC - AD 205	hazel brushwood	
	GU-3528	1570	50	AD 395 - 695	alder horizontal	
	GU-3529	1590	50	AD 350 - 600	alder pile	
	GU-3530	1540	50	AD 410 - 620	charcoal mixed	
	GU-3531	1530	50	AD 415 - 625	charcoal mixed	
	GU-3532	1610	50	AD 335 - 595	hazel withy	
Cults Loch 1	GU-10919	1790	50	AD 120 - 390	oak pile	Henderson et al 2006

Name	Lab No.	Det. B.P.	St. Dev.	Cal 2-sigma	Context/material	Reference
Cults Loch 3	GU-12138	2340	50	550 - 200 BC	oak pile	Unpublished
	SUERC-22906	2440	25	750 - 400 BC	oak pile	
	SUERC-22907	2375	30	710 - 380 BC	alder pile	
	SUERC-27660	2420	35	750 - 390 BC	alder horizontal	
	SUERC-27664	2405	35	750 - 390 BC	bracken	
	SUERC-27665	2355	35	720 - 370 BC	alder horizontal	
	SUERC-27666	2330	40	520 - 230 BC	hazel charcoal	
Dorman's Island, Whitefield Loch	GU-10917	2250	50	390 - 210 BC	alder pile	Cavers et al 2011
	SUERC-22914	2125	30	350 - 50 BC	charred spelt grain	
	SUERC-22915	2070	30	180 BC - 0 AD	hazel	
	SUERC-22916	2125	30	350 - 50 BC	oak horizontal	
	SUERC-22917	2515	30	780 - 550 BC	oak horizontal	
	SUERC-22918	255	30	AD 1520 - 1960	birch stake	
	SUERC-22919	2210	30	360 - 200 BC	oak post	
	SUERC-24644	2175	35	370 - 110 BC	birch charcoal	
Loch Arthur	GU-2643	2260	50	400 - 200 BC	birch pile	Henderson 2007
	GU-2644	2240	60	410 - 160 BC	birch pile	
	GU-12173	2240	35	400 - 200BC	alder horizontal	
	GU-12174	2275	35	400 - 200BC	alder horizontal	
	GU-12175	2215	35	390 - 170BC	alder horizontal	
Loch Heron I	SUERC-6742	2310	35	410 - 200 BC	pile	Cavers 2010
Loch Heron II	SUERC-6743	2390	35	760 - 390 BC	pile	Cavers 2010
Lochrutton	GU-2640	830	50	AD 1040 - 1280	pile	Barber & Crone 1993
	GU-2639	820	50	AD 1040 - 1280	pile	
Milton Loch 1	K-2027	2440	100	810 - 380 BC	pile	Guido 1974
	K-1394	2350	100	800 - 200 BC	oak ard	
	GU-2648	2080	50	360 BC - AD 30	pile	Barber & Crone 1993
Milton Loch 2	GU-2647	2060	50	200 BC - AD 60	pile	Barber & Crone 1993
Milton Loch 3	GU-2645	1470	50	AD 450 - 660	pile	Barber & Crone 1993
	GU-2646	1470	70	AD 430 - 670	pile	

Name	Lab No.	Det. B.P.	St. Dev.	Cal 2-sigma	Context/material	Reference
White Loch of Myrton	GU-10921	2080	50	350 - 30 BC	ash pile	Henderson et al 2006
Dubh Loch	GU-11924	2030	50	170 BC - AD 80	alder horizontal	Cavers 2010
Ederline	GU-2415	2220	45	400-190BC	oak	Henderson forthcoming
	SUERC-20200	2425	30	749 - 402 BC	oak	
	SUERC-20205	2510	30	789 - 538 BC	oak	
	SUERC-20206	2455	30	754 - 412 BC	hazel	
	SUERC-20207	1515	30	AD 433 - 617	alder charcoal	
	SUERC-20208	2450	30	753 - 410 BC	oak	
Loch Avich	GU-11920	2560	50	830 - 510 BC	alder offcut	Cavers 2010
Loch Eck	GU-11923	780	50	AD 1150 - 1300	wood offcut	Cavers 2010
Loch Glashan	GU-11394	1530	50	AD 420 - 640	E-ware residue	Crone & Campbell 2005
	GU-11395	1500	35	AD 430 - 650	E-ware residue	
	GU-11396	1415	35	AD 560 - 680	E-ware residue	
	GU-11397	1400	40	AD 560 - 700	E-ware residue	
	GU-11523	1780	35	AD 130 - 350	non-oak peg	
	GU-11524	1650	35	320AD-540AD	oak horizontal	
	GU-11525	1790	35	AD 130 - 350	alder trough	
	GU-11525	1815	35	120AD-330AD	oak horizontal	
	GU-11860	1650	40	AD 260 - 540	ash tub	
Loch Leathan	GU-11921	2480	50	790 - 410 BC	oak pile	Cavers 2010
Loch Seil	GU-11922	1500	50	AD 430 - 650	pile	Cavers 2010
Craggan	SUERC-6497	2420	35	560 - 390 BC	oak	Dixon et al 2007
	SUERC-6498	1270	35	AD 660 - 870	oak	
	SUERC-7155	2500	35	790 - 500 BC	oak	
	SUERC-7156	1300	35	AD 650 -780	oak	
Croftmartaig	GU-12342	2230	50	400 - 170 BC	alder pile	Dixon et al 2007
	GU-12343	2210	50	400 - 160 BC	alder pile	

Name	Lab No.	Det. B.P.	St. Dev.	Cal 2-sigma	Context/material	Reference
Dall Bay North	SUERC-6501	1245	35	AD 680 - 890	alder	Dixon et al 2007
	SUERC-6502	2400	35	550- 390 BC	alder	
	SUERC-7157	1330	35	AD 640 - 780	alder	
	SUERC-7158	2465	35	770 - 410 BC	alder	
	SUERC-7314	1435	35	AD 560 - 660		
Dall Bay South	SUERC-6499	2420	35	560 - 390 BC	oak	Dixon et al 2007
	SUERC-6500	2560	35	810 - 540 BC	oak	
Eilean Breaban	GU-12124	1520	50	AD 420 - 640	oak	Dixon et al 2007
	SUERC-7315	2430	35	600 - 400 BC	alder	
Fearnan Hotel	GU-1322	2475	55	790 - 410 BC	oak	Dixon et al 2007
Firbush	GU-1324	2140	55	370 - 50 BC	oak	Dixon et al 2007
Milton Morenish	GU-12123	2530	50	810 - 480 BC	oak	Dixon et al 2007
	SUERC-7305	2400	35	560 - 390 BC	alder	
Morenish	GU-12125	1940	50	50 BC - AD 220	alder pile	Dixon et al 2007
	SUERC-7310	1970	35	50 BC - AD 90	alder	
	SUERC-7306	1930	35	40 BC - AD 130	alder	
	SUERC-7311	1950	35	40 BC - AD 130	alder	
Morenish Boathouse	SUERC-6487	2425	35	560 - 400 BC	oak	Dixon et al 2007
	SUERC-6488	2400	35	550 - 390 BC	alder	
	SUERC-9746	2055	35	170 BC - AD 30	birch	
	SUERC-9747	2045	35	170 BC - AD 30	hazel	
Oakbank	GU-1323	2545	55	830 - 410BC	oak	Dixon et al 2007
	GU-1325	2410	55	770 - 390BC	oak	
	GU-1463	2360	60	800- 250BC	wood	
	GU-1464	2405	60	770 - 390BC	wood	
	GU-3468	2490	50	800 - 410BC	oak pile	
	GU-3469	2560	50	830 - 520BC	alder pile	
	GU-3470	2150	50	810 - 410BC	alder pile	
	GU-3471	2490	50	800 - 410BC	alder pile	
	GU-3472	2450	50	770 - 400BC	alder pile	

Name	Lab No.	Det. B.P.	St. Dev.	Cal 2-sigma	Context/material	Reference
Old Manse	SUERC-6491	2460	35	770 - 400 BC	alder	Dixon et al 2007
	SUERC-6493	2465	35	770 - 400 BC	alder	
Tombreck	GU-12126	1950	50	60 BC - AD 180	Alder pile	Dixon et al 2007
	SUERC-7312	1970	35	60 BC - AD 90	alder	
	SUERC-7313	2040	35	170 BC - AD 50	alder	
Edinample, Loch Earn	GU-12344	1090	50	AD 890 -1000	wood	Dixon et al 2007
Eilean nam Faolaig,	GU-12340	900	50	AD 1020 - 1250	oak	Dixon et al 2007
Loch Rannoch	GU-12341	730	50	AD 1210 - 1330	wood	
Loch Drumellie	GU-12345	1490	50	AD 530 - 640	oak	Dixon et al 2007
Loch Monzievaird	GU-12346	140	50	AD 1670 - 1950	oak	Dixon et al 2007
	GU-12347	2520	50	700 - 540 BC	wood	
Port an Eilean, Loch Tummel	GU-12339	130	50	AD 1800 - 1900	wooden post	Dixon et al 2007
Eaderloch, Loch Treig	SUERC-22908	315	30	AD 1484 - 1648	pine horizontal	Crone 2011
	SUERC-22909	315	30	AD 1484 - 1648	Birch pile	
	SUERC-22910	310	30	AD 1485 - 1650	Birch pile	
Migdale	NZA-18101	1957	40	40 BC - AD 140	oak plank	Unpublished
	NZA-18102	2515	40	800 - 420 BC	stake	
Ledmore	Beta-78833	700	50	AD 1220-1400		Holley & Ralston 1995
Eilean Ban	Beta-78832	2200	70	400 - 100 BC		Holley & Ralston 1995
Redcastle	AA-21248	2220	70	400 - 110 BC	leather	Hale 2004
	Beta-48763	2150	60	380 - 50 BC	alder	
	Beta-48764	1750	90	AD 60 - 530	alder	
	GU-4531	2510	50	810 - 410 BC	oak pile	
	GU-4542	2570	50	840 - 520 BC	oak pile	
	GU-4543	2550	50	820 - 520 BC	alder horizontal	

Name	Lab No.	Det. B.P.	St. Dev.	Cal 2-sigma	Context/material	Reference
	GU-4094	2310	50	460 - 200 BC	alder stake	
	GU-4095	2330	50	530 - 210 BC	oak stake	
	GU-4097	2480	50	775 - 415 BC	alder horizontal	
Carn Dubh	GU-4540	2530	50	810 - 410 BC	oak	Hale 2004
Cameron Bay	GU-2439	2160	80	400 - 30 BC		Hale 2004
	GU-2440	1990	50	110 BC - AD 120		
Phopachy	Beta-48765	1940	60	100 BC - AD 220	alder	Hale 2004
	Beta-48766	2030	60	200 BC - AD 90	alder	
	GU-4098	2060	50	199 BC - AD 54	alder	
	GU-4099	1990	50	110 BC - AD 120	alder	
Erskine Bridge	GU-2186	2210	50	400 - 160 BC	alder horizontal	Sands & Hale 2005
	GU-2187	1970	60	AD 160 - 190	oak pile	
	GU-2328	1950	50	100 BC - AD 150	pile	
	GU-2383	2170	60	390 - 100 BC	pile	
Dumbuck	GU-7470	2090	50	348 BC - AD 22	oak pile	Sands & Hale 2005
	GU-7471	1910	50	36 BC - AD 236	alder horizontal	
	GU-7472	2040	50	196 BC - AD 71	oak pile	
	GU-7473	2060	50	199 BC - AD 54	alder horizontal	

Table 6.1 List of radiocarbon dates from Scottish crannog sites.

The radiocarbon evidence

The increase in the number of radiocarbon-dated crannogs is the result of more active research into crannogs over the last two decades. This includes postgraduate studies by Graeme Cavers (2010), Alex Hale (2004), Mark Holley (Holley and Ralston 1995) and Matthew Shelley (2009), surveys in the Clyde (Sands and Hale 2005), excavation and survey in Perthshire (Dixon 2004, 2007), and the work of the Scottish Wetland Archaeological Programme (SWAP), which has undertaken both survey and excavation in south-west Scotland (Henderson et al. 2003, 2006; Henderson 2007; Cavers and Crone 2010; Cavers et al. 2011) and Argyll (Henderson forthcoming).

Figure 6.1 shows the distribution of those crannogs for which there are now radiocarbon dates. There are two main foci: in south-west Scotland and Perthshire, with a scatter of dates from Argyll and Mull; and in the estuaries of the Clyde and Beauly Firth. The majority of the radiocarbon dates come from structural timbers, mainly piling, most of them sampled during survey programmes rather than excavation. Consequently, these dates lack stratigraphic context, so at most all that can be inferred from them is that they reflect episodes of construction, repair or refurbishment. They cannot be used to provide unambiguous evidence for domestic occupation of the sites at the times indicated by the radiocarbon dates. Radiocarbon samples from excavated sites are derived mainly from structural timbers but also include material from occupation deposits such as charcoal, cereal grain and other macroplant remains, and on one site, wooden artefacts.

Perhaps the first question to be addressed of the mass of dates now available should be whether the apparent chronological distribution of activity has changed with the seven-fold increase in data (Figure 6.2), not least because this has a bearing on future research strategies (see below). The 1993 dataset appeared to show three distinct periods of crannog-building activity in Scotland. The first, and the most intensive (and here the numbers of radiocarbon dates are equated with intensity of activity which, given the near random processes by which most of the samples were recovered, seems reasonable), with 65% of the available dates falling in this period, lay between *circa* 850 BC and AD 200, a period spanning the Early Iron Age through to the Roman Iron Age in Scotland. After a short hiatus there was another bout of activity during the Early Historic period, the fifth – eighth centuries AD, and then, after a similar hiatus there was activity in the medieval period, from the eleventh to thirteenth centuries AD. Although the historical record documents the use of crannogs in the late medieval and the early modern period (Shelley 2009) this is not reflected in the radiocarbon chronology.

In the expanded dataset the floruit of crannog-building activity in the later prehistoric period continues to be emphasised, with 68% of all dates, and 71% of all sites, falling within the period *circa* 850 BC – AD 200 (Figure 6.2). However, the intervals between episodes of building activity now appear less distinct, particularly that between the second and fifth centuries AD. Single dates from Cults Loch 1 and the Black Loch, Sanquhar, both in south-west Scotland, extend into this period, while a cluster of dates from Loch Glashan, Argyll indicate activity some time in the second to fourth century AD. Doubt about the validity of these Loch Glashan dates had been expressed because samples from conserved wood had been

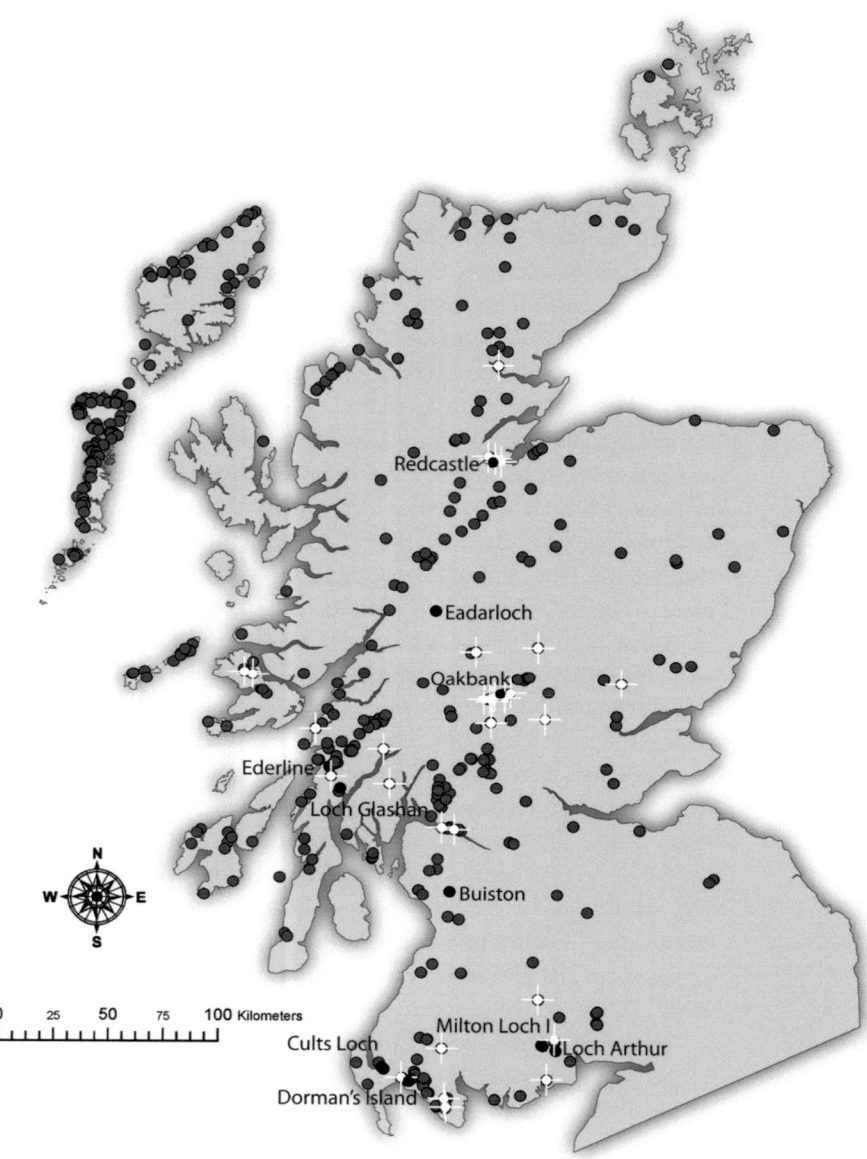

Figure 6.1 Distribution of all known crannogs in Scotland. Those crannogs that have been excavated are named; all other crannogs which have been radiocarbon-dated are identified by crosses.

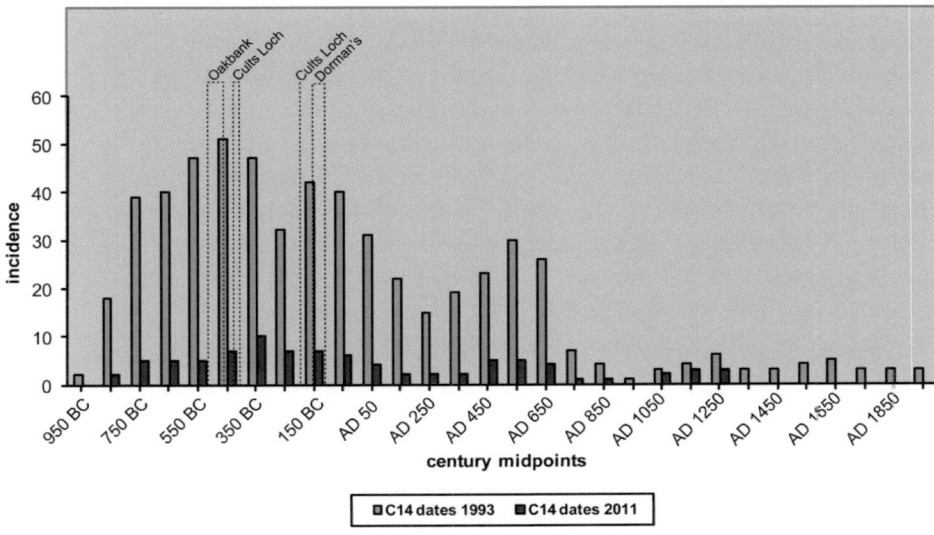

Figure 6.2 The chronological distribution of the radiocarbon dataset, with the number of dates on the Y axis whose calibrated ranges span the given centuries on the X axis.

used (Crone and Campbell 2005, 115), but a virtually identical date from an unfinished logboat recently found near the crannog suggests that there was indeed activity on the loch at this period (Crone forthcoming). Overall, the new crannog dates appear to indicate that, while crannog activity abates during the second to fifth centuries AD, it does not cease. In contrast, the period between the ninth and eleventh centuries AD remains a distinct hiatus in crannog activity, although the single date from Edinample, in Loch Earn, Perthshire, now falls within that period.

Finally, the radiocarbon dates from Eadarloch crannog, Loch Treig, Lochaber demonstrate that some crannogs were being built *de novo* as late as the sixteenth century AD (Crone 2011). Although they were used extensively in the early modern period (Shelley 2009), there are no unambiguous historical references to the actual construction of artificial islands at this time (ibid. 12-13). Many medieval and early modern crannogs have evidence of earlier foundations, for example Loch Arthur (Henderson 2007), Loch Migdale and Eilean nam Breaban, Loch Tay (Shelley 2009, 148), all of which have produced much earlier radiocarbon dates.

Early Historic re-use of later prehistoric crannogs

One pattern which has emerged more distinctly in the enlarged dataset is the re-use of later prehistoric crannogs in the Early Historic period (Figure 6.3). Of the eleven crannogs with evidence of building and activity in the Early Historic period, six also have evidence for an earlier foundation in the later prehistoric period, and the possibility cannot be excluded that this was also the case with the other Early Historic sites because, with the exception of Loch Glashan, Argyll, they are represented by only one or two dates each. Of the two excavated examples where such re-use has been observed there was no evidence of any continuity of use between the two periods. At Buiston, Ayrshire the abandoned Romano-British crannog had been sealed by a thick layer of sterile lacustrine mud before being used as the foundation for an elaborate palisaded construction in the late sixth century AD (Crone 2000, 16, Figure 3). At Ederline in Loch Awe, Argyll there was a similar stratigraphic sequence, with Early Historic deposits lying over a sterile layer of silt which sealed the later prehistoric structure (Henderson forthcoming).

The simplest explanation for this phenomenon is that it required less effort to use an old site as a foundation, but the two crannogs in Dall Bay, Loch Tay suggest that something more than indolence or expediency was involved (Figure 6.4). Both crannogs were built in the later prehistoric period, yet in the Early Historic period, Dall North, the crannog furthest out into the loch was selected for rebuilding; in other words the builders bypassed the larger crannog nearest the shore and deliberately selected the smaller, more distant one. Better security, or lower loch levels may explain this selection but it may equally reflect the fact that the site carried symbolic associations for the Early Historic community. For example, the builders might have been drawing on associations with persons or events important in local mythology to establish the legitimacy of their claims to power, a scenario evoked for other examples of re-use of earlier sites by later peoples (i.e. Hingley 1996, Driscoll 1998).

The historical context for this phenomenon is the emergence in Scotland of multiple independent Celtic kingdoms, each with differing, and changing political allegiances. Re-use of crannogs in the Early Historic period has been observed in Dal Riata (Argyll), Pictland (Perthshire), British Strathclyde and Rheged (south-west Scotland), so it is a common response across these various polities. It could reflect the jostling for power of local dynastic contenders, with the necessary corollary that all Early Historic crannogs in Scotland are statements of power. However, while the material evidence at Buiston suggests that it was indeed the settlement of a privileged elite (Crone 2000, 166), this is less evidently the case at the only

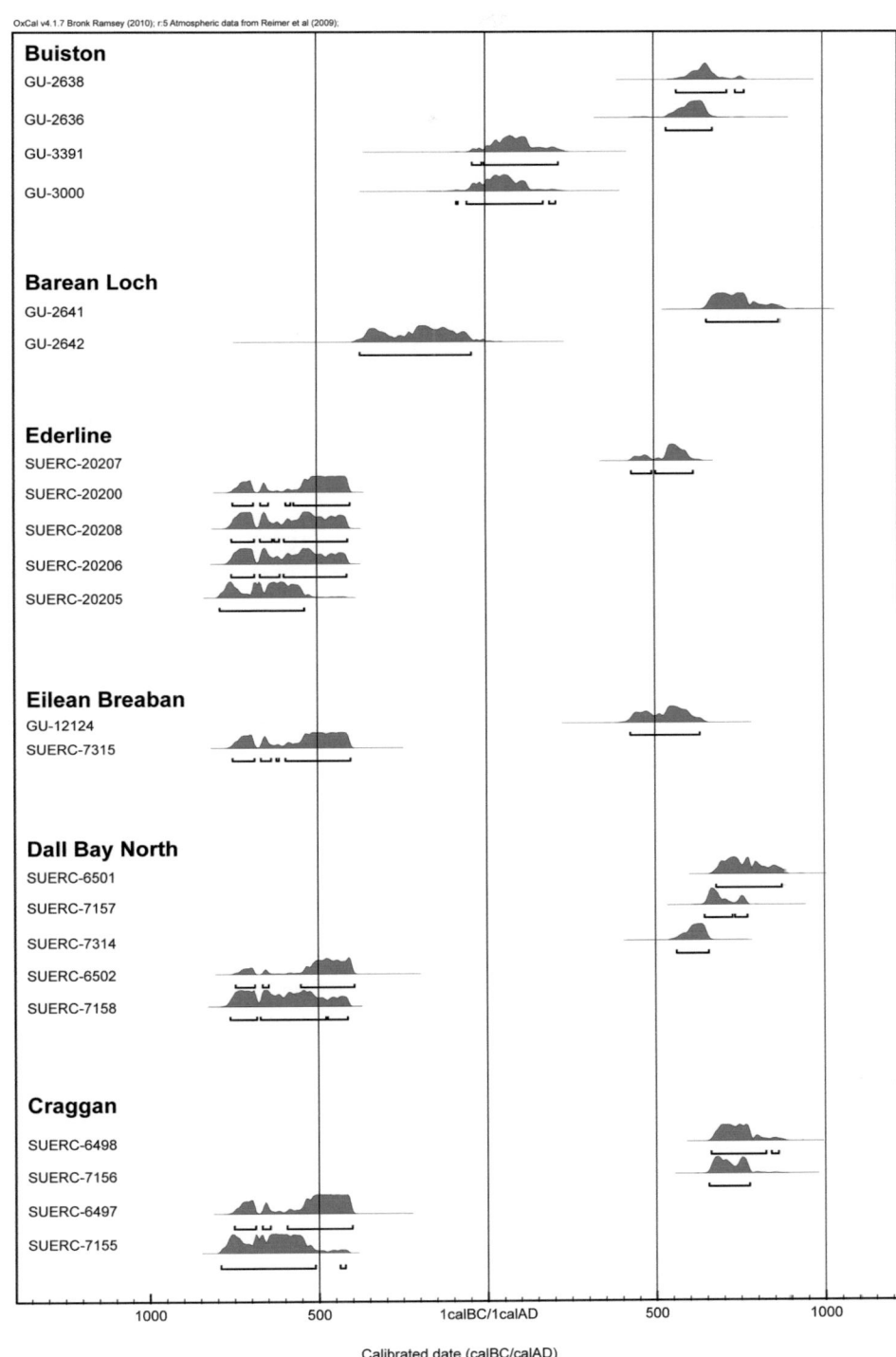

Figure 6.3 Crannogs with both later prehistoric and Early Historic radiocarbon dates (only a selection of the radiocarbon dates available from Buiston are shown).

Figure 6.4 The two crannogs in Dall Bay, Loch Tay (photograph by D.W. Harding).

other excavated Early Historic crannog, Loch Glashan, which may have been a craftworking site (Crone and Campbell 2005, 122-3).

Loch Tay

Loch Tay exemplifies the benefits of extensive dating, where the uses of the loch can be reconstructed h during different periods and the evolution of settlement patterns over time studied (Dixon 2007). Of the eighteen known crannogs in the loch, thirteen now have radiocarbon dates, and a further two have documentary evidence for episodes of activity in the medieval and later periods (ibid. 259-62). At least nine of the crannogs were in use during the period *circa* 800 – 400 BC, while the other four were in use during the period *circa* 400 BC – AD 200. Where multiple radiocarbon dates are available (and most of the dated examples in Loch Tay have at least two dates) there is no evidence that those built in the earlier Iron Age continued in use throughout the millennium; rather, they suggest distinct pulses of crannog-building activity with the construction of entirely new sites in the middle Iron Age. Then, after a period of several centuries in the early first millennium AD, during which there appears to have been no activity on the loch, at least three of the crannogs are re-used in the Early Historic period (Figure 6.3), part of the phenomenon discussed above.

Oakbank, the most intensively investigated of the Loch Tay crannogs (Dixon 2004, 125-68), has recently been the subject of a high-precision wiggle-matching programme (Cook et al. 2010). There are nine radiocarbon dates from timbers on the site, all of which span the period *circa* 800 – 400 BC. The wiggle-matching of a tenth timber, an oak pile which had retained its bark, predicts that the timber was felled around 500 BC (maximum range 520 – 465 BC).

The dendrochronological evidence

Using radiocarbon dates alone, the analysis of the Loch Tay data must necessarily remain crude, particularly for the first millennium BC, due to the effect of the 'Hallstatt plateau'- the flat part of the calibration curve between *circa* 800-400 BC. Macroscopic, landscape-wide pulses of settlement can be identified if they are widely separated in time, but it is impossible to come close to understanding the biographies of individual sites, as has been done at Buiston with the aid of dendrochronology (Crone 2000, 64-5; and see below).

Continental colleagues must be wondering why, in discussing the chronologies of sites with copious amounts of waterlogged wood, dendrochronology has not been a standard means of dating. Unfortunately, Scotland is not blessed with the extensive regional tree-ring chronologies available on the Continent which have made the dating of many of the sites described elsewhere in this volume relatively straightforward. Very few crannogs have been excavated, mainly because they are not under threat of imminent destruction (Crone and Clarke 2005, 9-10; although many crannogs have been lost since the nineteenth century, and many of those that survive are now in unstable, compromised environments; Barber and Crone 1993, Lillie et al. 2008). Consequently few large assemblages of timber suitable for dendrochronological analysis have ever been retrieved. Of the fifty-one crannogs that have been radiocarbon-dated, only ten have actually been excavated (Figure 6.1) and most of those have been very limited in scope. Dendrochronological studies have now been undertaken on assemblages from six of the excavated sites but Loch Glashan and Eadarloch were excavated in the mid-twentieth century at a time when extensive sampling was not routinely undertaken and it has not been possible to dendro-date the few timbers that had been retained (Crone 1998, Crone 2011).

Oakbank crannog

The first Scottish crannog to be studied dendrochronologically was that at Oakbank, but the analysis was unsuccessful (Crone 1988). It is worthwhile outlining the difficulties encountered in dendro-dating this crannog because they are likely to be encountered on other sites, particularly in the highland region. Firstly, the bulk of the structural timber was alder, a species which can be useful in building relative site chronologies but which, on its own, cannot be used to provide absolute dates for a site (Crone 1988, but see Crone 2000 and Billamboz 2003 for examples where it has been used to provide absolute dates in conjunction with oak). Furthermore, 84% of the alder from Oakbank was under forty years of age, the shortness of the sequences hindering reliable cross-correlations across the site. An alder chronology was constructed which suggested frequent episodes of building and repair, but it could not be substantiated (Crone 1988, 139-41). As alder is probably the commonest tree species fringing most Scottish lochs, it stands to reason that it will have been used extensively in crannog construction, an assumption which has been confirmed on other crannogs where more intensive timber sampling has taken place, ie Loch Arthur (Henderson 2007, 233), Ederline (ibid. 237) and Cults Loch (see below).

Some oak was present at Oakbank; it constituted 21% of the total sample, but again, most of the timbers were young, all but five of the oaks being under 90 years of age (Crone 1988, 134). Critically, the oak timbers displayed such asymmetric growth around their stems that even tree-ring sequences measured along different radii on the same tree compared poorly with each other, and consequently a dateable oak chronology could not be constructed (ibid. 162-3). This growth-pattern suggests a source in a stressed environment, possibly on steep, rocky, exposed hill slopes of the type that surround many highland lochs. Some difficulty in constructing chronologies with the quality of oak available on many crannogs must therefore be anticipated.

Nonetheless, the existence of robust regional tree-ring chronologies would enhance the chances of dating such difficult material though this remains a 'chicken-and-egg' situation; without sites producing large assemblages of dateable oak timbers, regional chronologies cannot be constructed. At present, there is no continuous dendrochronological coverage in Scotland earlier than the mid-ninth century AD (Crone and Mills 2002) and dendro-dating of prehistoric and Early Historic material must rely on comparisons with adjacent regions where there is better coverage. Not surprisingly then, the only crannogs that have so far been successfully dendro-dated lie in the south-west, that part of Scotland which lies geographically closest to northern England and northern Ireland - the sources of rigorously established dendrochronological master curves.

Buiston crannog

Buiston, in Ayrshire was the first crannog in Scotland to be successfully dendro-dated and it exemplifies the insights that can be gained by extensive sampling and analysis. It was first excavated by Munro in the nineteenth century (1882, 190 - 239) and re-excavated in the late twentieth century (Crone 2000). It is a testament to Munro's recording skills that his plans could be accurately placed over the twentieth century plans (ibid. Figure 132), ensuring that those structural relationships that had been lost to decay in the intervening century could still be understood.

As described above, there had been a crannog at Buiston during the Romano-British period, which was subsequently sealed below lacustrine muds and built upon in the Early Historic period. The structural remains from this later period were extensive, consisting of successive palisades, each with a quite distinct method of construction, and two roundhouses with stratigraphic evidence for multiple phases of subsidence and refurbishment (Figure 6.5). The complex stratigraphy led to the expectation that there would be a long duration for the settlement on the crannog (in line with the paradigm which assumes longevity for all settlements - see Halliday 2007, 50, and below). The radiocarbon dates obtained to provide an initial chronological framework did not refute these expectations, as they spanned 475 radiocarbon years.

In contrast, the dendrochronological analysis of nearly 400 oak and alder timbers indicated that most of the building activity occurred over a very short time-span, with building activity beginning in AD 583 and ceasing *circa* AD 668 (Figure 6.6; Crone 2000, 54-5). Within these eighty - ninety years of occupation, four palisades were built, each replacing the other, and at least two (and probably three) roundhouses were built, again, one replacing the other (ibid. 64-6). Within the houses, hearths and floors were frequently replaced, at least four times in one house within the space of fifteen years. The resolution afforded by the tree-ring chronology thus allows a view of the dynamics of the settlement at a very human scale. The almost constant struggle to keep the palisades in good repair can be envisaged, built as they were over an unstable substrate, and speculation as to why the occupants replaced their hearths and floors so frequently can be more profitably made. Insect, macroplant and structural evidence shows that, even during this compressed timescale, there were periods of a year or more when the crannog

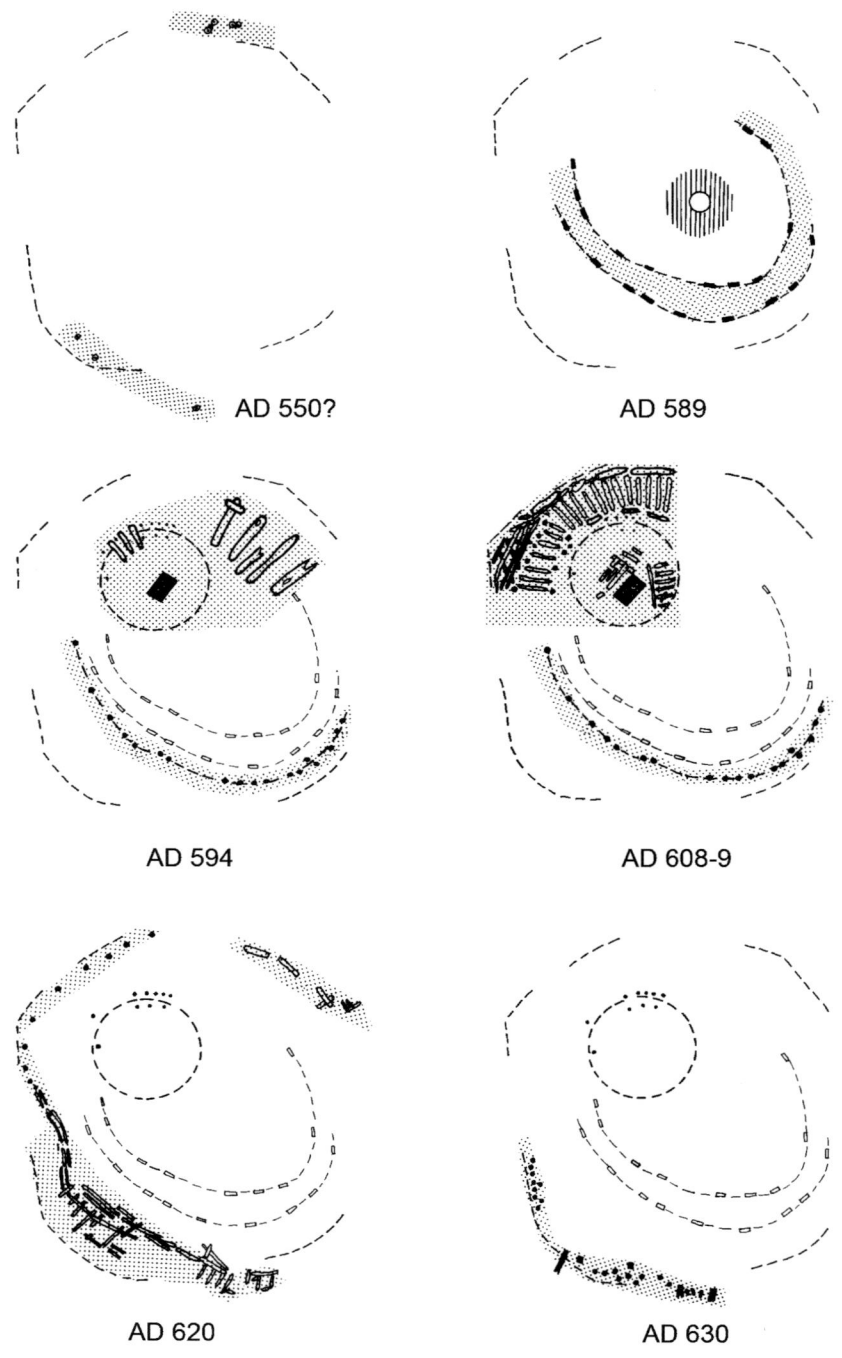

Figure 6.5 Summary plans showing dendro-dated phases of building activity on Buiston.

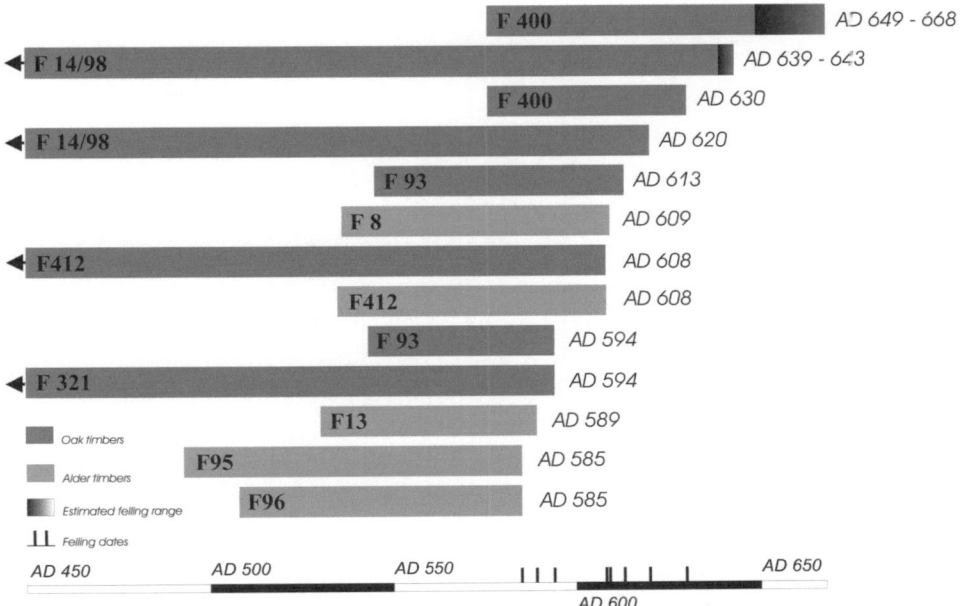

Figure 6.6 Summary bar diagram illustrating the chronological relationships between the oak and alder chronologies from the major contexts at Buiston.

must have been unoccupied (Crone 2000, 110). The insect evidence in particular indicates that occupation was discontinuous even in the short episodes identified from the dendrochronology (Kenward et al. 2000, 100-1). The replacement of hearths and floors may have been a form of 'spring-cleaning', part of the ritual of returning to the crannog after seasonal or longer absences.

Later prehistoric crannogs; Dorman's Island and Cults Loch

As crannogs were most popular during the first millennium BC, a period when chronological resolution is most elusive (see above), the ultimate goal has for some time been to excavate a crannog of that period and recover enough oak timber for dendro-dating. The SWAP programme in south-west Scotland has now afforded several opportunities, and although not as extensive a dating programme as that undertaken at Buiston, they are nonetheless, jointly yielding valuable insights.

At Dorman's Island, in Whitefield Loch (Figure 6.7a) limited excavation revealed occupation deposits consisting of deliberately laid clay surfaces, a floor of oak timbers and scatters of small stakes; no evidence for a superstructure was found but the small

Figure 6.7 a) Dorman's Island.

excavation trench probably lay within the structure (Cavers et al. 2011). Radiocarbon dates indicated building and occupation some time in the last four centuries BC, and activity much later in the early modern period when a small stake alignment was constructed. Artefactual evidence, in the form of re-used Roman glass, identified activity probably in the first/second centuries AD.

A small assemblage of ten oak timbers, mostly from the floor but including a few stakes, were analysed dendrochronologically, and seven were successfully dated against a suite of prehistoric and Roman chronologies from England and Ireland. Only one of the timbers retained any sapwood and this timber was probably felled sometime between 153 and 121 BC (Figure 6.7b). Although the absence of sapwood in any of the other timbers means that there cannot be precision regarding the chronological relationships between them, it is reasonable to assume that they were all felled at the same time as they form part of the same floor structure. The only exception is a stake which could represent a slightly later phase, though probably by a few decades at most. Thus, the late first millennium BC activity at Dorman's Island has been more closely defined as happening sometime during the last five decades of the second century BC.

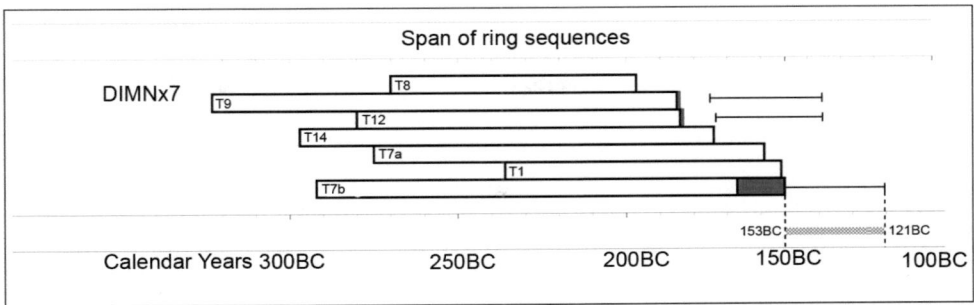

Figure 6.7 b) dendrochronological results from Dorman's Island.

On their own, the radiocarbon dates and the presence of Roman glass might have been seen as reflecting a continuous smear of activity on Dorman's Island from the latter half of the first millennium BC into the early centuries AD. However, the precision of the dendrochronological date makes it clear that the construction of the wooden floor and the deposition of the Roman glass were distinct events, separated by an interval of two to three centuries.

The other crannog which has now been successfully dendro-dated lies in Cults Loch, a few miles to the west of Dorman's Island. Although this crannog now survives as a promontory projecting out into the loch (Figure 6.8a) it was originally an island which was connected to the shore by a timber causeway (Cavers and Crone 2010). The halo of piling which surrounds the crannog was probably inserted to contain the crannog mound and did not form a defensive perimeter as such. On top of the mound were the remains of at least four structures, which were probably in use sequentially. The best-preserved of the structures consisted of a roughly circular 'platform' of gravel, interleaved with compacted organic deposits; these deposits probably represent frequently refurbished floor surfaces. The gravel/organic 'platform' was surrounded by a concentric framework of horizontal timbers, while in the centre of the platform was a roughly square timber feature, possibly a hearth base. Radiocarbon dates place all the activity on the crannog in the centuries between *circa* 750 BC and 200 BC.

As at Oakbank, the bulk of the structural timber was alder; of the 254 sampled timbers only 21% were oak, and of this small proportion only twenty two timbers had ring-patterns longer than seventy rings. Analysis is still in progress and the alder and shorter oak timbers have yet to be studied, so only the results from the longer oak timbers are reported here. Of this group, eight timbers have been successfully dated. The felling range for the timber with

Figure 6.8 a) Cults Loch promontory crannog,

the most sapwood indicates that it was probably felled sometime between 438 - 412 BC (Figure 6.8b).

Again, the absence of surviving bark edge on any of the dated timbers means that the precise chronological relationships between the timbers cannot be defined. Nonetheless, the close synchronicity between the heartwood/sapwood boundaries of these timbers suggests that, if there are numerous phases of building activity on the site, they are not separated by any great length of time - a few decades at most. There is therefore evidence at Cults for a phase of building activity in the second and third decades of the fifth century BC. There is also some later building activity on the crannog. A pile from the causeway connecting the crannog to the shore was felled in the spring of 193 BC. There thus appears to have been a revival of interest in the crannog in the early second century BC; the causeway may have been refurbished, or even constructed at this time.

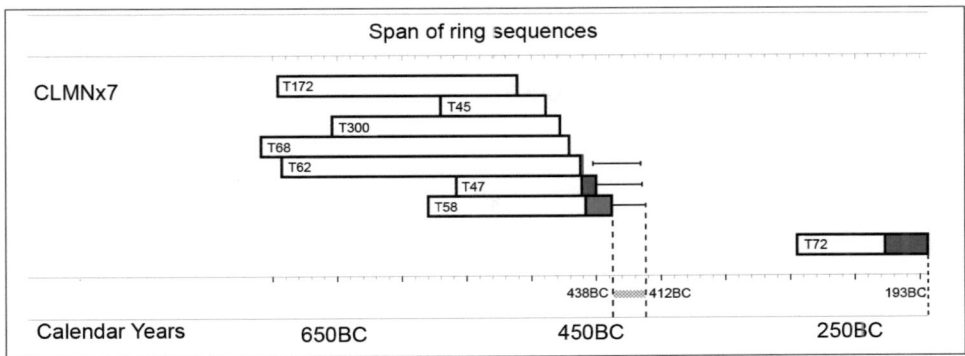

Figure 6.8 b) dendrochronological results from Cults Loch.

Discussion

At present Buiston remains 'special'; as the only precisely dated Early Historic crannog in Scotland, there is little else to compare it against and therefore its significance within the wider settlement patterns of this period remains largely speculative. Its chronological value lies mainly in its portrayal of a highly dynamic settlement, occupied episodically by three generations of a community which battled with the problems intrinsic to living out in the loch. In other words, it is the short duration of settlement which is highly significant at Buiston; not only does it make the human history of the site palpable, it also raises important issues relating to settlement mobility and social structure during the Early Historic period. The themes of duration of settlement and intermittent occupation will be returned to.

In the discussion that follows the first millennium BC crannogs form a focus as this is where the most significant patterns are beginning to appear. Two 'event horizons' appear to be emerging: one in the fifth century BC, identified by dendrochronology at Cults Loch, and by wiggle-matching at Oakbank; and one in the second century BC, when dendrochronology shows that Dorman's Island is occupied and Cults Loch is refurbished. With the increased sample size, the signal-to-noise ratio within the radiocarbon dataset has improved and two spikes of activity in the first millennium BC are also emerging (Figure 6.2), which appear to mirror those dendro-dated event horizons in the fifth and second centuries BC. This is crystallised at Loch Tay where, as noted earlier, the radiocarbon evidence suggests two discrete pulses of crannog activity during the first millennium BC; the crannogs there are active either in the middle of the millennium or late in the millennium, but never in both periods on the same site. It thus begins to look probable that, rather than continuous use of these site-types across the millennium, there may actually have been distinct pulses in crannog-building activity.

The chronological distribution of dendro-dated prehistoric sites in Ireland has long been known to be non-random. Baillie commented on the apparent clustering of dendro-dated prehistoric sites around 1500 BC, in the tenth century and second century BC (Baillie 1995, 67-8), and despite the increased number of sites investigated over the past two decades this non-random distribution is still visible. In fact, as more sites have been dated, more discrete clusters are emerging, in the seventh century and fifth century BC in particular (Baillie and Brown 2009, Fig 1). Similar phenomenon are now emerging in Scotland, with embryonic clusters developing at the same event horizons as in Irish prehistory, in the fifth and second centuries BC respectively.

Expressed at its most reductive, these clusters indicate that during the first millennium BC '…human activity that involved the placement of oak timbers in contexts wherein they could survive has not been uniform through time' (Baillie and Brown 2009, 17). In other words, these clusters indicate episodes when human activity changed, because during these episodes people were building with oak in lochs and bogs, i.e. in those very contexts where waterlogging ensured survival. During these periods in Ireland they built trackways and *fulacht fiadh* (burnt mounds) in and across bogs (Baillie and Brown 1996), settlements on the margins of lakes (O'Sullivan 1998, 91), and monumental earthworks across boggy areas (Baillie and Brown 1989). In Scotland they built crannogs in lochs.

Baillie and Brown (2009) have proposed that these apparent changes in human activity may have been stimulated by environmental change. In the case of the cluster of activity in the second century BC, this may have been influence by the after-effects of a volcanic dust-veil event in the last decade of the third century BC, which appears to have caused a major environmental downturn around the globe. Such long-range synchronicity of dendro-dated events on either side of the Irish Sea does indeed suggest an environmental stimulus, even if the cultural responses (as expressed in the various types of constructions) were different. This synchronicity also occurs later in the Early Historic period; construction began at Buiston in the latter half of the sixth century AD, at exactly the same time as there was an intensive spate of crannog building across northern Ireland (Baillie 1995, 59). This followed not long after a natural catastrophic event in 536 AD which affected the global climate for the following decades, as witnessed by contemporary records of crop failure, famine and plague (ibid. Chapter 6). What proxy records there are, hint that the weather in Scotland during the first millennium BC was colder, wetter and stormier than average (Dawson 2009, 89) so it must be wondered why people built out in the water at these times (see below).

The premise that there are discrete pulses of crannog-building activity in the first millennium BC is expressed cautiously here because it is based on three dendro-dated events and one wiggle-match dated event, with some support from the radiocarbon dataset. Nevertheless, it reflects a growing debate in Scotland about the longevity of occupation in individual structures and settlements (Barber and Crone 2001, Cowley 2003, Halliday 2007). Rather than the relatively static, long-term settlement patterns that have long been assumed for most periods in the history of the British Isles there is accumulating evidence of more short-lived episodic settlement, where the episodes of occupation are of varying duration, and are separated by intervals, themselves of varying duration. At the scale of the individual site, the assumption that crannogs were permanent, continuously inhabited residences has been challenged by the evidence from Buiston and the possibility of seasonal, episodic use must be included in the settlement models for these sites. On a landscape scale, settlements, whether they were isolated houses or villages, may not have been occupied for more than a few generations at most. Thus, crannog occupation need not be viewed as running synchronously with occupation on shore but must, to a degree, have interdigitated with it. There must have been terrestrial sites to which the crannog occupants moved in those abandonment periods, of years, decades or centuries, when they were not living out on the loch. The relationship between the occupation of crannogs and the broadly contemporary settlements in the surrounding landscape is at the core of the current research programme at Cults Loch (Cavers and Crone 2010).

Periodic, seasonal use must surely have a bearing on function. Running through the paragraph above is the assumption that all crannogs were domestic settlements but this is far from self-evident. The most extensively investigated examples - Buiston and Oakbank - display much of the evidence associated with domestic activities, but elsewhere this evidence is more ambiguous. Artefact assemblages comparable with terrestrial habitation sites have been found, along with the residues of food cultivation and preparation, but evidence for residential structures is sparse (see Cavers this volume). Some Early Historic crannogs in Ireland have been interpreted as craftworking loci (O'Sullivan 1998, 111, 122), as has Loch Glashan (see above). While some of the excavated later prehistoric crannogs of the Clyde and Beauly Firth do display evidence for occupation others may have been used as landing/launching points from which to control river traffic or exploit estuarine resources (Hale 2004, Sands and Hale 2005). Contemporary references to early modern loch settlements and placename evidence also highlight a range of other possible functions for crannogs including kennels, garrisons, refuges, traveller's lodges and feasting-houses (Morrison 1985, 64-8). If crannog-building is seen as an activity that happened at very particular points in time then this has ramifications for their role in contemporary society and how they were perceived and used.

Some researchers have posited a purely socio-cultural stimulus for crannog-building. Fredengren (2002, 242) has suggested that the actual process of building the crannog was what was important, binding a community together through communal effort, the resulting structure thereby expressing and strengthening communal identity. Cavers (2006, and this volume) offers a symbolic interpretation of later prehistoric crannogs; he sees them as representing the fusion of the ritual and domestic spheres of everyday life, living on the loch as a reflection of the Iron Age reverence for water. The accumulating evidence presented in this paper implies that an environmental stimulus must also be included in explanatory models for later prehistoric crannogs. Perhaps the impulse to build out on the water, either to make those spiritual connections with their protective deities, or to re-affirm and strengthen communal identity, or both, only occurred at times when the community felt unsettled by the changes in society being wrought by global environmental events.

What next?

The premise of episodic use now needs to be tested against a larger dataset. However, the overall structure of the radiocarbon dataset has not substantially changed despite an increase of data points by a factor of almost seven. This suggests that efforts would be better directed towards the chronological precision that can only be acquired through dendrochronology and wiggle-match dating, rather than the random sampling of uncontexted timbers which would only add more dots to distribution maps. To this end, a programme of work is currently under way in collaboration with SUERC (Scottish Universities Environmental Research Centre) which is testing radiocarbon wiggle-match dating on timbers dendro-dated to the earlier Iron Age from some of the south-west Scottish crannogs. The goal of the research is to determine the ideal sampling methodology needed to achieve sub-centurial precision in the region of the Halstatt plateau, which will not be an easy task given that much of the resource consists of material with short ring sequences (see above). In addition to the work being done on wiggle-matching in the earlier Iron Age, researchers at SUERC are also beginning to develop a programme of radiocarbon dating that seeks to develop robust Bayesian chronologies for Scottish crannogs (Derek Hamilton, personal communication).

Acknowledgements

I would like to thank my colleagues in the Scottish Wetland Archaeology Programme whose efforts over the past decade have made much of the work reported on here possible. I am especially grateful to John Barber and Graeme Cavers for reading and commenting on this paper.

References

Baillie, M.G.L. 1995, *A slice through time*. London: Batsford.

Baillie, M.G.L. and Brown, D.M. 1989, Further dates from the Dorsey. *Emania* 6: 11.

Baillie, M.G.L. and Brown, D.M. 1996, Dendrochronology of Irish bog trackways. In: B. Raftery *Trackway excavations in the Mountdillon Bogs, Co. Longford 1985-1991*. Dublin: IAWU Transactions 3, 395 – 402.

Baillie, M. and Brown, D .2009, A chronological glimpse into the later first millennium BC. In: G. Cooney, K. Becker, J. Coles, M. Ryan and S. Sievers (eds.) *Relics of Old Decency. Archaeological Studies in Later Prehistory*. Dublin: Wordwell, 17-24.

Barber, J.W. and Crone, A . 1993, Crannogs; a diminishing resource? A survey of the crannogs of South West Scotland and excavations at Buiston Crannog. *Antiquity* 67: 520-533.

Barber, J.W. and Crone, A . 2001, The duration of structures, settlements and sites: some evidence from Scotland. In: B. Raftery, B and J. Hickey (eds.) *Recent Developments in Wetland Research*. Seandálaíocht: Mon 2, Dept Archaeol, UCD and WARP Occasional Paper 14. Dublin: Department of Archaeology, University College Dublin, 69-86.

Billamboz, A. 2003, Tree-rings and wetland occupation in southwest Germany between 2000 and 500 BC: dendroarchaeology beyond dating in tribute to F H Schweingruber. *Tree-ring research* 59 (1): 37-49.

Cavers, M.G. 2006, Late Bronze and Iron Age Lake Settlement in Scotland and Ireland: the origins and development of the 'crannog' in the north and west. *Oxford Journal of Archaeology* 25(4): 389-412.

Cavers, M.G. 2010, *Crannogs and Later Prehistoric settlement in Western Scotland*. BAR Brit Ser 510, Oxford: Archaeopress.

Cavers, G. and Crone, A. 2010, Galloway crannogs: an interim report on work at Cults Loch and Dorman's Island by the Scottish Wetland Archaeology Programme. *Transactions of Dumfriesshire and Galloway Natural History and Antiquarian Society* 84: 11-18.

Cavers, G., Crone, A., Engl, R., Fouracre, L., Hunter, F., Robertson, J. and Thoms, J. 2011, Refining Chronological Resolution in Iron Age Scotland: excavations at Dorman's Island Crannog, Dumfries and Galloway. *Journal of Wetland Archaeology* 10: 71-108.

Cook, G.T., Dixon, T.N., Russell, N., Naysmith, P., Xu, S. and Andrian, B. 2010, High-precision radiocarbon dating of the construction phase of Oakbank crannog, Loch Tay, Perthshire. *Radiocarbon* 52(2–3): 346–355.

Cowley, D. 2003, Changing places – building life-spans and settlement continuity in northern Scotland. In: J. Downes, and A. Ritchie (eds.) *Sea change: Orkney and northern Europe in the later Iron Age AD 300-800*. Balgavies: The Pinkfoot Press, 75-81.

Crone, A. 1988, *Dendrochronology and the study of crannogs*. Univesity of Sheffield; unpublished PhD thesis.

Crone, A. 1993, Crannogs and chronologies. *Proceedings of the Society of Antiquaries of Scotland* 123: 245-54.

Crone, A. 1998, The development of an Early Historic tree-ring chronology for Scotland. *Proceedings of the Society of Antiquaries of Scotland* 128: 485-93.

Crone, A. 2000, *The history of a Scottish lowland crannog: excavations at Buiston, Ayrshire 1989-90*. Edinburgh: STAR Monograph Series 4.

Crone, A. 2011, Late beginnings; an early modern crannog at Eadarloch, Loch Treig, Lochaber. *History Scotland* 11(1): 33-7.

Crone, A. and Campbell, E. 2005 *A crannog of the 1st millennium AD; excavations by Jack Scott at Loch Glashan, Argyll, 1960*. Edinburgh: Society of Antiquaries of Scotland.

Crone, A. and Clarke, C. 2005, A programme for wetland archaeology in Scotland in the twenty-first century. *Proceedings of the Society of Antiquaries of Scotland* 135: 5-17.

Crone, A. and Mills, C.M. 2002, Seeing the wood and the trees; dendrochronological studies in Scotland. *Antiquity* 76: 788-94.

Crone, A. *forthcoming*, A logboat in Loch Glashan. *Discovery and Excavation in Scotland* 12.

Dawson, A. 2009, *So foul and fair a day: a history of Scotland's weather and climate*. Edinburgh: Birlinn.

Dixon, T.N. 2004, *Scottish crannogs: an underwater archaeology*. Stroud: Tempus Publishing Ltd.

Dixon, N. 2007, Crannog structure and dating in Perthshire with particular reference to Loch Tay. In: J. Barber, C. Clarke, M. Cressey, A. Crone, A. Hale, J. C. Henderson, R. Housley, R. Sands and A. Sheridan (eds.) *Archaeology from the wetlands: Recent perspectives*. Edinburgh: Society of Antiquaries of Scotland Monograph Series, 253-65.

Driscoll, S.T. 1998, Picts and prehistory: cultural resource management in early medieval Scotland. *World Archaeology* 30(1): 142 – 58.

Fredengren, C. 2002, *Crannogs. A study of people's interaction with lakes, with particular reference to Lough Gara in the north-west of Ireland*. Dublin: Wordwell.

Guido, M. 1974, A Scottish crannog re-dated. *Antiquity* 48: 54-56.

Hale, A. 2004, *Scottish marine crannogs*. BAR Brit Ser 369, Oxford: Archaeopress.

Halliday, S.P. 2007, Unenclosed round-houses in Scotland: occupation, abandonment and character of settlement. In: C. Burgess, P. Topping and F. Lynch (eds.) *Beyond Stonehenge. Essays on the Bronze Age in honour of Colin Burgess*. Oxford: Oxbow Books, 49 – 56.

Harding, D. 2004, *The Iron Age in Northern Britain. Celts and Romans, natives and invaders*. London: Routledge.

Henderson, J.C, Crone, A. and Cavers, M.G. 2003, A condition survey of selected crannogs in south-west Scotland. *Transactions of Dumfriesshire and Galloway Natural History and Antiquarian Society* 77: 79-102.

Henderson, J.C., Cavers, M.G. and Crone, A. 2006, The south-west crannog survey: recent work on the lake dwellings of Dumfries and Galloway. *Transactions of Dumfriesshire and Galloway Natural History and Antiquarian Society* 80: 29-51.

Henderson, J.C. *forthcoming*, Underwater excavation at Ederline Boathouse Crannog, Loch Awe, Argyll, Scotland. *International Journal of Nautical Archaeology*.

Henderson, J 2007 Recognising complexity and realizing the potential of Scottish crannogs. In: J. Barber, C. Clarke, M. Cressey, A. Crone, A. Hale, J. C. Henderson, R. Housley, R. Sands and A. Sheridan (eds.) *Archaeology from the wetlands: Recent perspectives*. Edinburgh: Society of Antiquaries of Scotland Monograph Series, 231-4.

Hingley, R. 1996, Ancestors and identity in the later prehistory of Atlantic Scotland: the reuse and reinvention of Neolithic monuments and material culture. *World Archaeology* 28(2): 231-43.

Holley, M.W. and Ralston, I.B.M. 1995, Radiocarbon dates for two crannogs on the Isle of Mull, Strathclyde Region, Scotland. *Antiquity* 69: 595-6.

Hunter, F. 2007, *Beyond the Edge of Empire – Caledonians, Picts and Romans*. Rosemarkie: Groam House.

Kenward, H. Hill, M., Jaques, D., Kroupa, A and Large, F. 2000, The Coleoptera. In: A. Crone 2000, *The history of a Scottish lowland crannog: excavations at Buiston, Ayrshire 1989-90*. Edinburgh: STAR Monograph Series 4, 99-101.

Lillie, M.C., Smith, R., Reed, J. and Inglis, R. 2008, South-West Scottish Crannogs: using *in situ* studies to assess preservation in wetland contexts. *Journal of Archaeological Science* 35: 1886-1900.

MacSween, A. 2000, Integrating the artefact assemblages from the 19th and 20th century excavations. In: A. Crone 2000, *The history of a Scottish lowland crannog: excavations at Buiston, Ayrshire 1989-90*. Edinburgh: STAR Monograph Series 4, 143 – 151.

Morrison, I. 1985, *Landscape with lake dwellings*. Edinburgh: Edinburgh University Press.

Munro, R. 1882, Ancient Scottish lake dwellings. Edinburgh: David Douglas.

Oakley, G.E.M. 1973, *Scottish crannogs*. University of Newcastle; unpublished M Phil thesis.

O'Sullivan, A. 1998, *The archaeology of lake settlement in Ireland*. Dublin: Discovery Programme Monograph 4.

Redknap, M. and Lane, A. 1994, The early medieval crannog at Llangorse, Powys: an interim statement on the 1989-1993 seasons. *International Journal of Nautical Archaeology* 23(3): 190-205.

Sands, R. and Hale, A. 2005, Evidence from marine crannogs of later prehistoric use of the Firth of Clyde. *Journal of Wetland Archaeology* 1: 41-54.

Shelley, M. 2009, *Freshwater Scottish loch settlements of the Late Medieval and Early Modern periods*. University of Edinburgh: unpublished PhD thesis.

Chapter 7

CRANNOGS AS BUILDINGS: THE EVOLUTION OF INTERPRETATION 1882 - 2011

Graeme Cavers[1]

Abstract

Crannogs are highly visible man-made statements in the Scottish later prehistoric landscape. The paper discusses the current understanding of crannogs, from their stereotypical model, through varied morphology of construction, to the island round house structures and farmsteads. It also considers the more promising avenues of research which are arising from recent work on Scottish lake dwellings, for example consideration of the domestic sphere of life and its relationship to the veneration of water, or modelling of social obligations through labour pooling, which can bring us closer to understanding the societies that built and used these sites.

Key words: Munro, crannogs, construction, occupation deposits, roundhouses

> 'However much variety or novelty may add to the interest attached to antiquarian discoveries, it must never be forgotten that their scientific value is to be determined by the extent to which they can be made to enrich our knowledge of the past phases of civilisation.'
>
> Robert Munro, *Ancient Scottish Lake Dwellings* (1882,240)

---

1 AOC Archaeology Group, Edgefield Industrial Estate, Loanhead, Midlothian, EH20 9SY, UK

Introduction

Crannogs have clear potential to flesh out prehistory- providing us with information on the form and use of materials that very rarely survive in other contexts. Since Munro's day, crannogs have been valued for this reason, the unparalleled clarity of the glimpse they give us of prehistoric domestic life being an obvious reason to hold them in this esteem. However, the clarity of this glimpse has never been matched by clarity in precisely what these structures looked like, and as a result, the impact of their contribution to Scottish archaeology has been reduced. The National Museums of Scotland's iconic portrayal of the material culture of prehistoric Scotland is greatly enhanced by a wide range of artefacts from crannogs from all periods, and while there are at least 400 known examples the sites themselves remain obscure and even in academic perception very few can be considered key sites of prehistoric or early historic Scotland.

At its most fundamental level of definition, a 'crannog' is merely an artificially created space: the fact that this may be a very well preserved space, made of materials that rarely survive elsewhere is inconsequential if we cannot understand what those remains tell us about what happened there. Waterlogged wood may be spectacular, but in and of itself, it tells us nothing, and it is an uncomfortable reality that very few crannogs have produced any substantial evidence of prehistoric buildings: even the best preserved and most thoroughly investigated examples have been surprisingly scanty in the details of their superstructures.

As always, the value of our conclusions is only a measure of the validity of the interpretive framework from which they were constructed, and almost 130 years after the publication of *Ancient Scottish Lake Dwellings,* it is pertinent at this juncture to review the historical context of our own view of crannogs. In this paper I aim to reappraise these frameworks and discuss our current understanding of crannogs as buildings, before turning to consider the most promising avenues of research which are currently arising from the most recent work on Scottish lake dwellings.

Crannogs in Scotland have now been clearly demonstrated to be predominantly later prehistoric in date (Henderson 1998, Crone *this volume)*, and it is with how crannog structures relate to the Iron Age (and principally pre-Roman Iron Age) settlement record more generally that I am principally concerned here. As I aim to explore, there is considerable variety in the format of crannog settlement, even within this Iron Age horizon; arguably the crannog stereotype has masked the importance of this variability and its relevance to the wider settlement spectrum of the later first millennium BC.

Robert Munro was aware of the need for serious archaeological research to extract more from lake dwelling studies than marvelling at their preservation (see introductory quote), and suggested some of the ways that this may be achieved. He was analytical of the evidence for crannog superstructures, and offered his own interpretations of how these lake dwellings might inform our view of prehistoric settlements more generally (Munro 1894a, 1894b). It is through proper contextualisation that crannog evidence can be brought to bear on our understanding of prehistoric society and contribute beyond merely providing that glimpse of the flesh on the bones that wetland archaeology is thought to provide; the following discussion considers how much closer we are to that contextualised appreciation of lake settlements than at the time of Munro's celebrated investigations.

The development of the Scottish crannog stereotype

Robert Munro's work was undeniably pioneering: he is to be admired for his skill in observation and his ability to document these observations, but also for his recognition of the limits of his own knowledge, of the demonstrable evidence, and therefore of the limits of reasonable speculation. He inspected a large number of crannogs personally, and systematically collated evidence from the investigation of many others that he did not personally supervise. His work at Lochlee and Buiston were his major excavations, and very formative in his description of the crannog construction model. This, and the publication of the plan of Buiston in 1882 were very influential in the formation of a Scottish crannog stereotype (Figure 7.1).

For his own part, Munro was always tentative in his conclusions: his interpretation of the Buiston 'dwelling house' was cautious and he considered the options of both a single large "pagoda-style" building (Munro 1882, 205), or a series of smaller individual huts, though he did prefer the former. He was clearly puzzled in the case of Lochlee by the non-correspondence of the base of the mound (which was circular) to the superstructure (a 'log pavement' which appeared to be rectangular). Perhaps contrary to common modern perception and commendably for the time, Munro was clearly aware of the likelihood of multiple phases of occupation and refurbishment of crannogs and how this might confuse the excavated plan, but using his plan and descriptions of Lochlee it does seem reasonable to postulate a superstructure quite different to the stereotypical crannog roundhouse at that site, even accepting

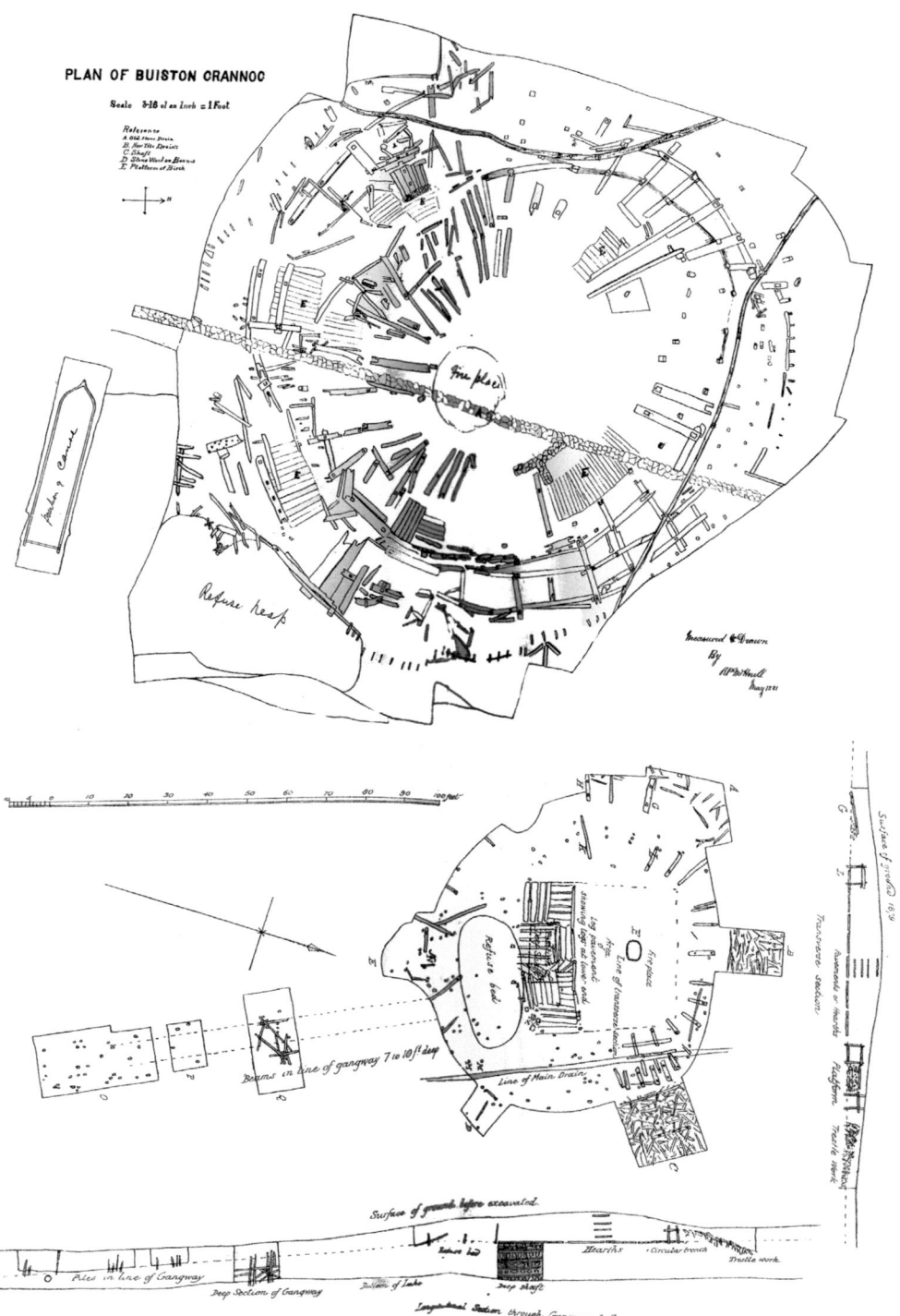

Figure 7.1 Plans of Buiston and Lochlee (Munro 1882).

that rectangular flooring arrangements can be found within both circular and rectangular structures.

Munro was certainly aware, then, of the variability in Scottish crannog morphology, and he considered the significance of the variable presence of the perimeter stockade, its occasional alternative in stone, and sites which seemed to combine both packwerk and piling modes (Munro 1882, 242-3), such as at Loch Dhu (Mackinlay 1862) and the Lochend crannog in Coatbridge (Monteith and Robb 1937). Despite Munro's recognition of the heterogeneous nature of lake settlements in Scotland, however, the perception of crannogs as large timber roundhouses, established by the evocative plan of Buiston, was to prove influential in the development of the crannog stereotype.

Mrs Piggott's excavations at Milton Loch 1 heralded something of a step change in the perception of crannogs as buildings (Figure 7.2). Although the variability in crannog structures was recognised by the efforts of the antiquarian investigators, Piggott's excavations served to embed the notion that most Scottish crannogs belonged to the Iron Age, and contemporary advances in the study of the Iron Age roundhouse [e.g. following Bersu's (1940) excavations at Little Woodbury and the development of models for the Iron Age of Wessex, but also by Piggott herself and her contemporaries working on defended settlements in SE Scotland, e.g. Piggott 1948] gave Piggott confidence in her conviction that her excavations at Milton Loch gave a clearer picture of the nature of crannog structures than had been offered before. She was frustrated at the lack of reliable parallels in the established literature for Milton Loch, stating that much of the published literature on crannogs was 'almost worthless' (1953, 150), a position that implied that Milton Loch had clarified the true character of crannog superstructures, and that other sites were either less well preserved or too poorly excavated to denote similar structures.

There seems little reason to doubt the validity of the Milton Loch crannog roundhouse (although there may be indications of multiple phases of activity that were not necessarily acknowledged in Piggott's report (see Cavers 2010)), and the single, large islet roundhouse is a model that seems to apply to two other sites investigated in the nineteenth century, at Lochan Dughaill, Argyll (Munro 1893) and Dumbuck on the Clyde (Bruce 1900). However, the simple equation of crannog to island roundhouse is not one that can be made reliably. Hyndford (Munro 1899) may illustrate how the term 'crannog' should be considered to denote a wide range of site types: rather than being a true island dwelling, Hyndford may have been an artificially enclosed roundhouse - the ditch - or artificial pond

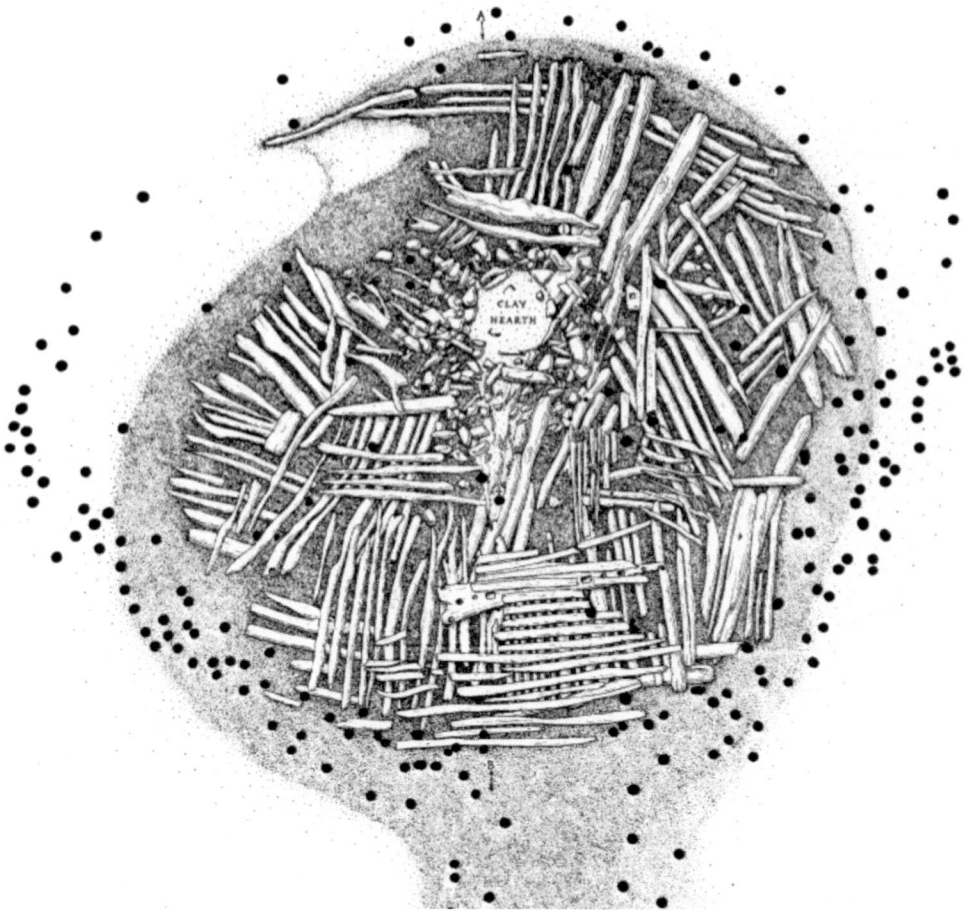

Figure 7.2 Plan of Milton Loch (Piggott 1953).

as Munro referred to it - being difficult to explain if the site were an archetypal crannog built in open water. Harding (2007) has also drawn attention to the possibility that many 'crannog islands' may rather have been promontories, the aerial evidence suggesting strongly that at least some were separated from dry land only by artificially dug channels. As has been noted before, crannogs - like 'duns' - suffer from such a vague definition that simplistic stereotypes are perversely taken, uncritically, as universally applicable (Harding 2000).

It is this author's opinion that there is little value in debating the validity of labels and terminology in the case of 'crannogs', since there is so little data with which to construct a reliable framework. The variability in the recorded evidence is such that attempts at classification based on form ('high cairn' and 'low cairn' (Fredengren

2002), constructional materials or geographical location (Henderson 1998) do not stand up to test. Terminology cannot help at this stage in crannog studies and is likely to be misleading; it is nonetheless important, once again, to highlight that there is the danger that sites are termed 'crannogs', and pigeon-holed as a consequence of the survival of organic materials alone.

The Milton Loch model of the Iron Age crannog as a large roundhouse was to persist as the dominant paradigm from the 1950s onward, and was reinforced by concurrent advances in the study of the terrestrial Iron Age settlement record, and this is how they are described in textbooks of northern British prehistory. Feachem's (1966) guide to prehistoric Scotland was particularly specific about what constituted a crannog, and the stereotype of the island roundhouse described there was to become very persistent; by the time of the publication of that volume the great degree of variability in crannog forms had effectively been masked by the image of the single island roundhouse (Figure 7.3).

This view of the crannog roundhouse has perhaps been further cemented by the model proposed for Oakbank by Dixon (Dixon 2004). Although structural evidence is plentiful from the site, there is very little in the way of demonstrably *in situ* structural remains, aside from the mass of vertical piling which, for the most part, does not respect the general impression of circularity given by the mound of stones under which it lies. The free-standing structure reconstructed at Croft-na-Caber on Loch Tay deals with many taphonomic problems posed by the excavated evidence, not least the problem of seasonally fluctuating water levels, but the arrangement and details of the superstructure are necessarily speculative, and it is certain that this can only have reflected one, very early, phase in the site's history (see discussion by Cavers 2010, 64-7).

Figure 7.3 Armit, Piggott and Feachem reconstructions (Armit 1997, Piggott 1953, Feachem 1966).

In support of the island roundhouse model are the large number of stone-built island settlements - often referred to as island duns - which were simply island variants of terrestrial roundhouses. It is far harder to establish a good basis for excluding these sites from the spectrum of artificial island forms than to include them within the same suite of sites. Sites such as Loch Leathan in Argyll and Rough Loch in Wigtownshire (Cavers 2010), as well as many in the Inner Hebrides which blur the distinction between crannog and 'island dun' (Holley 2000) show that large stone built roundhouses on artificial islands were widespread in Iron Age Scotland. The critical issue that these sites demonstrate is that island houses were a key component of the settlement landscape in later prehistoric Scotland, and hint that mainland timber crannogs should be considered alongside the dry land, terrestrial record.

Roundhouse structures

Milton Loch aside, two key sites best represent the evidence for substantial island roundhouses: the sites investigated by Munro at Lochan Dughaill (Munro 1893) and by Donelly at Dumbuck (Bruce 1900, Hale and Sands 2005). All of these sites confirm that buildings similar in form to terrestrial roundhouses were built on crannogs, but the details of the superstructures are very vague. Only a few proxy indicators, structural and palaeoenvironmental, hint at the character of the buildings that stood on these sites.

Dumbuck crannog on the Clyde was a remarkable structure (Figure 7.4), investigated by artist and archaeologist William Donnelly in the late 1800s. The structural details were recorded by Donnelly in a series of watercolours (collated and discussed by Hale and Sands 2005), and appear to denote a building reminiscent of a terrestrial ring-ditched house: the central platform of the structure was floored with roundwoods, locked in position by piling and mortised and forked timbers (Hale and Sands 2005, 20-6) and measuring around 20m in diameter. The central platform was surrounded by a ring of refuse material, although it is not clear from the excavation records whether this was contained in a ditch, or piled on the ground surface surrounding the platform. The site was accessed via a stone causeway, with a second leading to a dock where a large dugout canoe was recovered - it is possible that the two causeways suggest the superstructure had two entrances, a feature not uncommon in roundhouses in SW Scotland - with the platform surrounded by the midden or 'refuse bed' (Donnelly 1898). The platform was solidly built, retained by more substantial posts around the perimeter; the peculiar large oaks unevenly distributed in the floor do not seem to have been weight-bearing themselves, although it is conceivable that

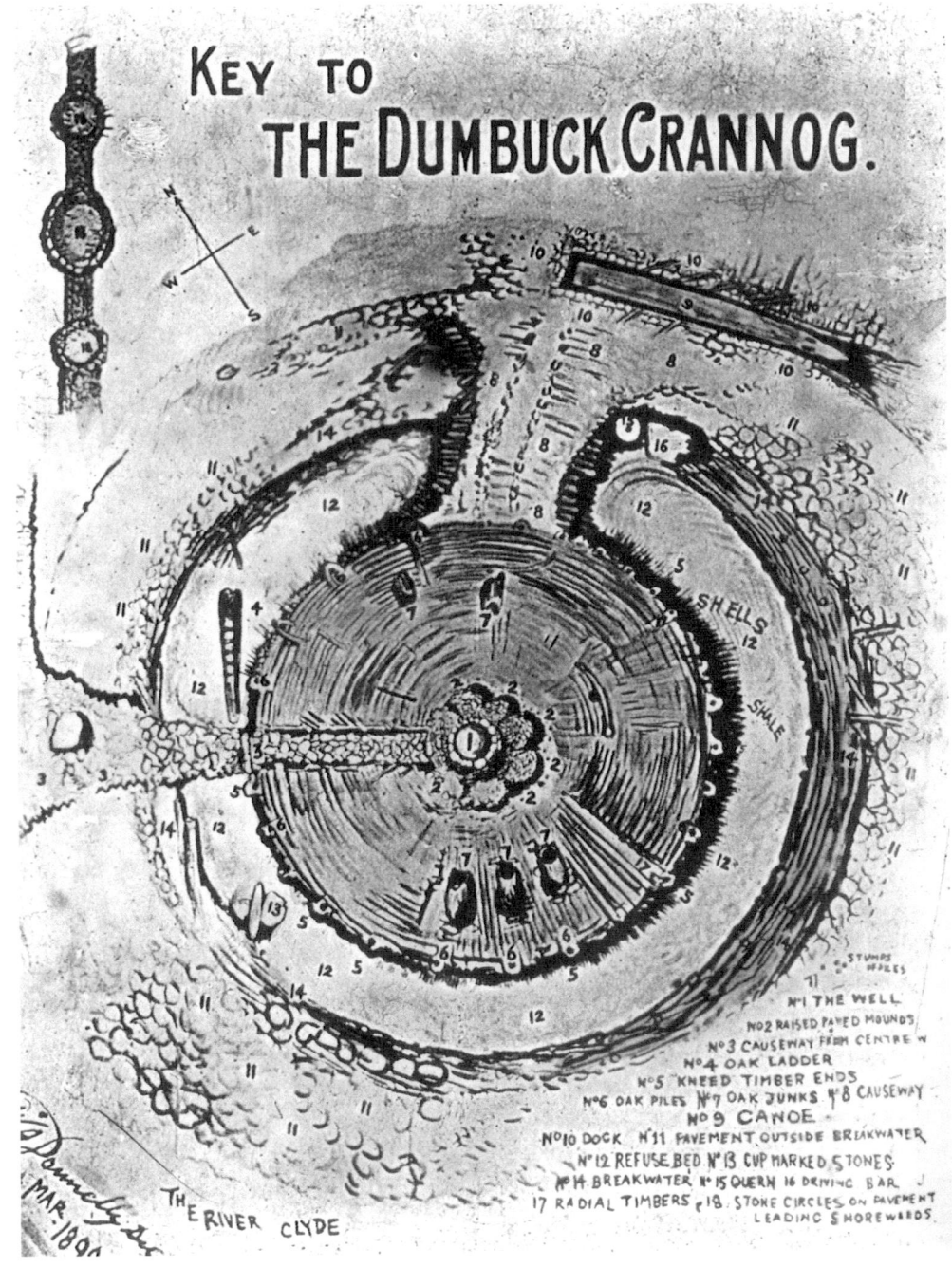

Figure 7.4 Dumbuck crannog, depicted by Donnelly (Hale and Sands 2005).

they functioned as bearers for free-standing posts that supported the bulk of the superstructure. The function of the central pit (or 'well') is not clear, but seems designed for some specific process, perhaps as mundane as heating water but equally possibly for some industrial process, such as tanning. Hale's investigation of similar stone-filled, wattle-lined pits on Redcastle in the Beauly Firth was inconclusive and many explanations are possible, although his consideration of the possibility that they may have been structural, designed to consolidate or bear weight on wet ground is not the least plausible (Hale 2004, 150-1), and this seems a possibility for the small stone 'pavements' surrounding the pit.

Nothing of the upper levels of the Dumbuck crannog survived, and nineteenth century techniques could not have been expected to collect proxy indicators of structural materials. The clue to the nature of the Dumbuck structure may be in the discovery of the large oak ladder, near the western causeway into the platform. A ladder within a building implies the presence of a first floor, suggesting that the Dumbuck roundhouse was indeed a substantial structure. A building with a first floor requiring a ladder some 4m in length must have occupied most or all of the circular platform, lending weight to the interpretation of the site as a single, large roundhouse. Hale's examination of the structural features of the sites and comparison to terrestrial roundhouses demonstrated that Dumbuck falls comfortably within the diametrical range of contemporary roundhouses (Hale 2004, 166) and his analysis of the finds, combined with the typical Iron Age evidence for mixed arable and pastoral economic basis (Hale et al. forthcoming) does not conflict with a domestic function for the site. The balance of probability then is in favour of the interpretation of Dumbuck as a single substantial roundhouse, probably built in the first century BC/AD.

Lochan Dughaill

Munro's excavations at the crannog in Lochan Dughaill, Kintyre, provide another seemingly unequivocal example of a single island roundhouse (Ralston 2003). At this site, radially arranged timbers formed a floor c. 12m in diameter (Figure 7.5), into which were built several 'sleeper beams': heavy timbers with recessed depressions near their ends, only in one case fully perforating the beam (Munro 1893, 216). There can be little doubt that the purpose of these beams was to act as sockets for substantial uprights that presumably formed a circular building occupying most of the crannog surface. The presence of the substantial central post at Lochan Dughaill is intriguing; this is not an essential structural component of

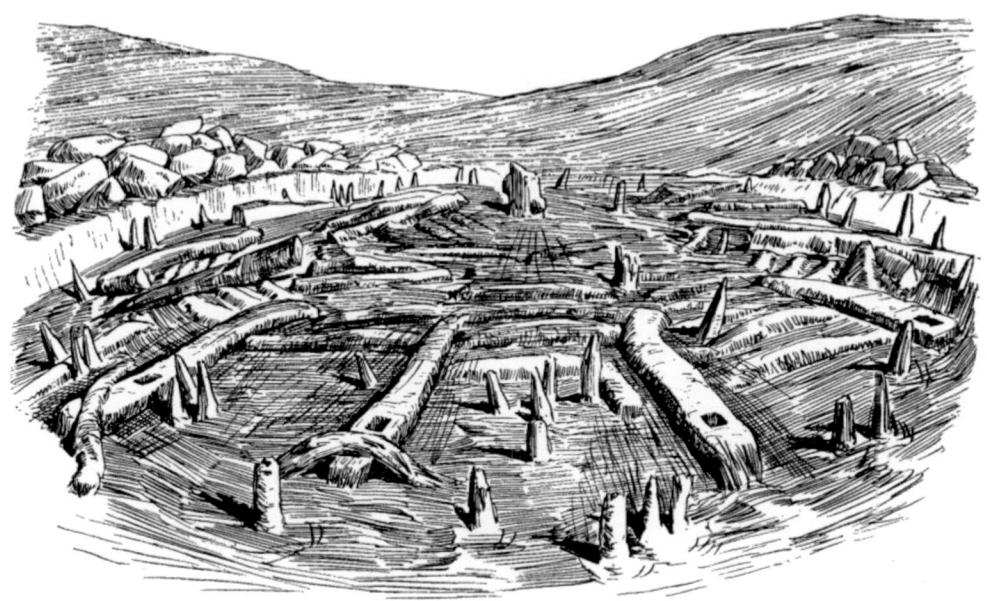

Figure 7.5 Lochan Dughaill (Munro 1893).

roundhouses and in most terrestrial examples is not present (see Harding 2009), and would have had the implication that the hearth could not have been located centrally within the building. Indeed, Munro suggests that the structure was divided into compartments, and that the hearth may have been located in the same compartment as the entrance (*ib id*). Although the site was already disturbed by the time of Munro's investigation, the impression given by the results of his work is of a complex and substantial building. The artefacts recovered from the work suggest the structure was probably in use in the earlier Iron Age.

Crannog roundhouses and domesticity: caveats

In combination with Milton Loch, the above examples are among the clearest examples of timber roundhouses found on stone and timber crannogs in Scotland. However, this interpretation is not beyond refute, and other reconstructions have been suggested. In particular, the possible lack of correspondence between what constitutes the substructure of a crannog and the building on top (*viz* Lochlee and Buiston) has led to suggestions that the ground plans of both Dumbuck and Lochan Dughaill are misleading. Hale's analysis of Dumbuck and other intertidal sites led him to suggest that they may have performed a specific function, and that they may not have been primarily domestic (Hale 2004, Sands and Hale

2001). While these possibilities remain valid, the presence of quern stones, palaeoenvironmental evidence for cereal processing and evidence for keeping animals on site on intertidal crannogs accords closely with our current understanding of domesticity in Iron Age Scotland. In general, where hearths are encountered the implication is of settlement, and accepting the possibility that some sites were seasonally or temporarily occupied, the greater weight of evidence is in favour of most Iron Age crannogs as domestic structures. Plainly, it would be unwise to assume that all crannogs were houses, or indeed that all were built for similar purposes (the variability demonstrated by survey alone makes this clear). However, while future research may refine this interpretation, currently, to question the domesticity of crannogs would be to question the interpretation of the vast majority of excavated 'roundhouses'.

Alternatives: crannogs as farmsteads

However, the likelihood is that although some crannogs were indeed island roundhouses, the range of structures on artificial islands was much greater than this. Crone's (2000) re-excavation of Buiston demonstrated that rather than the large roundhouse suggested by Munro, the buildings comprised a sequence of smaller, much slighter roundhouses enclosed within the perimeter breastwork.

Figure 7.6 One of the structures at Cults Loch crannog (AOC Archaeology Group).

Crone's work at that site highlighted the likelihood that crannog superstructures need not all conform to the single large island roundhouse stereotype that had developed through the twentieth century as a result of Munro's reconstruction and Piggott's work at Milton Loch. Although we should expect the format of crannog architecture to have evolved as significantly as terrestrial domestic architecture did through the late Iron Age and Early Historic periods, this may also be a more accurate reconstruction of some Iron Age sites. One of the crannogs investigated by Munro and surveyed as part of the South West Crannog Survey in 2002, at Barhapple in Wigtownshire, was very probably an island basis for a series of small roundhouses, in this case probably dating from the early Iron Age.

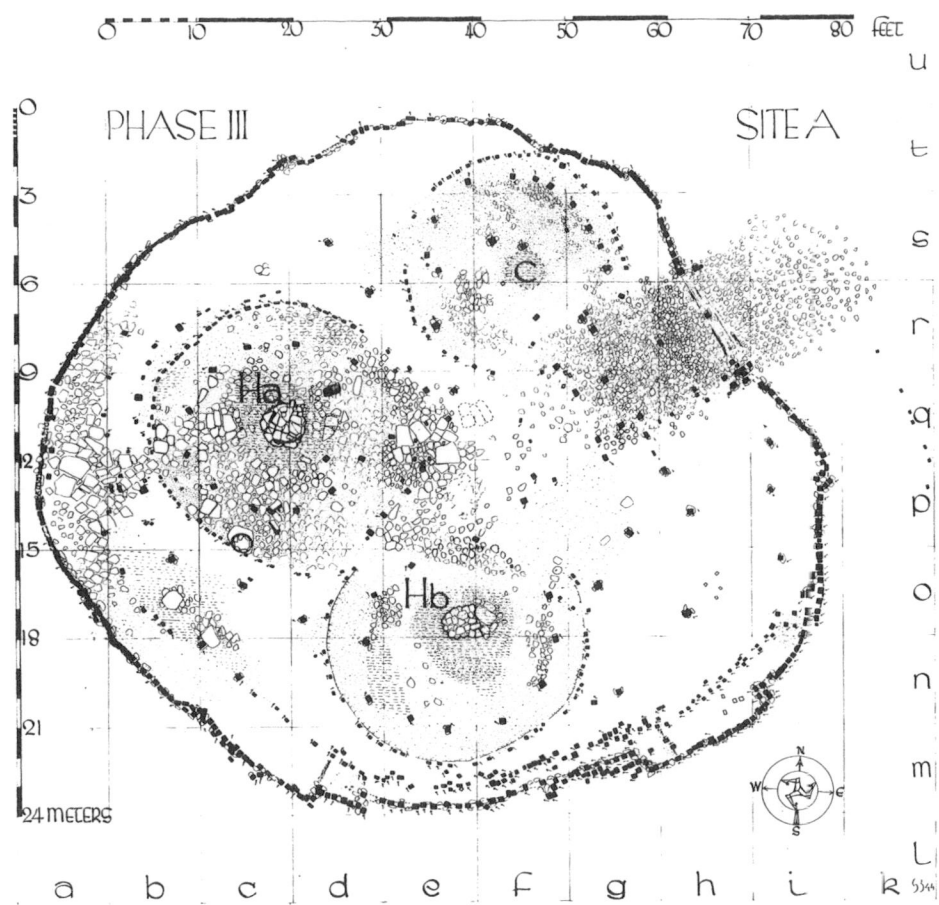

Figure 7.7 Ballycagen, Isle of Man (Bersu 1977).

Munro describes at least two circular huts on the surface of the site, enclosed by a perimeter stockade- an impression that is supported by modern survey (Henderson et al. 2003).

Similarly, recent excavations at Cults Loch are suggesting that the artificial promontory site - which dates to the early Iron Age - consisted of a series of structures, probably successive and situated on an artificially created platform, close to the shore of the loch. On this site, the floors of at least three structures have been identified (Figure 7.6), the circular arrangement of timbers in the southernmost of these possibly indicating that they were roundhouses in the region of 6 to 8m in diameter. In contrast to the single large roundhouse encountered at Milton Loch, it seems likely that the Cults site would have more closely resembled an enclosed farmstead similar to that excavated by Bersu at Ballycagen on the Isle of Man (Figure 7.7, Bersu 1977), or the late Bronze Age settlement at Clonfinlough, Co. Offaly (Moloney et al. 1993). The floors of the Cults Loch buildings were very well preserved, and the compressed organic flooring materials were in excellent condition, meaning it was possible to recover a range of deliberately-deposited artefacts from between the sub-flooring roundwoods, including an unused ard stilt very similar to that recovered from an identical context at Milton Loch (Piggott 1953), strongly suggesting that these buildings were blessed with foundation deposits and invested with ritual significance. We will return to discussion of the significance of this issue.

Methodological Implications

It is clear, then that there is greater variability in the morphology of Iron Age artificial islets than the substantial island roundhouse model might tempt us to believe. As always, the taphonomy of the sites we are looking at is critical to their interpretation. There is little doubt that the Munro *packwerk* model is correct for sites like Buiston, but in very many other sites the likelihood is that the 'crannog mound' is in fact an accumulation of very many phases of occupation and abandonment (see discussion by Crone et al. 2001 and Cavers 2007). In a recent example, from a small excavation on Dorman's Island in Wigtownshire, a 4 metre by 6 metre trench produced material of Iron Age and Roman and post-medieval date, with the classic problem of waterlogged preservation meaning that the original construction was indistinguishable from post-medieval stakes prior to radiocarbon dating (Cavers et al. 2011).

The truth is that despite the aspirations of wetland archaeologists to maximise the value of crannogs beyond analysis of their deposits, these grander narratives can only be constructed on the basis of a sound understanding of the physical form and development of the sites themselves. At this point it is valuable to consider some of the technical reasons why understanding crannog buildings can be challenging. Much of the difficulty involved in identifying crannog superstructures derives from the virtual impossibility of distinguishing sub-structural retention piling used to hold the crannog mound together from posts constituting the walls and structural posts of the buildings. Recent excavations at Cults Loch have clearly demonstrated this problem, where almost everywhere excavated was populated with vertical posts, but in some cases these were small roundwood stakes, in others massive posts, and the distinction was not always easy to make. Further complexity arose from the fact that what appeared in many instances to be horizontal flooring or make-up material was in fact fallen piling: again, these were virtually indistinguishable in many situations, partly because of the extent of decomposition of the wood in the upper levels of the site.

There are, furthermore, problems with the technicalities of identifying 'occupation'; this is relevant to roundhouse studies more widely (see discussion by Harding 2010). Work being undertaken as part of the Scottish Wetland Archaeology Programme - of which the excavations at Dorman's Island and Cults are part - has been approaching the problem of relating samples from waterlogged domestic contexts to their counterparts on dry land. In essence, it is difficult to compare like with like: the burnt bone fragments, hazel nut shells and charcoal, which are ubiquitous in crannog excavation, are taken as constituting a rich and well-preserved occupation deposit when encountered within a terrestrial roundhouse. Conversely, standard bulk samples of organic deposits can yield artificially low frequencies of plant macrofossils and other palaeoenvironmental material, partly due to the 'inflation' effect of their being more widely dispersed through a better preserved sediment matrix than would be encountered on dry land. The result is that characterising occupation deposits and distinguishing these from sub-structural foundations is difficult. Clearly, there are methodological issues for archaeologists to deal with when interpreting ecofactual assemblages from crannogs. The more research that is carried out, the more complex the taphonomic issues seems to become, leading to equal measures of sympathy for antiquarians who were unable to make sense of the complexity they encountered, and pessimism for the reliability and integrity of evidence from early, pre-scientific excavation.

This is not to say, however, that we can extract little from the evidence for building superstructures that we do have. At Cults Loch, a good range of evidence for the types of wood working employed in the construction of buildings has been recovered. The massive joints found in many large horizontal logs hint at their incorporation into a substantial building, and even where the domestic superstructures may have been relatively modest, the investment of labour in the Cults site was considerable, and the site would have represented a highly visible man-made imprint on the landscape. Creating a visible and impressive statement on the landscape must surely have been central to the intentions of Iron Age crannog builders.

Crannog buildings and prehistoric society

In what ways, then, do our interpretations of crannog buildings bring us closer to understanding the societies that built and used these sites, as Munro would have hoped? Establishing the range of form in crannog superstructures is essential to understanding the crannog phenomenon as a whole, which otherwise, at face value, seems like another illogical feature of an alien, inexplicable Iron Age. There can be little doubt that crannogs were a major facet of the settlement landscape of much of western Scotland through later prehistory, and it has been argued that the concurrence of the widespread flourish of crannog construction occurring during the late Bronze/early Iron Age transition, where the focus of ritual activity merges with the domestic sphere of life can be seen as analogous to the process now well described in the terrestrial settlement record (Cavers 2006). Where Atlantic roundhouses in the north and west represented major investments of labour by their occupants in what has been interpreted as a statement of the legitimacy of the occupants' claim to territory (Armit 1988, 2002), crannogs similarly represent a highly visible imprint on the landscape, clearly designed to look impregnable but also making a statement of presence. Through the later first millennium BC, domestic architecture became the principal investment of farming communities, standing in stark contrast to the monumental communal tombs and stone circles of earlier centuries. Concurrently, evidence for communal ritual activity declines and evidence for structured deposits within houses increases dramatically, suggesting that private, individual rites were prevalent, with the domestic sphere of life the principle arena for these activities. Within this context, crannog settlements can be thought of as 'domesticating' an established ritually significant environment, keying in to the power offered to the household by the Iron Age veneration of water.

This view perhaps leads to a more sophisticated avenue of exploration of the investment of social meaning in the materiality of a settlement. The labour requirements involved in constructing a substantial crannog - whether this effort was committed to the construction of buildings, or simply the island itself - are a crucial consideration in modelling the societies which produced them. Similarly, a considered assessment of woodland management necessary to provide the constituent raw materials to build these sites may give us a clearer view of Iron Age land and resource management. Labour provision can be through coercion (i.e. slavery), but also through collaborative pooling or through social obligations, the modelling of which might lead us to a more sophisticated understanding of the groups in which they operated. I have not attempted to approach these issues in this paper, but rather to identify the ways in which they might be explored based on the highly detailed, if equally complex structural evidence from crannog excavations.

It is in this respect, then, that the study of crannog architecture may be most informative, even where the structures themselves may be relatively ephemeral, or poorly preserved. The concept of monumentality is now fundamental to our theory of Iron Age society in Northern Britain, but the manifestation of monumentality may have been more sophisticated than stereotypes of the island roundhouse might suggest, and it is clear that there was significant variability within the crannog concept. It is possible that, like hillfort defences, the social obligations and labour organisation involved in the construction of a crannog may have been more important than any prescribed format of the final result.

The recent advances in Scottish prehistoric dendrochronology made by Anne Crone (this volume) are opening an extremely promising avenue of research for settlement studies, through which the conceptual origins and developments of Iron Age architecture might be explored in far higher resolution than ever before. These studies can hopefully bring crannog buildings out of archaeological obscurity and clarify our view of the forms, functions and meanings of prehistoric and early historic domestic architecture.

Acknowledgements

I am grateful to Anne Crone for our discussion of the themes of this paper, and for her editorial input, as well as to Alex Hale for his comments on the Dumbuck crannog and access to unpublished material.

References

Armit, I. 1997, *Celtic Scotland*. Edinburgh: Historic Scotland/Batsford.

Armit, I. 1988, Broch landscapes in the Western Isles. *Scottish Archaeological Review* 5: 78-86.

Armit, I. 2002, Land and freedom: implications of Atlantic Scottish settlement patterns for Iron Age land holding and social organisation. In: B. Ballin-Smith and I. Banks (eds.) *In the Shadow of the Brochs: the Iron Age in Scotland.* Stroud: Tempus Publishing Limited, 15-26.

Bersu, G. 1940, Excavations at Little Woodbury, Wiltshire. Part 1, the settlement revealed by excavation. *Proceedings of the Prehistoric Society* 6: 30 -111.

Bersu, G. 1977, *Three Iron Age Roundhouses on the Isle of Man.* Douglas: Manx Museum and National Trust.

Bruce, J. 1900, Notes on the discovery and exploration of a pile structure on the north bank of the River Clyde, east from Dumbarton Rock. *Proceedings of the Society of Antiquaries of Scotland* 34: 437-62.

Cavers, M. G. 2006, Late Bronze and Iron Age Lake Settlement in Scotland and Ireland: the origins and development of the 'crannog' in the north and west. *Oxford Journal of Archaeology* 25(4): 389-412.

Cavers, M. G. 2007, The complexity of crannog taphonomy: old evidence and new. In: C.Green (ed.) *Archaeology from the Wetlands: Recent Perspectives, Proceedings of the International WARP conference, 2005.* Edinburgh: Society of Antiquaries of Scotland, 243-252.

Cavers, M.G. 2010, *Crannogs and Later Prehistoric Settlement in Western Scotland.* Oxford: British Archaeological Reports, Brit Ser, 510.

Cavers, M.G., Crone, B.A., Engl, R., Fouracre, L., Hunter, F. and Robertson, J. 2011, Refining Chronological Resolution in Iron Age Scotland: excavations at Dorman's Island, SW Scotland. *Journal of Wetland Archaeology* 10: 71-108.

Crone, B.A. 2000, *The History of a Scottish Lowland Crannog: excavations at Buiston, Ayrshire, 1989-90,* Edinburgh: STAR Monograph 4.

Crone, B.A., Henderson, J.C. and Sands, R. 2001, Scottish crannogs: construction, conflation and collapse, problems of interpretation. In: B. Raftery and J. Hickey (eds.) *Recent Developments in Wetland Research.* Dublin: University Monographs, 55-67.

Dixon, T.N. 2004, *The Crannogs of Scotland: an underwater archaeology.* Stroud: Tempus Publishing Ltd.

Donnelly, W. A. 1898, Discovery of a crannog on the shore of the Clyde in Dumbarton. *Journal of the British Archaeological Association* (New Series) 5: 282-289.

Feachem, R.W. 1966, *A Guide to Prehistoric Scotland.* London: Batsford.

Fredengren, C. 2002, *Crannogs: a study of people's interaction with lakes, with special reference to Loch Gara in the North West of Ireland.* Bray: Wordwell.

Hale, A. 2004, *Scottish Marine Crannogs.* Oxford: British Archaeological Reports, Brit Ser, 369.

Hale, A. and Sands, R. 2005, *Controversy on the Clyde: archaeologists, fakes and forgers; the excavation of Dumbuck crannog.* Edinburgh: RCAHMS.

Hale, A., Sands, R., and Miller, J. *forthcoming* Palaeoenvironmental, sedimentological and dating evidence from Dumbuck crannog, Firth of Clyde.

Harding, D.W. 2007, Scottish crannogs: the aerial evidence. In: C. Green (ed.) *Archaeology from the Wetlands*, Edinburgh: Society of Antiquaries of Scotland, 267-273.

Harding, D.W. 2000, Crannogs and island duns: classification, dating and function. *Oxford Journal of Archaeology* 19(3): 307-17.

Harding, D.W. 2009, *The Iron Age Roundhouse: later prehistoric building in Britain and beyond.* Oxford: University Press.

Henderson, J.C. 1998, Islets through time: the definition, dating and distribution of Scottish crannogs. *Proceedings of the Society of Antiquaries of Scotland* 17(2): 227-44.

Henderson, J.C., Crone, B.A. and Cavers, M.G. 2003, A condition survey of selected crannogs in south west Scotland. *Transactions of the Dumfriesshire and Galloway Natural History and Antiquarian Society* 77: 79-102.

Holley, M. 2000, *The Artificial Islets/Crannogs of the Central Inner Hebrides.* Oxford: British Archaeological Reports, Brit Ser, 303.

Mackinlay, J. 1862, Notice of two 'crannoges' or palisaded islands, on Bute, with plans. *Proceedings of the Society of Antiquaries of Scotland* 3: 43-6.

Moloney, A., Jennings, D., Keane, M., and McDermott, C. 1993, *Excavations at Clonfinlough, County Offaly*, Transactions, vol.2. Dublin: Irish Archaeological Wetland Unit, University College.

Monteith, J. and Robb, J.R. 1937, The crannog at Lochend, Coatbridge, with a report on the osseous remains. *Transactions of the Glasgow Archaeological Society* 9(1): 26-43.

Munro, R. 1882, *Ancient Scottish Lake Dwellings, or Crannogs* Edinburgh: David Douglas.

Munro, R. 1893, Notice of crannogs or lake dwellings recently discovered in Argyllshire. *Proceedings of the Society of Antiquaries of Scotland* 27: 205-22.

Munro, R. 1894a, The structural features of lake dwellings, part I. *Journal of the Royal Society of Antiquaries of Ireland* 24: 104-11.

Munro, R. 1894b, The structural features of lake dwellings, part II. *Journal of the Royal Society of Antiquaries of Ireland* 24: 210-21.

Munro, R 1899, Notes on a crannog at Hyndford, near Lanark, recently discovered and excavated by Andrew Smith, Esq., F.S.A. Scot. *Proceedings of the Society of Antiquaries of Scotland* 33: 373-87.

Piggott, C.M. 1948, The excavations at Hownam Rings, Roxburghshire, 1948. *Proceedings of the Society of Antiquaries of Scotland* 82: 193-225.

Piggott, C.M. 1953, Milton Loch Crannog: a native house of the second century AD in Kirkcudbrightshire. *Proceedings of the Society of Antiquaries of Scotland* 87: 134-52.

Ralston, I.B.M. 2003, Scottish roundhouses: the early chapters. *Scottish Archaeological Journal* 25: 1-26.

Sands, R. and Hale, A. 200, Evidence from marine crannogs of the later prehistoric use of the Firth of Clyde. *Journal of Wetland Archaeology* 1: 41-5.